THE SPECTRUM OF SPORT COACHING STYLES

For the first time, this book applies The Spectrum to sports coaching to become a Spectrum of Coaching Styles. The non-versus approach to pedagogy taken by The Spectrum places athletes or players at the centre of their learning and clearly defines who (player or coach) is making pedagogical decisions in each style. This clarity allows players and coaches to have their teaching behaviours and decision-making clearly defined, and it provides a common language for players, coaches and practitioners to talk about coaching styles and the expected outcomes. For coaches interested in the holistic development of the player/athlete, The Spectrum provides a detailed framework for achieving multiple learning outcomes through cognitive, social, physical, ethical, emotional and social development.

Written by coaches for coaches, this book applies Spectrum theory in a coach-specific/friendly way to the following:

- Introduction to The Spectrum and the sport coach as educator;
- Summary and detailed description of the 11 coaching styles and their suitability to particular types of coaching episodes;
- Outlines of the strengths of each style with application examples; and
- Explanations of coaching to develop reflective practice, self-analysis and error correction, how to coach players to decide on appropriate practice levels or challenge points, player problem solving and solution generation ability.

The Spectrum of Sport Coaching Styles is important reading for coaches, athletes, students and lecturers of sports coaching across any sport.

Shane Pill, PhD, is Associate Professor in Physical and Sport Education at Flinders University, Australia.

Brendan SueSee, PhD, is Senior Lecturer at the University of Southern Queensland, Australia.

Joss Rankin, MEd, is Senior Lecturer in Health and Physical Education at Flinders University, Australia.

Mitch Hewitt, PhD, is Adjunct Lecturer at the University of Canberra and University of Southern Queensland, Australia.

THE SPECTRUM OF SPORT COACHING STYLES

Shane Pill, Brendan SueSee, Joss Rankin, and Mitch Hewitt

First published 2022
by Routledge
605 Third Avenue, New York, NY 10158

and by Routledge
2 Park Square, Milton Park, Abingdon, Oxon, OX14 4RN

Routledge is an imprint of the Taylor & Francis Group, an informa business

© 2022 Taylor & Francis

The right of Shane Pill, Brendan SueSee, Joss Rankin, and Mitch Hewitt to be identified as authors of this work has been asserted by them in accordance with sections 77 and 78 of the Copyright, Designs and Patents Act 1988.

All rights reserved. No part of this book may be reprinted or reproduced or utilised in any form or by any electronic, mechanical, or other means, now known or hereafter invented, including photocopying and recording, or in any information storage or retrieval system, without permission in writing from the publishers.

Trademark notice: Product or corporate names may be trademarks or registered trademarks, and are used only for identification and explanation without intent to infringe.

Library of Congress Cataloging-in-Publication Data
A catalog record for this book has been requested

ISBN: 978-0-367-48522-1 (hbk)
ISBN: 978-0-367-48518-4 (pbk)
ISBN: 978-1-003-04144-3 (ebk)

DOI: 10.4324/9781003041443

Typeset in Bembo
by Apex CoVantage, LLC

CONTENTS

List of Figures	*vii*
List of Tables	*viii*
About the Contributors	*ix*
Foreword	*xii*

	Introduction: Taking the Spectrum of Teaching Styles to Sport Coaching *Shane Pill and Brendan SueSee*	1
1	**The Spectrum; A Philosophy of Deliberate Coaching** *Shane Pill and Brendan SueSee*	7
2	**A Spectrum of Coaching Styles: Tenets of the Approach** *Shane Pill, Brendan SueSee and Joss Rankin*	14
3	**Coaching by Command: Style A** *Shane Pill, Brendan SueSee, Joss Rankin and Mitch Hewitt*	26
4	**Coaching by Task (Practice): Style B** *Shane Pill, Brendan SueSee, Joss Rankin and Mitch Hewitt*	36
5	**Reciprocal Coaching (Peer Coaching): Style C** *Shane Pill, Brendan SueSee, Joss Rankin and Mitch Hewitt*	42
6	**Coaching by Individual Programming (Self-Check): Style D** *Shane Pill, Brendan SueSee, Joss Rankin and Mitch Hewitt*	51

vi Contents

7 Small Group Coaching (Inclusion): Style E 58
Shane Pill, Brendan SueSee, Joss Rankin and Mitch Hewitt

8 Coaching by Guided Discovery: Style F 65
Shane Pill, Brendan SueSee, Joss Rankin and Mitch Hewitt

9 Coaching by Problem Solving (Convergent Discovery): Style G 74
Shane Pill, Brendan SueSee, Joss Rankin and Mitch Hewitt

10 Coaching for Creativity (Divergent Discovery): Style H 80
Shane Pill, Brendan SueSee, Joss Rankin and Mitch Hewitt

11 Player Designed—Coach Supported: Style I 87
Shane Pill, Brendan SueSee, Joss Rankin and Mitch Hewitt

12 Player Initiated—Coach Supported: Style J 94
Shane Pill, Brendan SueSee, Joss Rankin and Mitch Hewitt

13 Player Self-Coaching: Style K 101
Shane Pill, Brendan SueSee, Joss Rankin and Mitch Hewitt

14 Episodic Coaching 108
Brendan SueSee and Shane Pill

15 Game-Based and Direct Instruction Coaching Through a Spectrum of Teaching Styles Lens 123
Brendan SueSee and Shane Pill

16 From Physical Education to Alpine Ski Teaching and Coaching: A Figurational Study of The Spectrum 134
John Williams, John Arnold, James Crompton, Lesley Page and Luke Riddle

17 Future Directions: Using The Spectrum in Coach Education 143
Shane Pill, Brendan SueSee and Mitch Hewitt

Index *151*

FIGURES

2.1	The Spectrum is a continuum	15
2.2	Guided Discovery	17
2.3	Convergent Discovery	18
2.4	Divergent Discovery	19
2.5	The Spectrum of Coaching Styles—a model of the Landmark styles	21
2.6	The coaching process	23
5.1	Merian and Snyder's (2015) peer coaching model	43
5.2	Possible layout for front wheel lift practice using Reciprocal Coaching Style	46
5.3	An example of a Reciprocal Style task sheet	48
9.1	Positioning of attacker (X), defender (D), markers (M) and coach for Convergent Discovery episode	76
10.1	Third of a netball court	83
11.1	The decision distribution for the coach and player during Player Designed—Coach Supported: Style I	91
14.1	Example of 'lane work' activities	111
15.1	A Spectrum of Coaching Styles	124
15.2	A game-based version of a net session	126
15.3	Battlezone layout	130
17.1	Scenario description from the description inventory of teaching styles	144
17.2	Instrument for collecting coaches' self-identified beliefs in relation to the teaching styles they use during coaching sessions	145
17.3	An example of a section from the IFITS coding sheet to code a practice session	148
17.4	The Spectrum (Mosston & Ashworth, 2008) alongside A Varying Landscape of Affordances model (Chow et al., 2020)	149

TABLES

2.1	The Spectrum as an epistemological chain—teaching is a chain of decision-making	23
3.1	Applying Coaching by Command to delivering instructions for how to belay whilst a climber is top rope in a rock-climbing situation	30
5.1	Performance Criteria checklist for the Forehand Groundstroke	49
6.1	Self-Check task sheet for the set	54
6.2	Self-Check task sheet—setting up an attack using width self-check	55
7.1	Three challenge points for bowling	62
8.1	A sample of predetermined questions related to hitting a forehand groundstroke in a crosscourt direction	70
14.1	Australian football (AFL) coaching session plan as a series of teaching episodes	109
14.2	Football (soccer) coaching session plan as a series of teaching episodes.	112
14.3	Coaching session plan as a series of teaching episodes	114

ABOUT THE CONTRIBUTORS

John Arnold (Dip Sports Coaching) has been an educator for most of his professional career and currently works as a Well-Being coach, Life-Coach and Back Country skiing guide. In 2014 he completed an MSc in Mindfulness Studies at Aberdeen University, where his research field was mindfulness and coaching/learning Alpine Skiing. He is qualified in sports coaching, life coaching, mindful based stress reduction and neuro-linguistic programming. He is an internationally qualified Alpine Skiing coach, with many years of experience of coaching National Squad ski racers (from Scotland and New Zealand) and of coach and ski teacher training. He has developed mindfulness coaching and learning methods, which he uses with recreational and performance skiers, and he leads Mindfulness Retreats in the mountains of Northern Italy, where he now lives.

James Crompton (BA Hons, PG Dip) has worked as a professional ski instructor for 16 years, teaching 26 ski seasons in both the Northern and Southern Hemisphere. He is the only person ever to be a trainer and examiner for both BASI and the Australian Professional Snowsports Instructors (APSI) association. James delivers and assesses at every level for both associations and serves on the APSI's Technical Committee. James currently resides in NSW, Australia, and works for the largest snowsports school in the Southern Hemisphere. His European base is Morzine, France, where he is the Director of a boutique ski school.

Mitch Hewitt (PhD) has worked as a tennis coach, HPE teacher, and currently works for Tennis Australia in coach education. He completed his PhD in 2015 using The Spectrum to investigate coaching styles in tennis. He is the author of numerous articles on teaching styles and tennis. He holds an adjunct position at the University of Southern Queensland, and he has developed partnerships for the delivery of tennis programmes with more than 20 universities in Australia.

Lesley Page (BA Hons, PG Dip) is a professional ski instructor, an examiner and trainer for BASI and a PhD candidate at the University of Edinburgh. In 2019 she was selected to represent BASI as a speaker, educator and skier at INTERSKI (The International Snowsports conference). She is passionate about the professional development of snowsport instructors and is involved in the creation of BASI curriculum. Lesley is currently working on a PhD that explores professional learning in the workplace through the lens of BASI trainers' teaching practice.

Shane Pill (PhD) is Associate Professor: Physical Education and Sport, at Flinders University, Adelaide, Australia. He is Life Member and Fellow of the Australian Council for Health, Physical Education and Recreation. Shane researches in physical education, sport coaching, and coach development. Shane began coaching in 1988, coaching from U8-to-adult in multiple sports: Australian football (AFL), cross-country, football (soccer), touch football, rugby union, athletics-sprinting, swimming, triathlon, basketball, cricket, volleyball. Shane was twice nominated for the Australian Football Coaches Association (WA) Coach of the Year award (1993, 1994), and in 2013 he was awarded the SANFL Coach Award for services to coach education. Shane has worked with Tennis Australia, Cricket Australia, the AFL, NRL, Australian Rugby, SANFL, WAFL, SASI, Australian Lacrosse and many local sports clubs on coach education, research or resource development. He is author and editor of *Perspectives on Athlete-Centred Coaching* (Routledge, 2018), *The Spectrum of Teaching Styles in Physical Education* (Routledge, 2020), and *Perspectives on Game-Based Coaching* (Routledge, 2021).

Joss Rankin (MEd) is Senior Lecturer in Health and Physical Education and coordinates the Outdoor Education study stream at Flinders University, Adelaide, Australia. Joss currently holds a teaching specialist position, with scholarship investigating curriculum and pedagogy, embodiment and student engagement. He began his career teaching in secondary education as a Health, Physical Education and Outdoor Education teacher in schools across metro and regional South Australia, as well as Cambridgeshire, England. As a part of his role, Joss holds instructor and assessor qualifications in rock climbing, bushwalking and kayaking and an instructor qualification in mountain biking. He regularly engages with schools and organisations through student-led partnerships and is also a member of the Australian Council for Health Physical Education and Recreation, Outdoor Educators Association of South Australia and Australian Tertiary Outdoor Educators Network.

Luke Riddle is a BASI Level 3 Alpine Ski Teacher with 30 years' experience teaching in Austria, France, New Zealand and, most recently, in the Snowy Mountains of his adopted home, Australia. Luke has specialised at times as an Alpine Masters Coach and as a Moguls Coach for Perisher's Winter Sports Club. He has a passion for Telemark skiing and for ski mountaineering and touring. Luke has been able to combine these passions with his work as a guide for Snowy Mountains Backcountry, leading groups into the Kosciuszko National Park's main range.

Brendan SueSee (PhD) is Senior Lecturer at the University of Southern Queensland, Springfield, Australia. He was a high school teacher for 21 years and taught Health and Physical Education, Geography and History. He has coached at levels from U7-to-adult in cricket, netball, Australian football, baseball, athletics, cross country, volleyball, touch football, softball and triathlon. He has worked at the University of Southern Queensland (USQ) for five years. His research interests include teaching styles, alignment between HPE syllabus documents and reporting, and cognition. He is the author of numerous articles on teaching styles in physical education and most recently the author and editor of *The Spectrum of Teaching Styles in Physical Education* (Routledge, 2020).

John Williams (PhD) is Assistant Professor: Health and Physical Education at the University of Canberra, Australia, and is a National Board Director of the Australian Council for Health, Physical Education and Recreation. John has more than 30 years' experience as an HPE teacher educator and programme leader, former HPE teacher and tertiary senior lecturer/lecturer in sports coaching and sports management. John is also a British Association of Snowsports Instructors (BASI) Level 4 Alpine Ski Teacher and Snowsport Scotland Alpine Performance coach and has worked part-time and full time in Australia, New Zealand and Europe as a ski instructor/coach since the late 1980s.

FOREWORD

Although comfortably ensconced in an active retirement, it was an honour to be requested to supply a **Foreword** for this publication. I am seen as an elder leader in the use of the *Spectrum of Teaching Styles* within the Australian context. Dr Brendan SueSee, Dr Mitchell Hewitt and A/Prof Shane Pill, the principal authors of this book, are well known to me, and it was a pleasure to have been in a research team with such talented and conscientious practitioners, meticulous researchers and genuinely good people. All three are excellent role models, motivated to improve practice in teaching and sports coaching in more informed ways and at all levels. Combined, they have extensive experience in teaching and have been involved in the coaching of a wide array of sports involving all age groups and both genders for many years.

Background

In my own enormously satisfying career in the areas of sport, health and physical education (over four and a half decades), it was my privilege to meet, work with, observe, learn from, and mentor a great many wonderful people. I worked for over two and a half decades in the area of Health and Physical Education teaching and then several years as an academic in the tertiary area (sport, health and physical education and in sports science), retiring from the University of Southern Queensland (USQ) an Associate Professor. My teaching and leadership experience in health and physical education ranged from pre-school to upper secondary classes, tertiary sessions, and adult education classes. I taught at city and country schools, single-sex and mixed schools, government and non-government schools, and from pre-school to upper secondary. I was responsible for over ten thousand students during my career and thoroughly enjoyed every class. I taught over 70 discrete sports, games and other physical activity units as part of my teaching.

Closely associated with my teaching experience was a comprehensive involvement in a wide variety of sports (in excess of 40) in various roles. My sports coaching involvement encompassed school, club and elite-level sports and covered individual and team sports at levels ranging from beginner to elite level (single-sex and/or mixed gender).

During my professional life, I personally found the use of the *Spectrum of Teaching Styles* (whose earlier iteration I had encountered in the beginning years of my teaching career) as being of great practical application. In teaching and my leadership of staff, it provided an invaluable way to decipher and apply the plethora of teaching models and approaches described in curriculum documents and professional literature. My early years were inspired by elements of the experiential learning from the nascent environmental education movement, along with the fun and involvement offered by programmes such as New Games (with its less-competitive approach to learning through physical activity). Being aware of the early work of Muska Mosston encouraged me, along with the support of my staff, to use new and different approaches and to innovate and develop new units of work, which did not follow traditional ways of teaching. Much later, and in the sporting area, I found an awareness of the *Spectrum of Teaching Styles* supported my interest in developing the thinking skills of players (especially decision-making).

The Authors

I am fortunate to have known Dr Brendan SueSee since he was a teacher in training. In the early 2000s, I had the pleasure of supervising Brendan for a course during a master's level programme at Queensland University of Technology and then later co-supervising him for a time during his doctoral studies, where Brendan had decided to undertake research using the *Spectrum of Teaching Styles* developed by Muska Mosston (and later in association with Sara Ashworth). This research topic offered a fertile opportunity for Brendan to examine teaching practices, develop his research skills and improve his own teaching. A suggestion was made to contact Sara Ashworth (Muska Mosston had passed away) to seek her support and input—to which she readily agreed. This proved to be of immense value to Brendan's study and has developed into an enduring and productive relationship. Brendan's research focused on the teaching styles of senior school physical education teachers, and it, and later research related to it and other areas, has given him a significant national and international profile in the *Spectrum of Teaching Styles*.

While establishing a Sport, Health and Physical Education programme at USQ, Mitchell Hewitt was referred to me as a potential doctoral student. As the application of the *Spectrum of Teaching Styles* to coaching had only received cursory attention in the full gamut of sports, I convinced Mitch—based on the success of the study by Brendan SueSee—that such a study offered an immense opportunity to explore past and current practices and models and improve his own coaching performance and that of others. Mitch's study has revealed a largely untapped potential to inform coaches. He has effectively reimagined the work of Mosston and Ashworth into what might be seen as a **Spectrum of Coaching Styles**. This book and the research on which it is based has drawn inspiration and purpose from the opportunity that Dr Mitchell Hewitt saw by applying the *Spectrum of Teaching Styles* to coaching.

I was initially introduced to A/Prof Shane Pill, an academic at Flinders University, during a visit to Melbourne. I was already aware of extensive work that Shane had completed on the Games Sense Approach and in other areas of teaching and coaching pedagogy. I also knew of his prodigious publication record and enormous capacity for work. I was pleasantly surprised by his open-minded approach to ideas and information, especially with regards to the *Spectrum of Teaching Styles*, and his interest in disseminating research through publications. Shane is highly motivated and introduced to the team a range of new perspectives based on his background and experiences. Shane has contributed considerably to the preparation of academic papers, conference presentations, book chapters and books, which has resulted in a wider dissemination of the research conducted on the *Spectrum of Teaching Styles*.

A contributor to this book, Dr John Williams from the University of Canberra, is known to me as he was supervised by my twin brother, A/Prof Allan Edwards. I have met John a number of times and have come to know him through his work in an area of mutual interest, the traditional games of Aboriginal and Torres Strait Islander peoples. Uniquely, John has had a personal involvement in the use of the *Spectrum of Teaching Styles* in a sport, and his many interactions with the authors of this book will surely result in future cooperation.

The Spectrum of Teaching Styles

The *Spectrum of Teaching Styles* is based on the premise that teaching is a chain of decision-making (i.e., who makes the decisions and when and what are the intentions or purpose of those decisions). In suggesting a range of teaching styles, ranging from complete direction by a teacher to the situation where the student assumes responsibility for self-teaching, it does not propose the use of several (or all) of the styles described. People often misinterpret the *Spectrum of Teaching Styles* as requiring the use of most or all the styles. It is more a case of being aware of more effective ways to achieve outcomes and doing so by using more appropriate styles.

Although not its primary goal, this book reveals some research-informed refinements to the *Spectrum of Teaching Styles* in modelling it as a **Spectrum of Coaching Styles**. Although not detailed extensively in this book, Mitchell Hewitt has sought to examine and provide greater clarity related to each teaching style within the inconclusively explained micro-aspect called canopies. This work has the opportunity to observe individual styles in practice better and assist in better achieving desired coaching outcomes.

The authors have based their research (and hence this book) on the *Spectrum of Teaching Styles* and have preserved the integrity of all the styles, as well as the overall framework of the model. They have sought to appeal to the coaching fraternity by outlining research related to the application of the *Spectrum of Teaching Styles* across a wide range of sports. The information presented provides an opportunity to understand current practice and suggest ways of doing things a little differently—in order to motivate and/or improve performance and enjoyment for both the players and the coach. Besides presenting information and guidance to coaches of all sports, the book also provides incentives for a range of research possibilities within any sport.

Although the authors have preserved the integrity of the *Spectrum of Teaching Styles*, no model is perfect or has all the answers. The 'Spectrum Team' have sought ways to tweak, evolve and further develop the *Spectrum of Teaching Styles* based on a questioning approach, feedback and research. The authors believe that the *Spectrum of Teaching Styles* will continue to evolve as research informs the need for modification. As an integral part of this improvement process, they have interrogated the teaching styles of PE teachers and sports coaches and decided to place other models such as the *Games Sense Approach* (GSA) and the *Constraints-Led Approach* (CLA) within the *Spectrum of Teaching Styles* and show that they have relevance as a range of styles and not one style. The *Spectrum of Teaching Styles* can readily accommodate the basis of other models and approaches.

The opportunity to work with Brendan, Mitch and Shane has provided me with great satisfaction and immense pride. They are all widely published and sought after nationally and internationally to present and provide advice based on their research. I have always impressed on these outstanding academics that their work should be academic but have a practical application. I firmly believe that this book fulfils that purpose.

All coaches seek to be seen as effective in their role while allowing players to develop to their fullest potential. Because of their research and personal experiences as long-time sport coaches, the authors (as am I) are convinced about the benefits of the *Spectrum of Teaching Styles* in improving sport coaching performance. This book will be an indispensable addition to the coaching literature and provide an opportunity for sport coaches to learn more and to refine and further develop their coaching.

Dr Ken Edwards

INTRODUCTION

Taking the Spectrum of Teaching Styles to Sport Coaching

Shane Pill and Brendan SueSee

This book emerged from conversations the authors have had over many years about the application of the Spectrum of Teaching Styles (Mosston & Ashworth, 2008) (from here, referred to as The Spectrum) to sport coaching, specifically, conversations about how The Spectrum provides a different lens on coaching models as a canopy of teaching styles rather than a solitary or single style. Furthermore, the book discusses issues common with sport coaching, such as inconsistent use of terminology and idiosyncratic approaches to coaching (Mosston & Ashworth, 2008; Ashworth, 2020), leading to misconceived pedagogical applications to coaching as teaching. As an example, Mitch Hewitt's doctoral thesis used The Spectrum to consider whether tennis coaches adhered to the tenets of the game-based coaching approach identified by the coaches that they believed that they were implementing. This was the starting point for many of those conversations (Hewitt, 2015a). Hewitt's thesis not only provided a perspective on the alignment between a coach's espoused approach and what occurred in practice but also made obvious the benefit of a coaching styles analysis to coach development.

The Spectrum has established a strong and profound place in physical education and physical education teacher education and, therefore, sport teaching in physical education (SueSee, Hewitt & Pill, 2020) since the release of Teaching Physical Education in 1966 (Mosston, 1966). It is surprising that it hasn't transferred more often into sport coach education or development, as it is arguably the most enduring example of what is now referred to as models-based practice (Mosston, 1966, 1972, 1981; Mosston & Ashworth, 1986, 1994, 2002, 2008; SueSee et al., 2020). At this point in time, only Hewitt (2015a) and Hall (2016) have applied The Spectrum to sports coaching research. These pioneering scholars' work will be spoken about briefly to provide the reader with a background of research so far undertaken in this area.

Hewitt's application of The Spectrum to tennis coaching demonstrated the enormous potential of The Spectrum to evaluate coaching practice, as well as in the discipline of coach development. This work has shown that tennis coaching occurs in diverse learning conditions and experiences requiring the application of different teaching styles purposefully implemented to meet the needs of the player matched to the task requirements and intended learning outcomes. Although tennis coaches were found to self-align with key tenets of a

DOI: 10.4324/9781003041443-1

Game Sense coaching approach, for instance, the use of questions to enable player discovery and creativity towards developing thinking players (den Duyn, 1997; Hewitt, Edwards & Pill, 2016a), observation of junior development and club professional tennis coaches showed that the coaches used two main teaching styles: Coaching by Command Style A and Coaching by Task—Practice Style B (Hewitt & Edwards, 2013). These teaching styles share common and complimentary features with a direct instruction teaching model (Metzler, 2017). Coaches in Hewitt's study appeared to lack self-awareness regarding their own coaching performance and the ability to accurately describe why they enact coaching in a particular way. Hewitt's work has suggested a lack of intentional knowledge concerning the practical application of teaching styles in coaching (Pill, Hewitt & Edwards, 2016). Coaches are not alone here, as others have found physical education teachers in both Australia and Sweden have had trouble in accurately describing the teaching styles they are using for a range of reasons (SueSee et al., 2018; SueSee & Barker, 2018).

Hall's (2016) use of The Spectrum built on Hewitt's (2015a) work seeking to understand how equestrian coaches taught. She also examined their teaching perceptions, observing their teaching actions, and identified the role of the horse in their teaching. Hall stressed the importance and uniqueness of this topic as the horse is independently responsive to the player and coach and needed to be considered. Like Hewitt (2015a), Hall (2016) also found discrepancies between how coaches thought they coached (self-reported using Styles A, B and F the most) and what was observed (only recorded observing Styles A and B).

Contrary to the emphasis of many sport coach education materials, Hewitt's investigation of tennis coaches' teaching styles indicated that the coaches potentially offered players a limited range of developmental opportunities (i.e., motor skill development in the physical learning domain) due to a narrow use of teaching styles in their coaching (Hewitt et al., 2016). While two teaching styles dominated the coaching that Hewitt observed, coaching practice inevitably contained more than one teaching style, or a 'canopy design'. A 'canopy design' describes a teaching practice that shares similar features to one of Mosston's Teaching Styles but is a variation of the approximation of a particular style (Hewitt, Edwards & Pill, 2016b; Mosston & Ashworth, 2008). The concept of 'canopy design' will be explained in Chapter 2.

Since his thesis and subsequent publications, Hewitt has attempted to explain tennis as an athlete-centred coaching approach through The Spectrum, linking athlete-centred coaching to tenets of Inclusion Style E (Hewitt et al., 2018). He has also used The Spectrum to explain game-based tennis coaching (Hewitt, 2015b, 2020; Pill & Hewitt, 2017).

The Spectrum is both a philosophy and a model. The philosophy is that of deliberate or intentional teaching. According to Mosston, 'Teaching in all communities is deliberate' (1966, p. 4). As a coaching model, The Spectrum outlines an evolutionary process leading toward ever-increasing player independence in their learning and a recognition of the potential for shared decision-making in the learning process. The pedagogical maturity of the sport coach is then the understanding as to how to use each coaching style to attain an appropriate and intentional learning effect—in essence, knowing the coaching style that best works to achieve the task outcome/s the coach envisages. Moving along The Spectrum involves the progressive removal of elements from Coaching by Command Style A. This is shown in the sequence of the styles. These concepts will be explored further in Chapter 2.

Moving now to explain the layout of the book, which intentionally mirrors the structure Mosston used in Teaching Physical Education (1966) of working through each style, it is important to note that central to The Spectrum is the concept of a non-versus approach to pedagogy (from here, referred to as a teaching style) and an emphasis on the role of professional judgement of the coach in choosing the appropriate teaching style to meet the desired task outcome.

Chapter 1 explains the philosophy of deliberate teaching. It traces The Spectrum to the work of Bruner, Bloom and others to locate teaching as deliberate actions to structure the learning environment, the nature of subject matter and the style of teaching. This chapter positions the sport coach as a deliberate designer of coaching in the educational space. Chapter 2 outlines the operational structure of The Spectrum. Consideration is given to the decisions made by the deliberate sport coach as educator before the practice session, in delivery of the practice session and after the practice session.

Chapter 3 commences the section of the book viewing the application of specific Teaching Styles to coaching episodes. Each chapter will elaborate on the structure and purpose of the style. Practical examples from a range of sports will be provided to illuminate the styles.

Chapter 3 explains Coaching by Command Style A. The purpose of the Command Style is for the player/s to learn to move in a synchronous fashion with the coach or teammates. The style values precision, timing, fluency and accuracy of movement. When the 'command' is given, it is assumed a replicated and desired response occurs. In this style, all decisions are made by the coach, and the role of the player/s is to respond, and the closer the player/s response in both time and accuracy to the coach's stimuli, the more 'perfect' or ideal the practice session. Chapter 4 explains Coaching by Task, or Practice Style B. In this style, once a task has been demonstrated and explained, it assumes the player/s are independent enough to start the movement or activity, perform it for a number of repetitions or a period, and stop, on their own volition. The coach observes the performance and provides feedback to reinforce or correct the movement. We anticipate that these styles will be familiar to coaches as they form the 'backbone' of a historically common directive and replicative 'coach-centred' approach (Hewitt, 2015a).

Chapter 5 explains Reciprocal Coaching Style C—or peer coaching. In this style, 'the evaluation variable' is transferred to the player/s as it involves the coach entrusting partner observation of performance and then the partner provision of information about the performance of the task. The partner is placed 'in the role of an observer, corrector, and a reinforcer' (Mosston, 1966, p. 72). When successfully implemented, Mosston suggested a by-product of this style is to 'enhance the social climate in the class by creating this situation where one is actually dependent on the help from a peer. One learns how to receive criticism and evaluation from a peer' (1966, p. 90). Chapter 6 explains Self-Check Style D or Coaching by Individual Programming. In this style, player/s are performing a task and engaging in self-assessment. Player/s work independently and check performance against criteria prepared by the coach. Chapter 7 explains Inclusion Style E or small group coaching. The purpose of Inclusion Style E is to provide a differentiated practice environment to meet the range of challenge points of the players. Style E creates a learning environment where the players are required to develop skills by choosing the appropriate task challenge point appropriate for their respective abilities.

Chapter 8 begins a section introducing styles which move to more 'player-centred' coaching, in that the players assume increasing autonomy in their learning as the role of the coach transitions from a guide and facilitator to one of support when needed. Chapter 8 explains Coaching by Guided Discovery Style F. The purpose of the Guided Discovery style is to place the player/s in cognitive dissonance—a disturbance or irritation, deliberately created to prompt the player/s to seek a solution to remove the disturbance. Mosston (1966) proposed: Cognitive Dissonance leads to Inquiry, which leads to Discovery. Style F creates a learning episode, which requires the player to answer a series of questions posed by the coach that leads to the response.

Chapter 9 explores Convergent Discovery Style G or coaching by problem solving. The purpose of this style is to place player/s in a situation where they apply reasoning, questioning and logic to converge on a single correct response predetermined by the coach. Chapter 10 describes Divergent Discovery Style H or coaching for creativity, which rather than converge on a singular predetermined response, aims to place player/s in a situation where they discover or create multiple responses to a specific question, scenario or problem posed by the coach.

Chapter 11 illustrates Player Designed—Coach Supported Style I. This style moves the player from discovery to more self-direction and initiation. The purpose of the Player Designed—Coach Supported style is to position player/s in a situation where the coach has chosen a topic (that the player/s knows nothing or has limited knowledge about), and they are then required to make decisions about how to discover solutions and/or to demonstrate the performance. Chapter 12 explains Player Initiated—Coach Supported Style J. In this style, the player/s choose the topic/subject matter, and the player/s assume complete responsibility for designing their respective learning experience and choose how and when the coach is involved. The coach's role is to ask questions and check if the player/s are achieving their goals or to reinforce the behaviour the player/s are pursuing. Chapter 13 explains Player Self-Coaching Style K, where the defining feature is that the player/s assume responsibility for both the coaching and learning decision-making.

After this considered exploration at each of the Teaching Styles in sport coaching, we focus the reader's attention on how The Spectrum provides perspectives on other common coaching models. For instance, a coaching episode will be placed on The Spectrum, showing it to be not a 'style' but rather a cluster of teaching styles. In demonstrating this, we aim to detail the important pedagogical concepts and unify pedagogical decision-making that takes place in coaching sport.

Chapter 14 explains a coaching session as a series of teaching episodes—episodic coaching, that is, the content of the practice session is delivered by a multitude of episodes that each represent different coach-player learning intentions and therefore teaching styles (Mosston & Ashworth, 2008). In Chapter 15, we use The Spectrum to provide insights on a 'game based' model of sport coaching. This chapter examines a tactical or 'game-based' model coaching episode to identify the decisions being made between the coach and the player/s. Chapter 16 draws on the experience of one sport's use of The Spectrum in coach education. It shows the enduring effect of The Spectrum on the idea of coach education on the authors as coach educators. We conclude with Chapter 17—Future directions, outlining how to use The Spectrum to analyse coaching behaviour and explain how The Spectrum could be used in coach education.

This book is intended to engage undergraduate and postgraduate students in physical education and sport coaching, practising coaches and coach educators. The contributions, taken together or individually, will provide insight, learning and opportunities to foster the sport coach as educator proposition. Each chapter will raise issues that may resonate with the sport practitioner and researcher. In this way, the chapters can assist the practitioner to more comprehensively understand their own coaching, provide deeper insight into personal conceptualisations of the concept of coaching pedagogy, and stimulate reflections with the readers own coaching or the coaching contexts they are involved in. This book both summarises contemporary thinking and practical considerations about sport coaching as an educative endeavour, as well as providing direction for further practical, pragmatic and research consideration of the Spectrum of Teaching Styles and its precepts.

The Spectrum aligns agreeably with an 'athlete-centred' perspective (Pill, 2018) and notions of Physical Literacy in so far as developing the 'whole' player via social, emotional, cognitive and physical developmental channels (or in an educative sense, domains of learning). The use of 'canopies of teaching styles' to compliment different sports is also an aspect we engage with in this book. We show that some sports require more of a particular coaching style than another—which is considered 'perfectly ok' from The Spectrum perspective as we argue that the sport coach as educator (Jones, 2006) views planned and deliberate coaching episodes as caring about the clarity of learning objectives aligned to what the coach is attempting to develop with a player through a practice task. Therefore, consistent with Mosston's work, we adopt a non-versus approach to pedagogy descriptions and seek only to elucidate the alignment of coaching styles with task outcomes.

References

Ashworth, S. (2020). History and overview of the Spectrum. In B. SueSee, M. Hewitt, & S. Pill (Eds.), *The Spectrum of teaching styles in physical education* (pp. 14–26). Routledge.

den Duyn, N. (1997). *Game sense: Developing thinking players workbook*. Australian Sports Commission.

Hall, C. (2016). *The relational positioning of equestrian sports as a unique and specialist variant of sports pedagogy*. Unpublished thesis. School of Linguistics, Adult and Specialist Education, The University of Southern Queensland.

Hewitt, M. (2015a). *Teaching styles of Australian tennis coaches: An exploration of practices and insights using Mosston and Ashworth's Spectrum of teaching styles*. Unpublished thesis. School of Linguistics, Adult and Specialist Education. The University of Southern Queensland.

Hewitt, M. (2015b). How tennis hot shots is making sense of game sense. *Active & Healthy Magazine*, 22(2/3), 41–47.

Hewitt, M. (2020). Considering the application of a range of teaching styles from the spectrum that promotes the holistic development of tennis players in a variety of learning domains. In B. SueSee, M. Hewitt, & S. Pill (Eds.), *The Spectrum of teaching styles in physical education* (pp. 60–72). Routledge.

Hewitt, M., & Edwards, K. (2013). Observed teaching styles of junior development and club professional tennis coaches in Australia. *International Tennis Federation Coaching and Sport Science Review*, 59, 6–8.

Hewitt, M., Edwards, K., Ashworth, A., & Pill, S. (2016). Investigating the teaching styles of tennis coaches using the spectrum. *Sport Science Review*, 25, 350–373.

Hewitt, M., Edwards, K., & Pill, S. (2016a). Teaching styles of Australian junior tennis coaches. In J. Bruce & C. North (Eds.), *2015 Game Sense for Teaching and Coaching Conference* (pp. 40–52). Christchurch, New Zealand.

Hewitt, M., Edwards, K., & Pill, S. (2016b). Investigating the teaching style of a junior tennis coach using the spectrum of teaching styles. *ICHPER-SD Journal: Health, Physical Education, Sport & Dance*, 44(1), 5–32.

Hewitt, M., Edwards, K., Reid, M., & Pill, S. (2018). Applying the game sense approach and Mosston and Ashworth's Style-E to promote athlete-centred tennis coaching with junior novice players. In S. Pill (Ed.), *Perspectives on athlete-centred coaching* (pp. 193–205). Routledge.

Jones, R. (Ed.). (2006). *The sports coach as educator*. Routledge.

Metzler, M. (2017). *Instructional models for physical education* (3rd ed.). Routledge.

Mosston, M. (1966). *Teaching physical education*. Charles E Merrill Publishing.
Mosston, M. (1972). *Teaching from command to discovery*. Wadsworth.
Mosston, M. (1981). *Teaching physical education* (2nd ed.). Merrill.
Mosston, M., & Ashworth, S. (1986). *Teaching physical education* (3rd ed.). Merrill.
Mosston, M., & Ashworth, S. (1994). *Teaching physical education* (4th ed.). Maxwell Macmillan International.
Mosston, M., & Ashworth, S. (2002). *Teaching physical education* (5th ed.). Benjamin Cummings.
Mosston, M., & Ashworth, S. (2008). *Teaching physical education*. Benjamin Cummings.
Pill, S. (2018). *Perspectives on athlete-centred coaching*. Routledge.
Pill, S., & Hewitt, M. (2017). Tennis coaching: Applying the game sense approach. *Strategies: A Journal for Physical and Sport Educators*, *30*(2), 10–16.
Pill, S., Hewitt, M., & Edwards, K. (2016). Exploring tennis coaches' insights in relation to their teaching styles. *Baltic Journal of Sport & Health Sciences*, *3*(102), 30–43.
SueSee, B., & Barker, D. M. (2018). Self-reported and observed teaching styles of Swedish physical education teachers. *Curriculum Studies in Health and Physical Education*, *10*(1), 34–50.
SueSee, B., Edwards, K., Pill, S., & Cuddihy, T. (2018). Self-reported teaching styles of Australian senior physical education teachers. *Curriculum Perspectives*, *38*(1), 41–54.
SueSee, B., Hewitt, M., & Pill, S. (2020). *The Spectrum of teaching styles in physical education*. Routledge.

1
THE SPECTRUM; A PHILOSOPHY OF DELIBERATE COACHING

Shane Pill and Brendan SueSee

The Spectrum offers a framework for the application of a range of teaching styles (from here, referred to as coaching styles as this book is intended for the field of sport coaching). The framework explains the decisions of both the teacher, who in this book is the sport coach, and 'the learner', who in this book is the player.

Over 40 years, Mosston argued that pedagogy requires a framework for consistency to prevent discrepancy between (1) What academics might see as important and what practitioners (in this case, sport coaches) might see as important; (2) What academics say should occur and what really happens in the field; and (3) Claims social agencies or prominent people might seek to make, criticise or attack the profession or an individual's practice (Mosston & Mueller, 1969). In response to these three challenges, Mosston proposed The Spectrum. He defined a style of teaching by the decisions made before, during and after the act of teaching. We argue this is the same for the sport coach, and hence we can adapt The Spectrum to the field of sport coaching as it is an educative endeavour. To that end, the decisions made by the coach in the design of a practice activity create an order and give rise to a sequence of events within the practice activity. The decisions determine the limits of the activity and result in mutually exclusive outcomes. Thus, like teaching, sport coaching can be understood and explained as the deliberate act of pairing appropriately a coaching style with an activity outcome (Mosston, 1966a). As a result, a fundamental question arises for the coach in planning their coaching sessions: 'Which style(s) would be efficient with which activity?' (Mosston, 1966a, p. 4).

Mosston called on the work of Bruner (1966) to explain the philosophy of The Spectrum, and, specifically, the role of teaching as developing students to think for themselves (Mosston, 1966a). This in part explains the layout of The Spectrum 'from Command to Discovery', which will be explained further in Chapter 2. Borrowing from Bruner, player learning is viewed as involving the development of understanding of information through perceptual organisation, through manipulation and action, and through symbolic representation (Mosston, 1966a).

At this point in the chapter, it is relevant to note that ineffectual coaching practice can be passed on by informal learning of the experience of being coached, the 'everyday' experience of coaching or the observation of other coaches. Apart from sport accreditation courses that

DOI: 10.4324/9781003041443-2

may contain a component on teaching, historically, coaches mainly learn to coach informally (Nash & Sproule, 2012). Bruner's (1996) idea of 'folk pedagogies', the unevidenced personal ideas, assumptions and intuition about effective teaching or which approach has what specific effect on a learners' development, comes to mind. To avoid coaching behaviour being 'idiosyncratic' to 'the individual teacher's ability, fancy, whim, mood, needs, purposes, and so on' (Mosston, 1969, p. 2), we suggest that a coaching style must be congruent to the practice task (not to be confused with the Practice Style coaching) meeting the learning need of the player, a central tenet of The Spectrum.

Mosston had four reasons for the genesis of The Spectrum and a fundamental proposition, which we also believe apply to sport coaching:

1. To remove incongruities between sport coaching behaviour and player learning behaviour;
2. To remove incongruities between educational philosophies and the actual behaviour of sport coaches;
3. To bring together information and research about learning to affect sport coaching behaviour; and
4. To bring a focus on analysing the act of sport coaching.

(Mosston, 1969, 1992)

'The fundamental proposition of The Spectrum is that teaching is governed by a single unifying process: decision making. Every act of deliberate teaching is a consequence of a prior decision' (Mosston, 1992, p. 29). The Spectrum enables sport coaches to understand the possible combinations of coaching as teaching decisions by looking at the practice task as a coach-learner relationship. Each option in the coach-learner relationship has a structure of decisions that defines the role of the coach and the learner, which enables then, a coaching style to be described. This will be considered in detail in Chapter 2, where the operational structure of The Spectrum is explained, and consideration is given to the decisions made by the deliberate sport coach as educator before the practice session, in delivery of the practice session, and after the practice session. 'Teaching in all communities is deliberate' (Mosston, 1966b, p. 4).

Applying Mosston's philosophy of deliberate teaching to sport coaching, there are five decisions made by the coach before they go into a practice session:

1. The selection of subject matter;
2. The quantity of an activity;
3. The quality of the performance;
4. The degree of coach involvement; and
5. The degree of player involvement.

In execution of the practice session, five deliberate decisions are made by the coach. During practice, the coach makes decisions about:

1. Organisation;
2. Starting times of activities;
3. Duration of activities;
4. Pace and rhythm of activities; and
5. When to stop an activity.

Five deliberate decisions are made by the coach after a session:

1. Ongoing evaluation of the player;
2. Evaluation of tests of the player;
3. Evaluate the player against group norms (today we might call these standards, competencies, or outcomes);
4. Evaluate the player against the individual's growth and improvement; and
5. Evaluate the team (or squad) in relation to itself, other teams, or 'competition norms'.

The purpose of this decision-making is to be able to maximise individual opportunities for player learning by the sport coach being better equipped to encourage the players' concept of self, with the main purpose being to encourage the player towards becoming a 'fully functioning person'. Here we see again a connection to the contemporary understanding of athlete-centred coaching (Pill, 2018).

A Non-Versus Approach

Ideas about sport coaching models and approaches are often presented as alternatives, in opposition to each other, or in contrast with each other, for example, the cognitive perspective against the ecological perspective, direct versus indirect learning, non-linear versus linear pedagogy. Mosston described this as an education 'tug-of-war', creating fragmentation and separation of ideas as practitioners are asked to choose theories exclusively (Mosston & Ashworth, 2008). Mosston sought a non-versus approach that recognised the value of any style deliberately chosen to enable the task to meet the needs of the learner. The non-versus approach takes coaching beyond idiosyncratic preferences for theories and behaviours by examining the act of coaching as teaching from a structural perspective rather than personal preference (Mosston & Ashworth, 2008). The non-versus approach to The Spectrum logically and sequentially presents a structure providing any coach options in creating coaching as a teaching activity. This is explained in Chapter 2.

It is important to emphasise that The Spectrum does not present any style as good versus bad, as all styles have their place in what we might now call 'quality' coaching. The pedagogical skill of the sport coach is understanding how to use each style to attain a learning effect—in essence knowing the coaching style that best works to achieve the task outcome/s the coach envisages for the identified player/s learning need from that task.

> Fundamental to the structure of The Spectrum is that all teaching styles are beneficial for what they can accomplish; none is more important, or more valuable, than another. Rather than directing one's teaching toward any one behavior, the goal of the Spectrum for teachers is to demonstrate mobility ability. Proficient Spectrum teachers have the ability to shift among the behaviors, as needed, to accommodate learners' needs, content focus, time constraints, and the myriad goals of education.
>
> *(Mosston & Ashworth, 2008, p. 5)*

It is the configuration of deliberate selection of decisions that determines specific coaching behaviours. The Spectrum enables sport coaches to act with enhanced clarity of how to manipulate the deliberate selection of decisions as an intentional pattern of decision-making.

The Spectrum styles thus become tools and The Spectrum a coach's teaching 'toolkit' (Sue-See & Pill, 2018).

Developmental Channels

Sport, like any form of physical play, has the unique ability to deliberately contribute to developmental opportunities in cognitive (decision-making), physical (movement ability), social (interacting with others), emotional (self-control, joy, frustration) and ethical (fair play) development channels. The Spectrum theory postulates that all the developmental channels have an inseparable connection. Every learning experience 'provides opportunities for learners to participate in, and develop, specific human attributes along one or more of the Developmental Channels' (Mosston & Ashworth, 2008, p. 12). As athlete-centred coaches (Pill, 2018), we argue that sport coaches must engage players thought processes in all developmental channels and not simply think of sport as the provision of a form of physical activity.

Mosston adopted a cognitive orientation to The Spectrum theory, believing learning occurs when something triggers us to engage in memory, discovery or creativity. Mosston suggested that the search for answers started with cognitive dissonance, a state of 'needing to know' (Festinger, 1957). This search may involve memory (or recall), a discovery process, a creative process, or all three. When the search or the 'need to know' is over, a response has occurred—an answer, solution, idea or movement pattern has developed (Mosston & Ashworth, 2008).

The Spectrum premise that learning does not 'just happen', that it is planned for and the sport coach must aim and check for player success in making meaning of and further understanding the 'lesson' of a practice session (Mosston & Ashworth, 2008), is like one of the premises of a culture of thinking (Ritchhart, 2015). A culture of thinking is facilitated by visible thinking and learning. Visible thinking and learning are facilitated when sport coaches identify desired results from practice and are explicit with players about what the learning 'standards' are, what the success criteria is, and what the outcomes for each practice session are (Pill & SueSee, 2017; Wiggins & McTighe, 2012). We suggest that a culture of thinking required to develop players as decision-makers necessitates a coach to understand different thinking outcomes relevant to the tasks in a practice session in order to intentionally design appropriate tasks (Ritchhart, 2015).

Enacting The Spectrum as deliberate teaching is also like the idea of learning as Understanding by Design (UBD: Wiggins & McTighe, 2012). UBD asserts that educator planning begins with the identification of the needs of the learner before determining content and teaching style. We suggest that when sport coaches are better able to determine the necessary content of practice sessions pertinent to the players learning needs, there is enhanced player engagement in that learning because of the task and teaching style complementarity to the player/s needs (Pill & SueSee, 2017).

What Does It Mean to Develop 'Thinking Players'?

As the reader has perhaps already ascertained, The Spectrum is a model that attempts to avoid ambiguity by being specific about terminology. The idea of avoiding ambiguity as it relates to the use of the term 'thinking' is also clear when using The Spectrum theory (Mosston & Ashworth, 2008). Developing 'thinking players' in the context of The Spectrum is about a coach considering three cognitive processes: memory, discovery and creativity. When memory is used, it requires the reproduction of knowledge or skills. The discovery process requires players as learners to produce knowledge that was previously unknown to them. It involves a 'search' and cannot be achieved in one cognitive step. Creativity requires the player to produce something that is 'new, different, beyond commonly known or anticipated responses' (Mosston & Ashworth, 2008, p. 48). In summary, this explains that if you are questioning a player who has previously solved the problem in a game, they are likely recalling knowledge retrieved from memory in their response.

We suggest that it is the coach's responsibility to develop 'thinking players' as they must solve the problems of the moment in the game. This is achieved through the creation of experiences that require each type of thinking—recall retrieval (memory), discovery and creativity. For example, there are times when the coach or situation will require the recall or reproduction of a skill or strategy. For such times, it would be appropriate to apply a coaching style that requires the player to use recall from *memory* as the dominant conscious thought process in answering a coach's question/s or in meeting the problem of the task. Such styles exist in the Reproduction cluster of Styles A–E from The Spectrum. When a coach chooses to use these styles, the dominant conscious thought process in the coach's engagement with player/s will require the player/s to recall movement skills, tactics or strategies that they already know. They will recall how to kick, strike or throw a ball, perform a movement pattern (swim, run, jump, throw) or perhaps a known strategy. In many sports, this often occurs in the warm-up phase of a training session.

Regarding discovery thinking, there are three types to acknowledge in The Spectrum: guided discovery, convergent discovery and divergent discovery. Guided discovery involves a sequence of questions progressing to the intended 'discovery'. 'Convergent discovery involves the learner discovering a solution to a problem that has only one solution. Divergent discovery requires the learner to produce multiple solutions to a single question or situation' (SueSee & Pill, 2018, p. 22). The key concept to emphasise is the difference between *memory* and *discovery* processes that are centred around the production of new knowledge or previously unknown knowledge to the player. The creative process shares elements with the discovery process, which overlap, and at times, may seem blurred. The key difference between these two types of thinking is that when a player is using discovery, they are producing solutions to a problem and the coach has set the practice environment for the discovery to be made, whereas creativity brings unknown, possibly unforeseeable performance.

The creative process requires players to produce (again new to them) responses to a problem that is unique or original. The concept of uniqueness is contextual as it is referring to the individual, and it is new to them as they have not known the response before. This is suggested as you cannot truly 'solve' the same problem twice. The first time you solve the problem and the second time you recall the known strategy, tactic or action, or elements of it. The idea that creativity can be viewed as the formation of novel, original and high-quality ideas that are useful and adaptive is not new and has been supported by others (Runco, 2014; Runco & Jaeger, 2012; Stein, 1953; Sternberg & Lubart, 1999). Creative performance emerges when thinking leads to solving performance problems in unusual or unique ways (Santos et al., 2016). Creative practices are inherent in The Spectrum's Production cluster of Styles F–K.

Conclusion: The Sport Coach as Educator

It would be clear to the reader by now that we adopt the position of the sport coach as educator. Jones (2006) positioned the sport coach as educator as a reconceptualisation to highlight sport coaching as an educational enterprise, to foreground the premise that 'coaching is fundamentally intertwined with teaching and learning' (Jones, 2006, p. xiiii). Positioning the sport coach as educator is a departure from the behaviourist perspective of the sport coach as instructor and the rationalist scientific perspective of sport and coaching. Positioning the sport coach as educator accentuates the pedagogic function of the coach's role in creating specific learning experiences through the choice of appropriate coaching (teaching) styles.

Like Jones (2006), we believe that the writings of leading thinkers in education and the theories that they worked with may enrich the practices of coaches, coach educators and coach developers by providing them with increased opportunities to ruminate and reflect upon coaching practice—hence our desire to bring Mosston's Spectrum of Teaching Styles (1966b) to sport coaching. In this chapter we aligned with the idea that sport coaching is teaching as it is an educative endeavour. Bringing Mosston's idea to sport coaching, we suggest that The Spectrum enables a coach to:

- Reflect upon the concept of sport coaching as teaching, and the existence of options (coaching styles) in their coaching;
- Refine their coaching as player learning moments; and
- Revitalise their coaching through the deliberate use of coaching styles to work with players learning needs and to meet specific outcomes.

In bringing Mosston's ideas to the field of sport coaching, we have adapted terminology and nomenclature of The Spectrum to suit the field of sport coaching. In explaining the coaching styles, we have searched for literature from sport coaching that provides empirical support for the coaching style and the educative circumstances that the style is suited to. We have done this so that the work in this book resonates with sport coaches as coaching, while sharing pedagogical similarity with teaching particularly through the field of sport teaching in physical education, is its own field of research and its own academic discipline. Sport coaches who branch out to The Spectrum website and the Teaching Physical Education text explaining The Spectrum for physical education teaching (Mosston & Ashworth, 2008) will find a difference in nomenclature and terminology; however, the premise and anatomy of The Spectrum is unchanged in this book. Throughout each chapter in this book, we frequently refer to the body of work produced by Mosston to draw on explanation and elaboration of ideas. However, since the most recent version of Teaching Physical Education (Mosston & Ashworth, 2008), there is 13 years of additional research to be considered, and the idea of the sport coach as educator and coach education and development as a field of 'teaching' has grown, developed and increased in recognition as a profession and a field of study.

References

Bruner, J. S. (1966). *Toward a theory of instruction*. The Belknap Press of Harvard University Press.
Bruner, J. S. (1996). *The culture of education*. Harvard University Press.
Festinger, L. (1957). *The theory of cognitive dissonance*. Row, Peterson.
Jones, R. (2006). *The sport coach as educator*. Routledge.
Mosston, M. (1966a). *The integration of a style of teaching with the structure of the subject matter*. Paper presented to the National College Physical Education Association of Men, San Diego, CA. (United States).

Mosston, M. (1966b). *Teaching physical education*. Charles E Merrill Publishing.

Mosston, M. (1969). *Notes on the Spectrum of teaching styles*. Paper presented to the second and third general sessions of the 1969 SAPECW Conference, Memphis, TN. (United States).

Mosston, M. (1992). Tug-o-war, no more: Meeting teaching-learning objectives using the Spectrum of teaching styles. *Journal of Physical Education, Recreation, and Dance*, *63*(1), 27–31, 56.

Mosston, M., & Ashworth, S. (2008). *Teaching physical education* (1st online ed.). https://spectrumofteachingstyles.org/assets/files/book/Teaching_Physical_Edu_1st_Online.pdf

Mosston, M., & Mueller, R. (1969). *Mission, omission and submission in physical education*. Presented to the NCPEAM National Conference, Chicago, December 29.

Nash, C., & Sproule, J. (2012). Coaches perceptions of their coach experiences. *International Journal of Sports Science & Coaching*, *43*, 33–52.

Pill, S. (2018). *Perspectives on athlete-centred coaching*. Routledge.

Pill, S., & SueSee, B. (2017). Including critical thinking and problem solving in physical education. *Journal of Physical Education, Recreation & Dance*, *88*(9), 43–49.

Ritchhart, R. (2015). *Creating cultures of thinking: The 8 forces we must master to truly transform our schools*. Danvers, MA: Josey-Bass.

Runco, M. A. (2014). *Creativity: Theories and themes: Research, development, and practice*. Elsevier.

Runco, M. A., & Jaeger, G. J. (2012). The standard definition of creativity. *Creativity Research Journal*, *24*, 92–96.

Santos, S. D. L., Memmert, D., Sampaio, J., & Leite, N. (2016). The spawns of creative behavior in team sports: A creativity developmental framework. *Frontiers in Psychology*, August 26, 2016. https://doi.org/10.3389/fpsyg.2016.01282

Stein, M. I. (1953). Creativity and culture. *The Journal of Psychology*, *36*, 311–322.

Sternberg, R. J., & Lubart, T. I. (1999). The concept of creativity: Prospects and paradigms. *Handbook of Creativity*, *1*, 3–15.

SueSee, B., & Pill, S. (2018). Game-based teaching and coaching as a toolkit of teaching styles. *Strategies*, *31*(5), 21–28.

Wiggins, G., & McTighe, J. (2012). *The Understanding by Design guide to advanced concepts in creating and reviewing units*. ASCD.

2
A SPECTRUM OF COACHING STYLES
Tenets of the Approach

Shane Pill, Brendan SueSee and Joss Rankin

This chapter explores the structure, composition and anatomy of The Spectrum. We initially view The Spectrum in its original form, when it was introduced in 1966. We then articulate the various changes, adaptations and modifications that now represent some future considerations of The Spectrum (proposed by Hewitt, Pill & SueSee, 2020) as to how it may apply specifically to the sport coach as an educator. In this chapter we will directly refer to The Spectrum theory from its genesis, all the way through to its contemporary composition.

From Command to Creativity and Self-Coaching

The Spectrum is appropriately named as it displays teaching styles on a continuum, which involves the progressive removal of pedagogical decisions made by the coach using the first teaching style on The Spectrum—Command Style. This is illustrated in the sequencing of teaching styles that Mosston presented in 1966: Moving from Command to Creativity. When implementing the Command Style, the coach makes all the pedagogical decisions (Figure 2.1: in this diagram, minimum/maximum refers to player control of pedagogical decision-making related to the design and target outcome of the practice task). Typically, like other theories, The Spectrum has progressively evolved from the original conceptual framework developed in 1966. It has been progressively refined as research in relation to teaching and pedagogy has also advanced. Currently, The Spectrum presents as a series of teaching styles from Command to Self-Teaching (Coaching) (Mosston & Ashworth, 2008). Each style offers coaches and players with unique opportunities to develop different learning objectives and outcomes.

From this point forward, Chapter 2 refers to The Spectrum of Teaching Styles (Mosston & Ashworth, 2008) and specifically applies the styles to sport coaching to develop a Spectrum of Coaching Styles. This will be followed by an in-depth explanation of the coaching process (Figure 2.5) as a chain of decision-making (Table 2.1). Each of the styles will then be considered in reference to literature linked to the field of coaching, skill acquisition and motor skill learning. Coaching styles will then be further explored and explained as well as illustrated in practical examples from Chapter 3 to 13.

DOI: 10.4324/9781003041443-3

FIGURE 2.1 The Spectrum is a continuum. It shows minimum learner (player) pedagogical decision-making at Command Style and a progressive 'releasing' of coach pedagogical decision making to the learner (player).

Coaching by Command: Style A

The purpose of the Command Style is to elicit a response from one or more players: fifty pushes, 3 laps of the oval, spend 15 minutes practising lay-ups. When the 'command' is given, it is assumed the desired response occurs. In this style, all decisions are made by the coach, and the role of the player/s is to respond, and the more accurate the player/s response in both time and precision in relation to the coach's directions, the more 'perfect' the session. Coaching directives to both begin the activity and to conclude the movement may include the coaches voice, whistle, or handclapping, to name but a few. It is still assumed, however, that the player is a 'thinking' participant in the coaching session as acceptance and performance of what the coach requests require some cognition—understanding—of what the coach requires. There is also the very deliberate action of precision timing and movement in relation to the coach's cue, and with other player/players if the practice task involves others. Yet, in this style of coaching, the coach is the only one making all the decisions and the learning of 'what' is prescribed to the player/s.

In this style of coaching, Mosston suggested that demonstrations are a critical component as they reveal what is accepted and, therefore, what is not accepted. What this often looks like, in a sport coaching context, is Demonstration—Explanation—Execution—Evaluation (1966, p. 27) This is similar to Tinning's (2010) description of the common physical education method, which consists of demonstrate-explain-perform. In the Command Style, the role of the player is to 'listen, obey and execute' (1966, p. 29). It is important to stress that the Command Style does not represent a harsh or 'mean' form of interacting with the participants (Mosston & Ashworth, 2008). Additionally, this style does not involve punishing or reprimanding the player nor, importantly, taking away the one decision the player is making—to participate in the activity.

Coaching by Task (Practice): Style B

Coaching by Task removes a number of the elements, or decisions by the coach, in relation to the Coaching by Command Style. In this style, once a task has been demonstrated and explained, it assumes the player/s are sufficiently independent to start the movement for several repetitions, or time periods, and then stop when they decide. In this way, the players are making additional decisions in connection to the task without teacher stimulus. The coach's role is to observe the players performance and to provide feedback about the performance.

Coaching by Task is a concept 'avoiding one standard for all' (1966, p. 61). Both quantitative and qualitative differentiation is expected when coaching by task as the 'execution variable' is transferred to the player/s. The player/s behaviour will begin to change as the coach's behaviour changes. Individualised learning and independence from the coach may emerge as responsibility for the performance or movement is shifted to the player/s (Mosston, 1966). Some research suggests Coaching by Task to be the most observed style used by physical education teachers and sport coaches (Hewitt & Edwards, 2013; SueSee et al., 2019; SueSee & Barker, 2019).

Reciprocal Coaching (Peer Coaching): Style C

Reciprocal Coaching transfers 'the feedback variable' to the player/s as it involves the coach entrusting partner observation of the performance and then the partner provision of information about the performance of the task. The partner is placed 'in the role of an observer, corrector, and a reinforcer' (Mosston, 1966, p. 72). Although the partner acts as the observer and provides feedback, the feedback criteria are designed by the coach, who enacts their role through conversations with the observer. This coaching style has benefits for both the coach and players. For instance, the coach has many 'helpers' to provide immediate feedback regarding the performance. The performer of the task receives immediate and ongoing feedback in addition to the opportunity to learn the social skill of receiving and responding to feedback from a peer. The observer learns the skill of giving feedback, assisting a team-mate to improve, and becomes particularly familiar with the routines associated with desirable movements and error identification (Goldberger & SueSee, 2020).

Coaching by Individual Programming (Self-Check): Style D

Individual programming involves the coach setting a task and criteria in relation to the performance. The role of each player is to independently practice the task and make the decisions concerning the variables when, where, how much, and how well. When this coaching style is implemented, the player is now responsible for making additional decisions. These include individual practice, self-assessment, and the ability to correct one's behaviour. However, decisions concerning 'what' will be learnt are still determined by the coach. Importantly, individual programmes still contain specific subject matter, as well as a specific purpose determined by the coach. However, the player has additional self-responsibility for conducting self-assessment and correction of their performance. Therefore, within a session where individual programming occurs, there is a high degree of variability of progress and visibility of progress. It remains imperative that the coach provides clear and specific information about the 'final target' (objective), or what is referred to now as a 'success criteria'.

Small Group Coaching (Inclusion): Style E

This style requires more than simply placing players into groups. Rather, 'it calls for a specific designation of the role of each member in the group' (1966, p. 93). The progression from the previous coaching styles is the addition of role responsibility, such as the group leader to organise the discussion if the coach calls a 'tactical time-out' in play or differentiation of player challenge point/s. Style E may require the coach to design a task that has multiple levels of difficulty or challenge points and the player to select an appropriate level of difficulty. The Inclusion Style identifies that a task or outcome can be completed with a variation in the standard of achievement or degree of difficulty and that the 'success criteria' recognises this. As such, player/s with a range of experience or ability can enter the task at varying levels and complete with 'success' to differing degrees and within their respective challenge points. Byra (2020) suggested that instructional practices (such as Inclusion Style), which provide individuals with the opportunity for greater responsibility and autonomy over individual learning, enhances self-determined motivation.

Coaching by Guided Discovery: Style F

In previous styles, Mosston would suggest that the 'intellectual activity' of the player was 'limited'—'The learner has been in a condition of cognitive acquiescence' (1966, p. 144). Coaching by Guided Discovery aims to place the player/s in a state of cognitive dissonance—a disturbance or irritation deliberately created to prompt the player to seek a solution to remove the disturbance. Mosston proposed that cognitive dissonance leads to inquiry, which leads to discovery.

For this style to achieve its designed objectives, the coach must resist the temptation to provide the answer to the player. The key communicative behaviour of the coach, when using Guided Discovery, is the application of questioning. However, each question posed by the coach is designed to produce a specific response for a deliberate purpose. Determining the sequence of questions is central to the successful use of this style of coaching. The posing of questions is not random but a determined sequence of steps progressing from the general to the specific. The dependency of the player/s expected responses rests upon the coach's design of the questions (Figure 2.2).

Episodes using Guided Discovery are commonly brief and require a series of questions (Mosston & Ashworth, 2008). The questions can only be posed if and when the player does not know the answer to the problem. This point is particularly relevant to this style of coaching, as players are unable to discover something they already know. Research has revealed that some coaches and teachers believe they apply this style during sessions; however, it has been shown

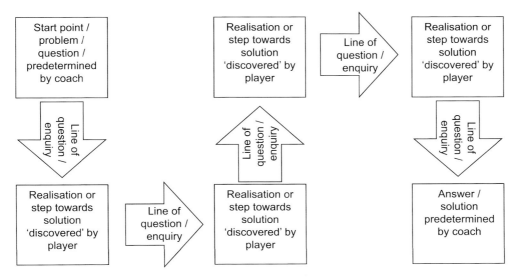

FIGURE 2.2 Guided Discovery: pre-determined start and end point with a line of questioning and exploration designed by the coach.

that the questions are typically open-ended questions rather than a process of discovering new and unknown knowledge (Hewitt, 2015; Hewitt & Edwards, 2013; Mosston & Ashworth, 2008; SueSee et al., 2018, 2019; SueSee & Barker, 2019).

Coaching by Problem Solving (Convergent Discovery): Style G

When Coaching by Problem Solving, the coach remains in control of designing the task and associated problem to solve; however, the expectation is for the player/s to seek out the one correct answer independently. The coach introduces the problem and the player/s receive the problem. While Guided Discovery zones in towards a specific answer or solution, Coaching by Problem Solving involves encouraging the ability to find alternatives, explore options, and then illicit the appropriate solution or answer. There is additional choice and flexibility in player thinking encouraged in coaching by problem solving than offered in Coaching by Guided Discovery, as alternative solutions are entertained in the discussion with the coach. The distinction between Guided Discovery and Convergent Discovery is evident in the previous style (Guided Discovery), whereby the questions were prepared, specifically arranged, and asked by the coach whereas now, in Convergent Discovery, the player/s produce and ask the questions (Mosston & Ashworth, 2008). The distinction from Guided Discovery is that the discovery process, in Convergent Discovery, allows the player/s to work with the possibility of multiple solutions and engage in the questioning process with the coach to reach one solution. As a part of this, however, 'converging' on the previously unknown, yet still pre-determined, answer or solution (designed by the coach) is a paramount outcome. The avenues to the answer may vary in Convergent Discovery (Figure 2.3).

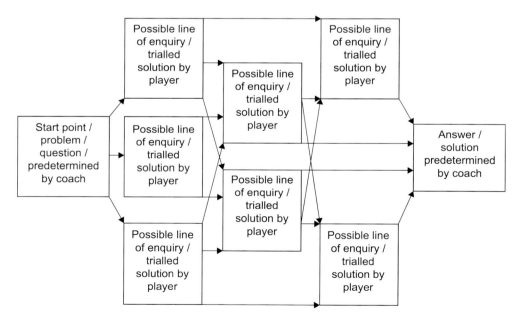

FIGURE 2.3 Convergent Discovery: pre-determined start and end point with a line of questioning and exploration initiated and chosen by the player/s. Various possible lines of inquiry are guided to a singular answer or solution.

Coaching for Creativity (Divergent Discovery): Style H

Coaching for Creativity is distinguished by the player asking the questions stemming from the identified problem, in addition to designing the relevant subject matter to question. As The Spectrum developed, this style emerged as Divergent Discovery. Divergent Discovery begins with a pre-determined starting point with a series of questions. This is followed by the player/s initiating and choosing a pathway to solving the problem, which requires numerous answers, solutions or possibilities. Coaching by Divergent Discovery differs from Convergent Discovery in two ways. First, the problem set by the coach has multiple solutions (not just one solution as in Convergent Discovery) and second, the players will be involved in producing multiple options with the task. Various lines of inquiry encourage creativity in establishing a range of answers or solutions (Figure 2.4).

Player Designed—Coach Supported: Style I

In this style, the coach provides the player/s with a task, topic or problem (skill, movement, strategy, etc.) that the player has limited knowledge of and then proceeds to instruct them to design their own set of learning episodes to develop (or learn the movement) or to solve a problem. The challenge and associated answers to any questions or problems must be unknown; otherwise, the player/s will not be producing new knowledge. The role of the coach, in this style, is to pose questions when they observe discrepancies between what the player is trying to achieve and their decisions or behaviours. The coach must embrace and

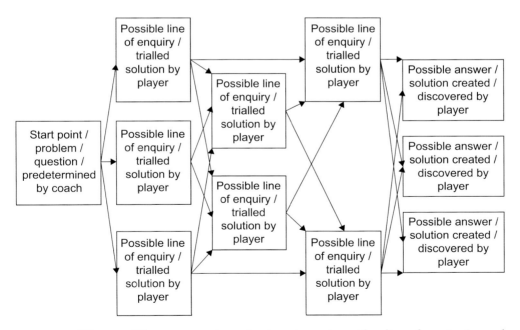

FIGURE 2.4 Divergent Discovery: pre-determined starting point with a line of questioning and exploration initiated and chosen by the player/s. Various avenues of inquiry encourage creativity in establishing a range of answers or solutions.

promote the player's autonomy and self-assessment and avoid providing feedback before the player has self-assessed. Failure to adhere to this coaching behaviour will result in a Practice Style learning experience.

Player Initiated—Coach Supported: Style J

This coaching style is characterised by the player/s 'initiation of, and responsibility for designing the learning experience' (Mosston & Ashworth, 2008, p. 283). It differs from the previous coaching style in that the player chooses the subject matter or topic they wish to learn about. The player will decide when, where and how the coach is involved. This behaviour does not mean that the coach is obsolete in the learning process. Rather, the coach has a significant obligation to initiate questions when discrepancies arise between the player's intent and related actions.

Player Self-Coaching: Style K

In this coaching style, the coach is not present during the session—unless the player/s decides to include them in the process. Otherwise, the player is, essentially, both player and coach and responsible for making all the decisions in connection to the objectives, coaching experiences and even the criteria for success or completion. Arguably, the most recent well-known example of player self-coaching is Kenyan Julius Yego—Javelin Gold Medallist at the World Athletics Championships, 2015. Julius observed online videos to coach himself initially using sharpened sticks he cut from trees. After a period of training in Finland prior to the 2012 Olympics, he returned home to the Rift Valley, stayed connected with his Finnish coach by Skype and continued to use self-coaching through YouTube.

> I do not have a coach. My motivation comes from within. Training without a coach is not an easy thing. . . . I watched YouTube and it really paid off for me, to see the training techniques and skills they are using.
>
> *(Yego in Davis, 2015)*

The Spectrum of Coaching Styles—A Model

When a coach designs a practice session, they need to consider three factors: (1) The Player/Learner; (2) The expectation of player learning; and (3) The pedagogical decisions that the coach will make (Figure 2.5). We suggest these three factors must be considered by the coach to help them choose which coaching style they will use. Designing a practice session without considering where the player/s are positioned in terms of their learning and development could result in the choice of a coaching style incongruent with the desired outcome for the player. If a coach decided they wanted to use Coaching by Problem Solving (Convergent Discovery) Style G without considering the level of knowledge of their players, there could be issues. For example, if the players had been playing for many years and were well aware of strategies to beat the opposition in a two versus one scenario, and the coach asked them to conduct an experiment to conclude what is the best way to beat an opponent, then it is most likely the players will recall a known strategy rather than discover one. In this case, ignoring the knowledge players have could result in a choice of coaching style that is incompatible in that situation, as the coach was intending convergent discovery. As Hewitt et al. (2020) suggested, if a coach does not consider the player's characteristics

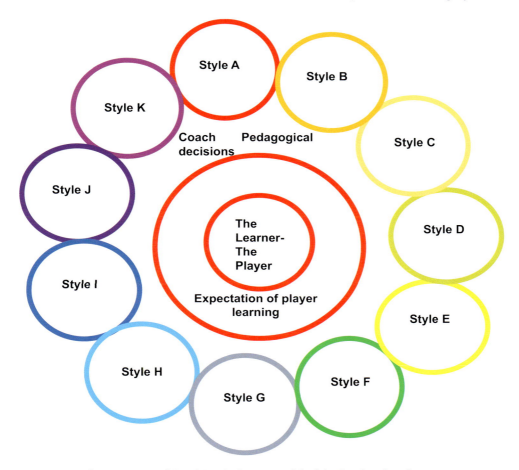

FIGURE 2.5 The Spectrum of Coaching Styles—a model of the Landmark styles.

Source: Adapted from SueSee et al. (2020)

and the desired learning outcomes, and chooses a coaching style incompatible with the decisions required (e.g., asking for creativity when players know the answer), then the result is likely not achieved and the likelihood of effective learning by the player is diminished.

Clusters of Teaching Styles

The Spectrum is organised into two clusters. Styles A–E represent Reproduction styles and Styles F–K represent Production styles. In the Reproduction cluster of styles, all styles have in common some form of modelling of the task or task elements by the coach and practising the modelled task by the player/s. In the Production cluster of teaching styles, all styles have in common some degree of player-driven production of new knowledge or capability. This concept of Reproduction and Production clusters of coaching styles is based on a model of cognition that suggests there are 'three basic processes of thinking: memory, discovery, and creativity' (Mosston & Ashworth, 2008, p. 48). Memory involves the process of recalling or reproducing past knowledge or skills. Discovery engages players in the process of the production of new knowledge (previously unknown to the player) via the solving of problems or tasks where the solution is unknown. Lastly, creativity 'refers to responses that are perceived as unique or original—something that is new' (Mosston & Ashworth, 2008, p. 48). More simply when coaches ask players to reproduce known skills, tactics, strategies, or movements, the players are using memory. Conversely, when the coach sets a task where the players do not know the answer or solution, then the player will be using discovery or creativity. These elements will be explained and illustrated with practical examples in following chapters.

Canopy Coaching Styles

When a coaching style is implemented with an approximation of all its relative characteristics, objectives and outcomes, however, with slight deviations and differences that are not quite representative of that style but are an approximate of it (Styles A–K are known as the Landmark styles), it is referred to as a Canopy Design of the style. The term Canopy Design is also applied where two styles may have blended into a coaching episode. The application of the label Canopy Design, therefore, communicates that an intentional modification has been made to the structure of a coaching style. This will be examined in Chapters 14 and 15. It is important to emphasise, in line with The Spectrums non-versus philosophy, that a Canopy Design is not inferior to, or better than, the A–K Styles; it is just a variation created by the coach based on the desired outcome and needs or characteristics of the players (Figure 2.5).

Episodic Coaching

All coaching sessions can be conceived, planned, and implemented as a series of intentionally designed teaching episodes. This is known as episodic coaching. Episodic coaching may be a sequence of the same coaching style, or the sequence of episodes may represent different coaching styles. A whole coaching session of production cluster episodes would make no sense as players are required to recall known skills and strategies during games. Similarly, an entire session of Reproduction cluster episodes would not benefit players who may at times be required to solve new problems in a game. This is one reason the non-versus approach is so important as one coaching style cannot address all the needs of all the players all the time. Thinking about a practice session as a series of teaching episodes brings a thorough scrutiny onto the content of practice beginning with the learning needs of the player/s. Episodic coaching will be explained in detail in Chapter 14.

An Epistemological Chain

Grecic and Collins (2013) used the phrase *epistemological chain* to describe a logical decision-making framework for planning, reflection, and review of coaching. Epistemology is concerned with knowledge, how it is acquired, its scope, and nature. An epistemological chain links a coach's philosophy, belief and understanding of learning and how it occurs, and practice of coaching. We argue that The Spectrum provides an epistemological chain from belief and understanding of the 'how' and 'what' of learning to the pre-impact planning phase of a coaching task and its intended learning outcome, the impact delivery of the task on the player's learning, and the post-impact reflection and review of the task. We suggest this is provided by the *axiom of a teaching style*. The 'anatomy of any style' of teaching is described by Mosston (1981) as three sets that represent the sequence of professional judgement and decision-making of teaching: pre-impact, impact and post-impact decision-making. The three sets provide what Mosston (1981) called an *axiom* about the act of teaching, which is that **teaching is a chain of decision-making** (Table 2.1; Figure 2.6).

TABLE 2.1 The Spectrum as an epistemological chain—teaching is a chain of decision-making.

Epistemological chain

Belief about knowledge and learning	Non-Versus—select the coaching style that will invite the corresponding player learning that is identified as the objective of the task
	Deliberate—the coach intentionally creates the climate for player learning
Pre-impact (planning)	- Objective of a coaching episode
	- Subject matter to teach
	- Selection of coaching style to teach content
Impact (delivery)	- Implementation of coaching episode adhering to coaching style
	- Observation of players and gathering information about performance of the players during the coaching episode
Post-impact (reflection and review)	- Reflecting on the information gathered about player performance during the impact phase
	- Feedback to players
	- Assessing alignment of the teaching style and player achievement of the objective of the coaching episode

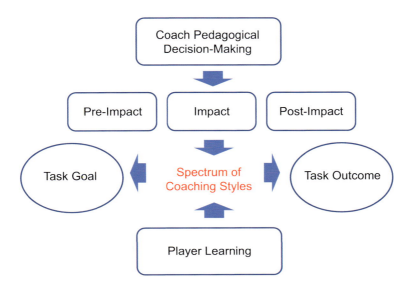

FIGURE 2.6 The coaching process.

Professional judgement and decision-making appear central to coach practice design and implementation. However, it has been identified that many coaches are prone to draw on theoretically naive and uncritical reflections to inform their coaching (Abraham & Collins, 2015). To identify coaching practice rhetoric alignment with the reality of the implementation necessitates going beyond what can be described by the coach to what is critically observed and a consideration of the process of decision-making that led to what is observed (Abraham & Collins, 2015; Collins, Carson & Collins, 2016; Hewitt, 2015). The Spectrum provides a means of the analysis of coach alignment between assumed coaching style and learning environment (Hewitt, 2015). This will be looked at in more detail in Chapter 17.

We agree with Abraham and Collins (2011) that there is persistent theoretical posturing about the 'best' model for coaching practice; however, professional judgement and decision-making can be a unifying focus for sport coaching pedagogy. The Spectrum provides a framework through which to achieve a unifying focus through alignment of the cluster of coaching styles used through a practice session to the dynamic and complex demands inherent in each coaching episode learning objective. Furthermore, The Spectrum offers the potential for coach development of and for 'thinking about their thinking about' coaching, or commonly what is referred to as *metacognition: the active control of their cognitive process of professional judgement and decision-making* (Abraham, Collins & Martindale, 2006). As an epistemological chain (Table 2.1), The Spectrum provides an integration of declarative and procedural coaching knowledge. Collins et al. (2016) explained that the professional judgement and decision-making of coaching relies on a coach's understanding of 'what needs to be done' (declarative knowledge) and 'how it needs to be done' (procedural knowledge), which links back to the coach intentions: that is, knowing why (declarative knowledge) instructional action(s) should be taken in response to the dynamics and complexity of a learning situation (Figure 2.6).

Conclusion

This chapter has outlined the basic tenets of The Spectrum and how it applies to sport coaching. The chapter was specifically written to provide the reader with the introductory knowledge, principles, models and overall philosophy of The Spectrum so that the reader not only understands the concepts in isolation but additionally in the specific context of sport coaching. Some of the concepts presented may challenge coaches' understanding; however, we remind that the ideas have mostly been presented without elaboration. That is because in the following chapters we will seek to 'bring to life' each coaching style by providing sports specific applications. Further to this, in the following chapters we discuss in greater detail the numerous ways each style can contribute to the development of the player beyond just the physical/psychomotor domain.

References

Abraham, A., & Collins, D. (2011). Taking the next step: Ways forward for coaching science. *Quest*, 63(4), 366–384.
Abraham, A., & Collins, D. (2015). *Professional judgement and decision making in sport: Coaching: To jump or not to jump*. International Conference on Naturalistic Decision Making 2015, McLean, VA. http://eprints.leedsbeckett.ac.uk/2256/1/AbrahamCollins042615.pdf
Abraham, A., Collins, D., & Martindale, R. (2006). The coaching schematic: Validation through expert coach consensus. *Journal of Sport Sciences*, 24(6), 549–564.

Byra, M. (2020). Inclusion style of teaching: Student autonomy and responsibility. In B. SueSee, M. Hewitt, & S. Pill (Eds.), *The Spectrum of teaching styles in physical education* (pp. 116–127). Routledge.

Collins, L., Carson, H. J., & Collins, D. (2016). Metacognition and professional judgment and decision making in coaching: Importance, application and evaluation. *International Sport Coaching Journal*, *3*(3), 355–361.

Davis, S. (2015). The javelin thrower who won gold at the World Championships learned how to throw from YouTube videos. *Business Insider Australia*, August 27, 2015.

Goldberger, M., & SueSee, B. (2020). Effects of the reciprocal teaching style on skill acquisition, verbal interaction and ability to analyse in fifth grade children in physical education. In B. SueSee, M. Hewitt, & S. Pill (Eds.), *The Spectrum of teaching styles in physical education* (pp. 116–127). Routledge.

Grecic, D., & Collins, D. (2013). The epistemological chain: Practical applications in sports. *Quest*, *65*(2), 151–168.

Hewitt, M. (2015). *Teaching styles of Australian tennis coaches: An exploration of practices and insights using Mosston and Ashworth's Spectrum of teaching styles*. Unpublished Doctoral dissertation. University of Southern Queensland, Springfield, Australia.

Hewitt, M., & Edwards, K. (2013). Observed teaching styles of junior development and club professional tennis coaches in Australia. *ITF Coaching and Sport Science Review*, *59*, 6–8.

Hewitt, M., Pill, S., & SueSee, B. (2020). Future considerations on the spectrum. In B. SueSee, M. Hewitt, & S. Pill (Eds.), *The Spectrum of teaching styles in physical education* (pp. 166–177). Routledge.

Mosston, M. (1966). *Teaching physical education*. Charles E Merrill Publishing.

Mosston, M. (1981). *Teaching physical education* (2nd ed.). Charles E Merrill Publishing.

Mosston, M., & Ashworth, S. (2008). *Teaching physical education* (1st online ed.). Spectrum Institute for Teaching and Learning. https://spectrumofteachingstyles.org/index.php?id=16

SueSee, B., & Barker, D. M. (2019). Self-reported and observed teaching styles of Swedish physical education teachers. *Curriculum Studies in Health and Physical Education*, *10*(1), 34–50.

SueSee, B., Edwards, K., Pill, S., & Cuddihy, T. (2018). Self-reported teaching styles of Australian senior physical education teachers. *Curriculum Perspectives*, *38*(1), 41–54.

SueSee, B., Edwards, K., Pill, S., & Cuddihy, T. (2019). Observed teaching styles of senior physical education teachers in Australia. *Curriculum Perspectives*, *39*, 47–57.

SueSee, B., Hewitt, M., & Pill, S. (Eds.). (2020). *The Spectrum of teaching styles in physical education*. Routledge.

Tinning, R. (2010). *Pedagogy and human movement: Theory, practice, research*. Routledge.

3
COACHING BY COMMAND

Style A

Shane Pill, Brendan SueSee, Joss Rankin and Mitch Hewitt

Coaching by Command is characterised by an expectation of a predicted response or performance. It is often associated in the coaching literature as an 'authoritative' style of coaching. This may be because the role of the coach is to make all decisions about the teaching and learning environment, and the role of the player is to follow those decisions as instructed. Coaching by Command may become or be perceived as if it is the only style or dominant style of a coach, as opposed to a style used for specific teaching-learning objectives. Also, we recognise that Command Style instruction is often associated with 'progressive part pedagogy' colloquially referred to as 'skill and drill', but more accurate is 'drill to skill'. Command Style coaching is not limited though to 'drill to skill' as it can also be applied to a 'whole task' practice, such as a match simulation or game form practice of 'simplified' yet still representative of the 'full game' as the logic of play is retained, game practice.

We suggest that Coaching by Command is suitable for the following types of teaching-learning objectives:

- To reproduce a technical model of performance;
- To achieve a synchronised performance, such as synchronised swimming, ballet, or line dancing;
- To teach a historical 'data base' of standard moves in a required form or pattern, such as a martial art poomsae or kata;
- To achieve specific aesthetics standards, such as in a marching drill performance;
- To develop consistency of responses or movements; and
- To instil safety procedures, such as the 'shooting line' and 'safety line' procedures in coaching javelin, discus, shot, archery and shooting.

Coaching by Command might also be called precision practice, cued response, or imitation practice (Mosston & Ashworth, 2008) or explicit instruction. We suggest that sports requiring accuracy, synchronicity and precision in body shape, body position/s and movement sequences require a coach at some point to use Coaching by Command with player/s. The use within those scenarios is determined by the objectives the coach has determined as suitable to the tight alignment

DOI: 10.4324/9781003041443-4

between stimulus (command) and a response (player/s behaviour). We need to emphasise that the pedagogical use of Coaching by Command is not the use of commands for authority and disciplining of behaviours. Coaching by Command is a pedagogical choice for effective learning.

Explicit instruction has been explained using Anderson's (1982) theory of cognitive skill acquisition. Smeeton et al. (2005) explained that Anderson's theory is that knowledge is initially stored in a declarative (to know) form and interpreted using if-then statements. The prescriptive nature of explicit instruction is believed to accelerate early learning by providing a framework for subsequent knowledge development and reducing the time spent searching for relevant information. Coaching by Command may therefore be particularly useful during what has been called *skill establishment*. Skill establishment refers to the structures or representations of movement on which other factors such as emotion, information perception, and attentional focus act. Skill establishment is not the same as skill level, which is a measurable performance outcome. Skill establishment encompasses processes concerning motor responses developed over time through repeated training experiences (Carson & Collins, 2015). Relevant to Coaching by Command, research has found that 'verbal information in addition to visual cues enhances perceptual representation and retention of modelled activities to improve task reproduction capabilities' (Janelle et al., 2003, p. 825). Studies have shown that learning is enhanced if feedback is provided after good, rather than poor, trials (Chiviacowsky & Wulf, 2007). An important consideration for coaches is that a player's existing skills play a role in the player understanding the instructions or feedback and performing the desired movement (Hodges & Franks, 2002; Janelle et al., 2003).

Combining verbal cueing with modelling has shown skill acquisition benefits (Doody, Bird & Ross, 1985; Janelle et al., 2003; Landin, 1994; Masser, 1993; Roach & Burwitz, 1986). For example, research by Janelle et al. (2003) found:

> The beneficial aspects of verbal cueing extend beyond sequencing aspects of motor skills, permeating not only the outcome of the movement for a discrete motor task, but also the critical form necessary for skill reproduction. In addition, the augmented information provided through verbal cues apparently enhanced information processing beyond that which could be achieved through the sole provision of visual cues.
>
> (p. 835)

The mechanism by which verbal cues assist skill acquisition is the directing of a player's attention towards what to pay attention to in a movement performance. From a cognitive perspective, 'commands' are there to condition a response by a player. This is achieved by constraining selective attention[1] by directing a player's focus on assumed to be important task cues. 'Commands' assist retention of understanding by reducing subjective cognitive load[2] (Janelle et al., 2003). From an ecological perspective, visual and verbal cues provided by a coach might be considered constraints on players opportunity to behave and in doing so help their learning of affordance[3] recognition. The benefit of an information constraint provided to the player/s by coach visual or verbal commands is that the player/s have information from which to query their performance.

Implementation of Coaching by Command

The following steps describe how to use Coaching by Command with deliberate intention, through the pre-impact, impact, and post-impact set.

The Pre-Impact Set (Planning)

The coach decides the specific teaching-learning task, requiring the behaviour of the player that occurs in Coaching by Command and sequencing the expectations of the player through the coaching episode. The teaching-learning behaviour is determined by the objective or outcome the coach wishes to achieve.

The Impact Set (Implementation)

The teaching implementation begins by the coach clearly outlining roles and expectations on player/s. The coach establishes the 'subject matter' to be mastered by demonstration to the player/s often supported by an aligned series of key cues for performance, establishing a model for the performance and the success criteria. Logistics, procedures and behaviour expectations are then identified by the coach. Now, the player/s can begin the activity governed by the command signals, movement cues and other feedback mechanisms favoured by the coach.

The Post-Impact Set (Feedback to the Player/s)

At the end of the practice, feedback is provided to the player/s about the performance of the task and how well the player/s followed the command signals.

A useful way of thinking about a Coaching by Command teaching episode is as follows:

- Demonstrate
- Explain
- Execution-Practice
- Evaluate (feedback)

(Mosston, 1981)

All teaching-learning decisions are made by the coach and conveyed by the coach to the players. Players listen, comply, and execute. A metaphor for Coaching by Command may be 'instructor'.

Being able to instruct a player what to do, how to do it, and how to do it well is a defining role of a coach (Hodges & Franks, 2002). When Coaching by Command, it is assumed that a movement template provided as part of pre-practice information is important for learning. Whether optimal or stylised movement patterns exist and are beneficial or limiting to player performance in some sports is a debate in the field of skill acquisition. According to some theories of skill acquisition, attention to a modelled action is necessary for the representation of the movement in memory to serve as a reference for movement performance (Hodges & Franks, 2002), in particular, the representation of the biomechanical markers of performance that have been cued through verbal information from the coach. This does not imply the need to always require a player/s to exactly replicate a movement model but may involve using the movement model as a template to find out what works and does not work for the player. However, what is inherent in Coaching by Command is a demonstration and explicit feedback from the coach. Individual difference is not invited in so far as the coach decides what is to be learnt, how it is to be learnt and what success looks like (Mosston & Ashworth, 2008). That does not mean the coach must demonstrate; it means the coach must decide who should provide the demonstration and what information should be presented (Williams & Hodges, 2005).

Demonstrations

In skill acquisition literature, consideration of demonstrations often comes under the banner of observational learning or imitation. It is assumed that observation can result in new movement behaviours (Horn & Williams, 2004)—in other words, learning. However, observational learning may not align well to situations where Coaching by Command is used for the purpose of retrieval and refinement of existing (learned) performance skills and abilities: in other words, situations where the player/s know what to do but haven't reached the performance standard criteria or level yet (Ste-Marie et al., 2012). From a cognition perspective, providing player/s with an image of performance is an important element in building a cognitive representation to guide performance understanding and expectation. Considering an ecological perspective on performance, a player's cognitive representation may be an individual player constraint on performance and so enhancing that mental representation should improve performance. Also, observing the relative motion of body parts in relation and configuration to each other may provide the player salient information constraints for the emergence of a movement pattern in the early stages of skill learning, and later may provide salient information about the required dynamics that constrain the movement pattern for movement efficiency and effectiveness (Al-abood, Davids & Bennett, 2001; Ste-Marie et al., 2012). From whichever skill acquisition theory is considered, essential is the thought that demonstrations provide a player/s information specifying what the player/s should do. Demonstrations in a Coaching by Command context are a pedagogical consideration about the intent or purpose of the coach for the player/s observing the demonstration.

Feedback

Feedback is a factor well considered in sport coaching research. It is sometimes referred to as knowledge of results (information about the movement outcome) or knowledge of performance (information about the movement pattern). It is sometimes referred to as augmented feedback or extrinsic feedback provided to the player/s, and intrinsic feedback obtained by a player kinaesthetically by observation of the movement or by feel of the movement. In addition to the volume and accumulation of feedback to provide attentional focus on an aspect of performance, the affective quality of feedback, timing and frequency can affect learning.

In a Coaching by Command scenario, feedback provides guidance to a player/s learning. Research suggests that feedback focussed on movement effect, or an external focus, has been shown to enhance learning compared to feedback focussed on how to control one's body movements, or an internal focus (Shea & Wulf, 1999; Wulf et al., 2002). Research on frequency of feedback is less clear as to whether frequent external focussed feedback or less frequent is more effective in promoting learning (Wulf et al., 2010). However, feedback precision and the scheduling of feedback have an influence on learning (Abernathy, Masters & Zachry, 2008; Chiviacowsky & Wulf, 2007). Feedback after relatively good trials has been shown to result in greater intrinsic motivation and greater perceived competence than after poor trials (Badami et al., 2011).

Using Coaching by Command assumes either a need for efficiency or speed of learning, or routine consistency—consistency of group (synchronisation) or an individual and their movement patterns (technique).

Examples of Coaching by Command

Example 1—Outdoor Pursuits (Rock Climbing)

Outdoor pursuits often require individuals to apply a range of interpersonal and intrapersonal skills in combination with technical competencies. Adventurous activities such as rock climbing, hiking, kayaking and mountain biking are often used as a medium in which learning is designed (Froude & Polley, 2011). Many of these activities have specific techniques that must be performed by participants to ensure the safety of themselves and other group members, and as such Command Style can be applied to ensure reproduction of these techniques. One example is the instruction of the belaying technique that is used to control the climber's safety rope in a top-rope climbing setting. Before participants begin rock climbing, an instructor demonstrates tie in procedures, safety checks and the belaying technique, including required communication. The instructor selects a participant or assistant instructor to tie in as a climber for the demonstration, conducts required safety checks and begins the required communication. As an example of the Command Style, Table 3.1 outlines the set of instructions to 'Command' participants on the correct method for belaying. Although the exact wording of the instruction varies between

TABLE 3.1 Applying Coaching by Command to delivering instructions for how to belay whilst a climber is top rope in a rock-climbing situation.

Instructions for belayer	*Example of common language when coupled with the demonstration*
Step 1. Position one hand high on the climber's line and the other hand close to the belay device on the live end of rope.	Begin in ready position
Step 2. Brush knuckles of hands past each other by taking rope through the belay device.	Take in with a 'V'
Step 3. Lock the live end of rope off by dropping your hand with the live end of rope to your knee.	Lock to the knee
Step 4. Take your hand from the climbers' line and place this on the live end of rope, which is still in locked position, next to the belay device	Reset whilst locked with a one . . .
Step 5. Slide your hand that is at your knee up along the rope, with the rope still in locked position, until it is next to your hand by the belay device.	two . . .
Step 6. Return the hand next to the belay device to its original position high on the climbers' line of rope. Continue to repeat so that the line remains tight without slack.	three.
Note. The live end of rope must always be held; keep the rope tight with the climber and unless taking rope in, keep the rope in a locked position with two hands on the live end of rope until the climber begins to move again.	Remember that you must always hold the live end of rope; keep the rope tight and lock your climber off if they aren't moving.

instructors, the actions remain constant and in each version the requirement is for exact replication by participants with direct supervision and feedback for adjustment of performance provided by the instructor. Exact replication for the purpose of safe participation is required to meet duty of care and risk management expectations associated with this sport.

Although this example does not encompass every component of the climbing, belaying and lowering involved in this activity, it does demonstrate how the Coaching by Command can be effectively applied to ensure exact replication for the purpose of safe participation. The pre-impact set was undertaken by the instructor without any input from participants to determine what instruction and demonstration would be given, how participants would perform the task and the role of the instructor in observation and feedback. The impact set allows participants to perform the required technique under close observation and the post-impact set provides an opportunity for any feedback to be given by the instructor. It is important to note that if safety is compromised at any point, an instructor will intervene to prompt an adjustment. This is a good example highlighting the value of Coaching by Command with regards to safety. The person belaying cannot decide on the speed of their actions as the rope near the climber would get too loose. If this happened, and the climber slipped, an injury could result. Thus, by the instructor deciding the speed of movement by counting or cues, safety objectives are also met.

Example 2—Baseball

In the sport of baseball, Coaching by Command is sometimes seen during warm-up sessions. The team will be asked to form one line on the foul line. All runners will then run 90 feet (or 27 m—the distance between 1st and 2nd base). They will repeat this back to the foul line. The coach will use a clap signal to cue them to begin each run-through. Depending on the size of the team and how much scrutiny they wish to place the players under, the coach may decide to have more than one line. This allows the coach to watch each player closer and be more time efficient than if each player did it one at a time. By everyone doing it together (or at least in large groups), the coach may be able to detect injuries or lack of effort.

Coaching by Command can also be applied to coaching base running. A coach may instruct a player to stand on first base and take their lead. He may then say he wants the player/base runner to take their shuffle steps (2–3 steps) towards second base and on the coach's signal (usually a clap) they will steal second. If there is no clap, the base runner returns quickly to a safe proximity of first base. Again, this can be done in groups or individually. This choice of Coaching by Command is cued in this situation as the coach may wish to see the movement as demonstrated repeated by the players. The coach wants the players to take a three-step lead (always watching the pitcher), get set with feet spread at an appropriate width, take their three shuffle/side steps towards second and steal (or go back to first) on the cue (the clap). This coaching episode has two cues—the cue to begin to take your lead and the clap to steal. The Coaching by Command Style allows the coach to reduce the other cues (in this case a real pitcher) and focus just on the movement.

Example 3—Cricket

Mosston and Ashworth (2008) suggested that one reason for choosing to use Command Style is 'to elicit an immediate response so that certain tasks can be learned accurately and in a short period of time' (p. 82). Due to the very challenging nature of the laws of bowling, it would be very easy for the beginner player to feel frustration at the lack of success. The bowling action is unique and challenging for beginners, and the development of poor bowling mechanics can lead to injury (Cronin & Portus, 2014; Stretch, 2003).

In the scenario that follows, Coaching by Command may allow the player to experience some success (even if it is just the 'basic' movement pattern of bowling) in a very short amount of time. In the pre-impact set the coach would decide to teach the players to bowl and identify the cues (commands) which they will use. In the impact set the coach may begin the episode by explaining that the player is going to learn how to bowl. The coach would explain the content (the cues or steps to bowl) and then the behaviour (following on-cue or the coach's voice and actions). The coach would demonstrate the whole task (also known as the delivery stride), which gets the bowler side-on to bowl in the delivery stride. The demonstration would involve the coach standing facing the player's, first with a ball in their right hand, and feet together (ball in left hand for a left hander). The coach would then say:

Step 1—Lift right leg and right hand at the same time or lift the right leg and 'bite the apple'.
Step 2—Put right leg down and face foot and turn out/away from body slightly. Right arm comes down at the same time as right foot.
Step 3—Lift left knee up and grab the sky with left hand.
Step 4—Pull down with left hand so it swings beside left hip and step towards batter with left foot.
Step 5—Twist torso as you bowl to batter, brush your right ear with right arm and put right hand in left pocket.

The coach would then say, 'Let's try this but you will move when I move and copy the movement and the commands I give. Everyone begins with their feet together and arms by their sides. Ok, (1) lift right leg and arm and 'bite the apple'. (2) Down with right and right. (3) Up with left and left. (4) Grab the sky and pull down. (5) Twist and deliver'. The post-impact set would involve giving feedback to the players about the performance of the task and the players role in following the coach's decisions (Mosston & Ashworth, 2008). However, this feedback may also be self-evident to the player as they see they are not doing the same as everyone else, and the player by imitation tries to self-correct. Whilst self-correction is not one of the elements of the Command Style, no coach would discourage a player realising and self-correcting. If a player notices they are not doing the same thing as everyone else in the group but does not change, the coach can ask (for example): 'Mary, do you have the same leg and arm up? Please have the same leg and arm up'.

By Coaching by Command in this episode, the coach can see who is struggling with the movement mechanics. The synchronicity of the movement highlights those 'who can, and those who cannot'. For the learner, there is the possibility of some form of 'immediate' success of 'getting' the nascent movement pattern of the delivery stride.

Example 4—Tennis

Command Style coaching is defined by the coach making all the decisions and the player responding in a synchronised and precise manner. This style is designed to produce precision performance while reproducing a predicted response. Practice and performance on cue while adhering to a controlled set pace and rhythm is essential. For this example—which reflects on tennis—an assumption is made—with novice tennis players—who possess no or very limited knowledge of elements in the psychomotor domain (or the technical movements related to various tennis strokes). For instance, the continental grip—which is used during the performance of the serve—can be practiced—in a step-by-step instructional manner, using Command Style coaching. The purpose behind the use of the style is to begin to consolidate in the player's memory the precise position of the player's dominant hand holding the racquet. To buttress the skill, the coach may stimulate a coaching episode, which is performed in a synchronised (and on cue) learning episode, followed by a controlled 'performance' episode, with the coach determining the 'finishing' time for the skill. The performance is orchestrated and synchronised. The role of the player is to exactly reproduce and replicate an anticipated response or performance so that the motor skill of serving using a continental grip may be practised.

In another example related to tennis, the coach may perform an orchestrated demonstration of the service action. In this way, the coach moderates and controls all elements of the swing shape and motor performance of this serve. In this example, the player copies and replicates in a synchronised performance the precise and exact actions of the coach. In this example, Command Style coaching provides the player with both a visual and relevant explanatory example of a complex movement—the tennis serve.

Conclusion

Coaching by Command is a teaching style focused on the coach and the subject matter they wish to teach or reinforce (Mosston, 1966). The role of the player/s is to copy and 'remember'. The purpose of the commands is to direct the player's attention to what the coach assesses to be the critical components of the movement behaviour and retention of the observed skill. Verbal instructions have been found to be beneficial to the sequencing of skills in a task performance (Doody et al., 1985; Roach & Burwitz, 1986; McCullagh, Stiehl & Weiss, 1990). Beginners may particularly benefit from visual and verbal modelling (Weiss, 1983), and adults skill learning has been found to benefit from verbal cues (Meaney, 1994). Historically, 'high levels of technical instruction, feedback, reinforcement and supportive behaviour have been associated with higher player perceptions of competence, enjoyment, self-esteem and self-confidence' (Borrie & Knowles, 2003, p. 189). Whilst sometimes maligned as authoritative, this chapter has highlighted numerous ways Coaching by Command can meet an array of needs from safety, precision movement to meeting the requirements of beginners learning complex skills, to name but a few. As with all styles on The Spectrum, Coaching by Command has its place and value for coaches and players.

Notes

1. Selective attention is the process of selectively giving our attention to stimuli in our environment. It is theorised that we have limited capacity for attention and so learning to attend to what is most relevant or important prevents an information 'bottleneck' and leads to faster and more accurate decision-making more often.
2. Cognitive load refers to the amount of information that the working memory can 'handle'. Working memory is theorised as having limited capacity for information, and so instruction should avoid overloading working memory by focusing explicitly on 'what matters'.
3. Affordances are visual cues that provide the viewer with an 'intuitive' indication of possibilities for action.

References

Abernathy, B., Masters, R. S. W., & Zachry, T. (2008). Using biomechanical feedback to enhance skill learning and performance. In Y. Hong & R. Bartlett (Eds.), *Routledge handbook of biomechanics and human movement science* (pp. 581–593). Routledge.

Al-abood, S. A., Davids, K., & Bennett, S. J. (2001). Specificity of task constraints and effects of visual demonstrations and verbal instructions in directing learners' search during skill acquisition. *Journal of Motor Behavior, 33*(3), 295–305.

Anderson, J. R. (1982). Acquisition of cognitive skill. *Psychological Review, 89,* 369–403.

Badami, R., VaezMousavi, M., Wulf, G., & Namazizadeh, M. (2011). Feedback after good versus poor trials affects intrinsic motivation. *Research Quarterly for Exercise and Sport, 82*(2), 360–364.

Borrie, A., & Knowles, Z. (2003). Coaching science and soccer. In T. Reilly & A. M. Williams (Eds.), *Science and soccer* (2nd ed., pp. 187–197). Routledge.

Carson, H. J., & Collins, D. (2015). The fourth dimension: A motoric perspective on the anxiety-performance relationship. *International Review of Sport and Exercise Psychology, 9*(1), 1–21.

Chiviacowsky, S., & Wulf, G. (2007). Feedback after good trials enhances learning. *Research Quarterly for Exercise and Sport, 78*(2), 40–47.

Cronin, J., & Portus, M. (2014). Part 1: Biomechanics, injury surveillance and predictors of injury for cricket fast bowlers. *Strength and Conditioning Journal, 36*(4), 65–74.

Doody, S. G., Bird, A. M., & Ross, D. (1985). The effect of verbal and visual models on acquisition of a timing task. *Human Movement Science, 4,* 271–281.

Froude, C., & Polley, S. (2011). *Outdoor education: Foundations for tertiary and senior secondary education* (2nd ed.). Impact Publishing.

Hodges, N. J., & Franks, I. M. (2002). Modelling coaching practice: The role of instruction and demonstration. *Journal of Sports Sciences, 20*(10), 793–811.

Horn, R. R., & Williams, A. M. (2004). Observational learning: Is it time we took another look? In A. M. Williams & N. J. Hodges (Eds.), *Skill acquisition in sport: Research, theory and practice* (pp. 175–206). Routledge.

Janelle, C. M., Champenoy, J. D., Coombes, S. A., & Mousseau, M. B. (2003). Mechanisms of attentional cueing during observational learning to facilitate motor skill acquisition. *Journal of Sports Science, 21*(10), 825–838.

Landin, D. (1994). The role of verbal cues in skill learning. *Quest, 46,* 299–313.

Masser, L. S. (1993). Critical cues help first-grade students' achievement in handstands and forward rolls. *Journal of Teaching in Physical Education, 12,* 301–312.

McCullagh, P., Stiehl, J., & Weiss, M. R. (1990). Developmental modelling effects on the quantitative and qualitative aspects of motor performance acquisition. *Research Quarterly for Exercise and Sport, 61,* 344–350.

Meaney, K. S. (1994). Developmental modeling effects on the acquisition, retention, and transfer of a novel motor task. *Research Quarterly for Exercise and Sport, 65*(1), 31–39.

Mosston, M. (1966). *Teaching physical education*. Merrill.

Mosston, M. (1981). *Teaching physical education* (2nd ed.). Merrill.

Mosston, M., & Ashworth, S. (2008). *Teaching physical education* (1st online ed.). https://spectrumofteachingstyles.org/assets/files/book/Teaching_Physical_Edu_1st_Online.pdf

Roach, N. K., & Burwitz, L. (1986). Observational learning in motor skill acquisition: The effect of verbal directing cues. In J. Watkins, T. Reilly, & L. Burwitz (Eds.), *Sport science: Proceedings of the VIII Commonwealth and International Conference on Sport, Physical Education, Dance, Recreation and Health* (pp. 349–354). London.

Shea, C. H., & Wulf, G. (1999). Enhancing motor learning through external-focus instructions and feedback. *Human Movement Science, 18*(4), 553–571.

Smeeton, N. J., Williams., A. M., Hodges, N. J., & Ward, P. (2005). The relative effectiveness of various instructional approaches on developing anticipation skill. *Journal of Experimental Psychology: Applied, 11*(2), 98–110.

Ste-Marie, D. M., Law, B.. Rymal, A. M., Jenny, O., Hall, C., & McCullagh, P. (2012). Observation interventions for motor skill learning and performance: An applied model for the use of observation. *International Review of Sport and Exercise Psychology*, *5*(2), 145–176.

Stretch, R. A. (2003). Cricket injuries: A longitudinal study of the nature of injuries to South African cricketers. *British Journal of Sports Medicine*, *37*, 250–253.

Weiss, M. R. (1983). Modelling and motor performance: A developmental perspective. *Research Quarterly for Exercise and Sport*, *54*, 190–197.

Williams, A. M., & Hodges, N. J. (2005). Practice, instruction and skill acquisition in soccer: Challenging tradition. *Journal of Sports Sciences*, *23*(6), 637–650.

Wulf, G., Chiviacowsky, S., Schiller, E., & Avila, L. T. G. (2010). Frequent external-focus feedback enhances motor learning. *Frontiers in Psychology*, November 11, 2010. https://doi.org/10.3389/fpsyg.2010.00190

Wulf, G., McConnel, N., Gärtner, M., & Schwarz, A. (2002). Enhancing the learning of sport skills through external-focus feedback. *Journal of Motor Behavior*, *34*(2), 171–182.

4

COACHING BY TASK (PRACTICE)

Style B

Shane Pill, Brendan SueSee, Joss Rankin and Mitch Hewitt

Whereas Coaching by Command limits recognition of individual player difference by presenting a movement model for all to replicate as the coach desires a predictable, repeatable performance, Coaching by Task (Practice) is characterised by the coach setting the player/s to practice under the player/s timing and pacing. In Coaching by Task, one element of the pre-impact/impact/post-impact decision-making seen in Coaching by Command is moved to the player/s. The coach's role remains to make all the decisions in pre-impact task design and post-impact feedback, reflection and evaluation of player/s task performance. In a Coaching by Task scenario, after demonstration and explanation by the coach, the player/s move to initiate practice within the parameters established by the coach. The idea of player/s undertaking practice identifies the essence of the coach–player/s relationship in this style of coaching (Mosston & Ashworth, 2008).

Coaching by Task (also referred to in this book as Practice Style coaching) is observable by the coach presenting expectations for the task, the logistics of the task and allotting a unit of time in which player/s undertake the practice task. Player/s then practice while the coach observes the performance of the task and provides feedback. When this style is executed well, the coach provides group or squad feedback at the end of the practice if necessary; however, the expectation is that individual feedback is provided to each player. This requires the coach observe practice to ensure the expectations for the task are met and to observe the individuals performing the task to offer individualised feedback—not only to those who need 'help' or 'correction', also affirming feedback to those who are performing to expectation or the required standard of performance (Mosston, 1981). Performance expectations may have a qualitative-descriptive or quantitative-numerical description (Mosston, 1966). For example, a quantitative measure may be a practice task for football/soccer goal kicking penalty, requiring the player/s to kick from a set spot on the pitch with the aim to hit a marker at the back of the goal on the goal net ten times using the players preferred kick. A qualitative measure may be to practice a given movement, or an element of a given movement, in a particular way. For example, novice Australian Football (AFL) player/s learn to handball with a fist where the thumb is positioned on the fingers (on the outside) and not tucked into the fingers as striking the football with a fist where the thumb is inside the fingers may lead to a sprained or broken thumb.

DOI: 10.4324/9781003041443-5

Practice has traditionally been regarded as an important determining factor in motor skill learning, related to the observation that volume of practice is a requirement in mastery of motor skills, such as sport-specific movement abilities. Evidence is also emerging that practice influences observable 'physical' movement abilities and a cognitive effect as well, for example, enlargement of cortical maps, recruitment of brain networks and synaptic reorganisation (Trempe & Proteau, 2012). It appears that changes in brain physiology and structure accompany movement skill learning (Mang et al., 2020). Motor skill learning memories appear to stabilise through a process post-practice in an interval allowing the occurrence of consolidation. The complexity of the practice task is a factor to consider in determining the interval time required for consolidation of memory (Lugassy et al., 2018). The requirement of an interval to allow cognitive consolidation processes to occur seems to align with the idea that generally learning benefits from more, shorter, interleaved or variable, and distributed practice sessions (Coker, 2018; Magill, 2011; Simon & Bjork, 2001). However, it is not just the duration and frequency of task that influences learning; it is the quality of the practice. Quality of practice task includes the relevance of the activity to improving an aspect of performance, the effort invested by player/s in the task, the structure of the task design, the nature and type of feedback provided by the coach, and player/s readiness for challenge point of the task (Ford et al., 2017). It is also relevant for coaches to note that autonomy-supportive language has been shown to enhance learning compared with controlling language. Hooyman, Wulf and Lewthwaite (2014) showed that providing learner's autonomy appears to give them confidence in their ability, diminish the need for control of negative emotional responses, and create more positive feelings, which from a cognitive perspective on learning may help consolidate motor memories.

Task cards are often used as an example of Coaching by Task (Mosston, 1981; Mosston & Ashworth, 2008). Task cards are a tool combining illustration with written instruction. In the sport of tennis, Iserbyt et al. (2011) found task cards accomplished motor goals almost as well as a direct instruction. However, there isn't much research in the use of task cards in sport coaching.

Iserbyt and Byra (2013) suggested six principles for designing effective task cards:

1. Spatial contiguity—written instructions are placed close to corresponding pictures;
2. Signalling—written instructions are connected to parts of corresponding pictures: for example, using an arrow;
3. Coherence—the instructional message is coherent, which is enhanced by conciseness and preciseness of language and images without extraneous and distracting background;
4. Personalisation—the use of first person and second person statements to create a direct connection with the user;
5. Segmentation—the deconstruction of complex movement patterns into segments over multiple pictures, such as breaking a movement into preparation, contact and follow through phases of the movement; and
6. Design considerations—these considerations include the prior knowledge and experience of the user, the age of the user, and the utility of embedding multimedia tools in the task card if creating a digital task card.

Two examples of task cards used in sport coaching that we are aware of are the Tennis Australia match play cards for the Hot Shots and Tennis for secondary schools' programme and the Coaching Lab (n.d.) Match Play cards. When using task cards, if the player/s 'know the answer' or solution to the question/task, then it is Coaching by Task. However, if players do not 'know the answer' or solution and creativity is required to find new or novel answers/solutions, then convergent discovery, or divergent discovery if asking for more than one answer/solution, is the objective. Coaching for convergent and divergent discovery is explained in later chapters.

Examples of Coaching by Task (Practice)

Example 1—Baseball

An example of Coaching by Task (Practice) could be any movement in the game. For example, in the pre-impact set the coach may decide that a player needs to work on hitting the inside pitch off a tee. During the impact set, the tee would be placed out in front of the batter on the inside of the plate. Another player may be asked to 'feed' the ball onto the tee to be economical with time. The coach will instruct the batter with the relevant cues (e.g., contact the ball arms extended) and to practice for 5 minutes (or a nominated time). The batter practices hitting the ball and implementing the cues they were instructed to. In the post-impact set, the coach will provide feedback to either reinforce the behaviour (e.g., 'Nice job extending your arms') or to correct or refine the movement (e.g., 'You need to step towards the pitcher, not away').

Fielding ground balls hit by a coach is also an example of Coaching by Task (Practice). In the pre-impact set the coach may decide that they want the players to work on this skill. Depending on how difficult or easy the coach wishes to make the task, they could hit the ball directly to the fielder who is required to field the ball and throw to first base. Again, the coach may give the player cues to replicate (e.g., 'attack' the ball, wide base of support, hands out in front, etc.), and the player will attempt to perform the movement according to the cues each time they field the ball. All of this would occur during the impact set. The post-impact set would involve the coach providing feedback about the performance which either reinforced the behaviour or corrected it.

Example 2—Outdoor Pursuits (Downhill Snow Skiing)

When a novice downhill skier first takes to the slopes, there are many aspects of skiing that pose an unfamiliarity to the learner and very few activities that provide a transfer of direct movement application. It is common for novice learners to initially apply the snowplough technique to control their descent by turning, slowing and stopping. Application of the Coaching by Task Style of coaching provides learners with the visual representation and key cues through a demonstration provided by the coach from which they can then replicate and adjust through a series of turns over a distance or time frame set by the coach. In the pre-impact set, the coach has determined where and for how long this task will be performed to provide a clear demonstration, safe learning space and ample opportunity for practice and feedback. The coach initiates the impact set by demonstrating the position of the body and equipment in a stationary position close to the learner, supported by key cues and followed by a demonstration of what is expected in body control and positioning, transfer of weight and use of equipment to link a series of controlled snowplough turns before coming to a controlled stop. Once the learner attempts to practice the snowplough technique, the coach enters the post-impact set by providing feedback on performance with the intention of influencing the next stage of instruction, demonstration and reproduction. Learning in movement (Arnold, 1979) is emphasised as the learner begins to make sense of the way in which their body 'feels' in motion and what happens when they adjust their movements. In applying a Coaching by Task style of coaching, rather than replicating the exact number of turns or exact path of the coach, the intention is for the learner to apply the snowplough turn and make decisions about how they control their descent safely and with correct technique to reach the desired location.

Example 3—Netball

Coaching through Practice Style is useful for many skills in sport, and some have shown that it is the most used style in physical education (SueSee, 2020) and by coaches (Hewitt, 2020). In this example, we show how Practice Style can be used to coach the skill of netball shooting.

In the pre-impact set the coach would make the decision to practice this skill. If the team was comprised of intermediate level players, it could be assumed that the players are aware of the cues to perform the skill. However, perhaps the team had shot poorly in a recent game, and the coach decided that a portion of the session needed to be dedicated to shooting. In the impact set the coach may restate the cues or ask the players to help co-recall the cues for good shooting—(e.g., Ready position—Feet shoulder width apart facing the goal; balanced position with equally weighted feet; ball in shooting hand, held high above head, with non-shooting hand supporting the ball on its side. Execution—Focus sight above the ring. Straighten knees and elbows and flick your wrist ('close the lid') to create backspin). They may then ask the players to divide into equal numbers and go to each end of the court and practice their shooting for 10 minutes. The coach would then walk around, observing the performance and give feedback based on the subject matter or cues recalled at the beginning of the session. These cues are either to reinforce behaviour (i.e., those who are performing the task correctly) or offer feedback corrective feedback to those who are making errors. It is important to give both types of feedback if necessary and not just become the coach who tells the player when they are doing something wrong. Giving feedback to athletes who are performing correctly can also be opportunities to create positive interactions between coach and player. Similarly, whilst giving corrective feedback is not negative, waiting until the player has performed the behaviour correctly and giving feedback which reinforces the behaviour should also be viewed as an opportunity for positive interactions between player and coach.

Example 4—Tennis

While we provided an example of the application of Command Style coaching for a specific learning episode using the game of tennis as an example in an earlier chapter, the objective now is to illustrate how a coach may apply Practice Style coaching or Coaching by Task. Using this style of coaching practice, the coach transfers a series of decisions to the player to produce a variety of different learning outcomes than when using a Command Style of coaching. For instance, in Command Style coaching all pedagogical decisions in the planning, implementation and feedback phases of the coaching episode is determined by the coach.

However, in Practice Style or Coaching by Task, a shift in the accountability of decisions occurs. The anatomy of decisions relating to Practice Style-B or Task Coaching are:

- Pre-impact (planning): The coach makes all the subject matter and logistical decisions about the task;
- Impact (implementation): The player privately practices the memory/reproduction task. The player practices, for instance, hitting a forehand groundstroke in a crosscourt direction with a partner. In contrast to Command Style coaching, however, the players determine the starting time for the task, the pace and rhythm in addition to the initiation of questions to the coach for clarification; and
- Post-impact (feedback and assessment). During the implementation phase, the coach circulates and provides private feedback to each player in regard to how they are performing the task (i.e., observing their performance to hit a forehand groundstroke in perhaps a crosscourt direction and assisting players to achieve this outcome).

We demonstrated in the previous chapter a Command Style tennis example of coaching a player to use the continental grip and associated service action. In continuing to use this example, the coach implements Coaching by Task by requesting players to grip the racquet correctly (using a continental grip) and serve an additional ten times, individually and at their own starting and finishing time in addition to rhythm and pace. This learning episode is contrasted with Command Style, whereby the coach is responsible for all the decisions and primarily focused on skill development in the psychomotor domain.

Conclusion

Coaching by Task (Practice) is a style focused on the player replicating a movement which is either known (has been practised before) or the coach has modelled and explained cues which are to be performed. It allows the coach to watch the performance and provide feedback to reinforce the movement or correct and refine the movement. Coaching by Task (Practice) places the player in an opportunity to reproduce the required movement in a variety of situations. Coaching this way can provide the opportunity for large volumes of practice of movement to take place. Coaching by Task (Practice) is not limited to closed or isolated movement skills and closed drills and can even take the form of a game if the players know the movements and strategies to be implemented and are asked to replicate them. Game-based coaching approaches can also be forms of Coaching by Task (Practice) or contain moments of Coaching by Task (Practice) (see SueSee, Pill & Edwards, 2016).

References

Arnold, P. J. (1979). *Meaning in movement, sport and physical education*. Heinemann.
Coaching Lab. (n.d.). *Match play cards*. www.thecoachinglab.org/
Coker, C. (2018). *Motor learning and control for practitioners* (4th ed.). Routledge.
Ford, P. R., Coughlan, E. K., Hodges, N. J., & Williams, A. M. (2017). Deliberate practice in sport. In J. Baker & D. Farrow (Eds.), *Routledge handbook of sport expertise* (pp. 347–362). Routledge.
Hewitt, M. (2020). Considering the application of a range of teaching styles from the Spectrum that promotes the holistic development of tennis players in a variety of learning domains. In B. SueSee, M. Hewitt, & S. Pill (Eds.), *The Spectrum of teaching styles in physical education* (pp. 60–72). Routledge.

Hooyman, A., Wulf, G., & Lewthwaite, R. (2014). Impacts of autonomy-supportive verses controlling instructional language on motor learning. *Human Movement Science*, *36*, 180–198.

Iserbyt, P., & Byra, M. (2013). Design and use of task cards in the reciprocal style of teaching. *Journal of Physical Education, Recreation & Dance*, *84*(2), 20–26.

Iserbyt, P., Madou, B., Vergauwen, L., & Behets, D. (2011). Effects of peer mediated instruction with task cards on motor skill acquisition in tennis. *Journal of Teaching in Physical Education*, *30*(1), 31–50.

Lugassy, D., Herszage, J., Pilo, R., Brosh, T., & Censor, N. (2018). Consolidation of complex motor skill learning: Evidence for a delayed offline process. *Sleep*, *41*(9), 1–7.

Magill, R. A. (2011). *Motor learning and control: Concepts and applications* (9th ed.). McGraw Hill.

Mang, C. S., Borich, M. R., Wadden, K. P., Boyd, L. A., & Siengskon, C. F. (2020). Motor skill learning and its neurophysiology. In N. J. Hodges & A. M. Williams (Eds.), *Skill acquisition in sport: Research, theory and practice* (3rd ed., pp. 293–312). Routledge.

Mosston, M. (1966). *Teaching physical education*. Merrill.

Mosston, M. (1981). *Teaching physical education* (2nd ed.). Merrill.

Mosston, M., & Ashworth, S. (2008). *Teaching physical education* (1st online ed.). https://spectrumofteachingstyles.org/assets/files/book/Teaching_Physical_Edu_1st_Online.pdf

Simon, D. A., & Bjork, R. A. (2001). Metacognition in motor learning. *Journal of Experimental Psychology Learning Memory and Cognition*, *27*(4), 907–912.

SueSee, B. (2020). Using the Spectrum to interrogate the teaching styles of physical education teachers. In B. SueSee, M. Hewitt, & S. Pill (Eds.), *The Spectrum of teaching styles in physical education* (pp. 48–59). Routledge.

SueSee, B., Pill, S., & Edwards, K. (2016). Reconciling approaches: A game centred approach to sport teaching and Mosston's Spectrum of teaching styles. *European Journal of Physical Education and Sport Science*, *2*(4), 69–96.

Trempe, M., & Proteau, L. (2012). Motor skill consolidation. In N. J. Hodges & A. M. Williams (Eds.), *Skill acquisition in sport: Research, theory and practice* (2nd ed., pp. 192–210). Routledge.

5

RECIPROCAL COACHING (PEER COACHING)

Style C

Shane Pill, Brendan SueSee, Joss Rankin and Mitch Hewitt

The change in the role of the coach in Reciprocal Coaching (Peer Coaching) Style is that instead of the coach being the sole person responsible for feedback to player/s, the coach creates an environment where player/s provide feedback to each other. Player/s are therefore placed in the role of observers of each other's performance. When using this coaching style, the role of the coach is to make the pre-impact decisions regarding the design of the learning environment, explain the task and expectations to the players, then observe the performance of the player/s (but not provide feedback to the player/s) and the observer/s, and be available to the observer/s. It is important to note at this time that the coach only provides feedback to the observer/s that further support the development of the player (Mosston & Ashworth, 2008).

Merian and Snyder's (2015) research with collegiate athletes found that peer coaching improved team dynamics, encouraged reflective activities, developed confidence, and enhanced player learning. They also produced a structured model of peer coaching similar to The Spectrum's Reciprocal Style (Figure 5.1). In another study, Legrain, D'Arripe-Longueville and Gernigon (2003) found the potential benefits of reciprocal peer coaching to be a more desirable performance form, self-efficacy, interest-enjoyment, and feeling less pressure compared with physical practice led by the coach in a boxing programme. Other research by Atkins et al. (2015) in the effects of parents and peers influence on sporting involvement found that peer behaviours that are supportive and encouraging of effort and improvement, despite setbacks, resulted in greater levels of enjoyment and intention to continue in sport. The Reciprocal Coaching style, when implemented accurately, should be one which creates such an environment. Further to this, Holt, Kinchin and Clarke's (2012) research suggested that 10–12-year-old football players who were taught to observe, assess and record the performance of their peers found an improved 'level and consistency of performance in all five participants, which, for most players and skills, was maintained when the intervention was removed. Players were willing and able to reliably assess their peers and collect objective data on each player's performance' (p. 231).

In coaching settings, it has been found that peers can assess each other accurately and reliably (Engelmann, 2016; Marty, Henning & Willse, 2010). In sport teaching in physical education, it has been acknowledged that with primary/elementary school age players

DOI: 10.4324/9781003041443-6

FIGURE 5.1 Merian and Snyder's (2015) peer coaching model.

using observational assessment protocols with a high number of observation variables can be challenging to implement and peer coaches may forget or not be clear about the differences in some observational variables (Richard et al., 1999). This reminds coaches that the use of observational assessment protocols for player peer coaching needs to be taught to players like any other skill a player may require. However, research in a school sport programme setting showed that where players understood the observational assessment protocols, high school age players could effectively use the protocol for peer coaching (Nadeau, Richard & Godbout, 2008).

Observation of another player may give the observer unique opportunities to extract important information concerning appropriate movement coordination patterns and requirements of the movement task or to evaluate the effectiveness of movement strategies that would be difficult to reflect on during play. When players alternate between physical and observational practice in pairs: that is, two players alternate between observing and physically practising the task, studies have shown that on retention tests players perform as well as, or better than, players who undertake only physical practice. This is despite paired players undertaking only half the physical practice trials of the players in the physical practice group (Wulf, Shea & Lewthwaite, 2010).

Mosston and Ashworth (2008) argued that application of Reciprocal Style is likely to create a learning episode that can develop socialisation skills, communication skills, the giving and receiving of feedback from peers, and permit the development of empathy and manners. Further to this, Reciprocal Style may build trust by interacting and socialising with others, allowing players to experience the reward of seeing others succeed and knowing you contributed, and promoting a player's experience in connection to the effect you have on the feelings and learning of others (Mosston & Ashworth, 2008). Using Reciprocal Style allows the coach to focus on more than just the physical development of the player, thus developing a focus on other aspects of player development as feedback on 'physical performance' is handed to a player's peer. Attention provided to various domains of learning, such as social and emotional, through the physical practices, is representative of Peter Arnold's construction of learning 'in', 'through' and 'about' movement interactively to further enhance the players' development (Pill, 2016)

Examples of Coaching by Reciprocal (Peer Coaching) Style

Example 1—Touch Football

In the game of Touch Football, the coach could create a small game of 5 versus 5 in a reduced playing area. The coach may have the 'doer' playing and the observer standing on the sideline observing. The coach may have said the objective is to work on body positioning when implementing a 'touch', working on touching the opponent on the side of the hip (allowing the defender the opportunity to use force when implementing the touch to put the attacker off balance) and for the defender to be moving in a backwards direction when implementing the touch (so they are on side quickly). The 5 versus 5 games would be played for a specified time (10 minutes) and the 'observer would record the success of the 'doer' on a coach-prepared criterion sheet, noting how often or well the 'doer' performs these two tasks. At the completion of the game the coach would instruct the observer to provide feedback to the doer about how well they met the objectives.

It is important for the coach to remember that social skills need to be taught and practised for improvement. Presuming that every player has the skills to observe, provide feedback and receive feedback would be naïve. Therefore, it is important to teach these skills. Providing sentence starters such as 'I like the way you. . . .', or 'Next time you need to . . . ' can provide scaffolding for success the first few times. The 'doer' may also need to be taught how to receive and respond to feedback ('I'm not sure what you mean, can you show me' or even just thanking the observer for their feedback). Leaving the learning of any skills (whether they be physical, social, cognitive or emotional) to 'osmosis' does not always result in the outcomes desired and is not aligned with The Spectrums tenant that teaching is a deliberate act.

Example 2—Baseball

A learning experience which could be used in Baseball could relate to baserunning after a base hit to the outfield. The coach may decide, in the pre-impact set, that the subject matter to be practised involves the following behaviour or skills after a batter hits a line drive to leftfield:

- Runs an arc to first base;
- Spots the inside corner of the base;
- Spots the ball in leftfield;
- Touches the inside corner of the base with a good body lean in towards the infield; and
- Spots the ball/leftfielder and either accelerates to second base or sidesteps back towards the first base whilst keeping an eye on the fielder for clean pick or a 'bobble' of the ball (where they will take 2nd base).

During the impact set the doer would perform this behaviour whilst the observer would provide feedback to the doer, either providing feedback to reinforce the behaviour ('I like the way you hit the inside of the base with your foot') or feedback to correct the behaviour ('When you round 1st base you need to touch the inside corner of the bag and lean in'). When the observer is providing feedback, it is occurring in the post-impact set. If the doer does not understand the feedback or requires clarification, they are permitted to ask questions of the observer. Again, for the first few Reciprocal episodes, sentence starters ('I'm not sure I understand, can you show me'?) may be helpful to prevent inappropriate social interaction ('That's wrong!' or 'No it's not, wrong—you are'). An adaptation to the Reciprocal Style that can be added (and moves the learner player along the decision-making journey) occurs if the observer asks questions which require the doer to self-reflect on their performance. In the next chapter we cover the Self-Check Style; however, a brief episode could be added to the Reciprocal episode if the observer was challenged by the doer about feedback given. For example, if the observer said, 'Next time you need to run more of an arc to first base' and the doer disagreed, the observer may ask the doer a question which required reflection such as 'Where did you think you ran? Can you show me?' The doer is now required to self-reflect on their performance.

Mosston and Ashworth suggested that a common misconception with this style is the coach is 'not working' (2008) because the coach is focusing on the social skills of players, giving and receiving feedback (as well as the technical and tactical game skills) and interacting with the observer using questioning. For example, the coach will guide the observer's feedback by asking questions such as 'What is one thing the doer is performing well?', 'Did you tell them'? Similarly, the coach can ask the observer, 'What is one aspect which the doer needs to work on'? If the coach does notice inappropriate conflict or social interaction, then they must step in. Mosston and Ashworth (2008) suggested asking, 'who is the doer and who is the observer?' Then stating, 'I want to see the doer performing the task and the observer giving feedback as per the criteria sheet'. I would also like to hear the sentences begin with 'I like the way you are . . . ' or 'next time you need to . . .'. The practicing of social communication skills is one of the outcomes desired from this coaching style.

Example 3—Outdoor Pursuit (Mountain Biking)

There are many examples of activities that require students to practice refined and technically demanding movements and receive feedback to inform adjustments to their practice to demonstrate skilful performance. In applying a 'traditional' approach to coaching, a coach would often set athletes into lines to ensure they observed performance and provided participants with feedback to apply adjustments to performance. Mountain biking has previously lent itself to this approach to coaching due to the perceived risks involved and the physical nature of many single or narrow tracked environments. The use of the Reciprocal Style of coaching, however, enables an increased level of participation and time for meaningful reflection as the doer and observer engage in conversation and analysis of performance based on observation. There is also the opportunity to combine with other styles, which may lend themselves to enable for differentiation to be applied to the learning environment so that the peer feedback received is based on observation of performance that is appropriate to the level of the doer. For instance, in applying the Reciprocal Style of coaching with the learning of the front wheel lift, the combining of the Inclusion Style can also influence the way the doer engages with the task. For example, the performance checklist remains the same; however the challenge of the obstacle may be increased or decreased to help provide a 'benchmark' for the quality of the performance of the 'doer'.

This example will focus on the front wheel lift, which can be used to clear the front of the bike from hitting objects such as rocks, tree roots or depressions on a track. The selection of a technique such as the front wheel lift enables the creation of a performance checklist that participants can easily refer to, to compare the performance to, and provide directed and specific feedback. In aligning with the Reciprocal Style, the coach would then present subject matter to be performed by the rider via a demonstration that may be performed by one of the participants in the group. In this demonstration, the coach must also include information about the role of the observer by fulfilling this role during the demonstration, ensuring to use the performance criteria and provide an example of how the observer can provide feedback. In this example, the coach will have made a series of pre-impact decisions such as the area defined for practice, participants' assent to work in pairs as a doer and observer, the timeframe for doing and observing, and the performance criteria to work from. A range of decisions are then made by the participants in both the impact and post-sets of performance, such as how many times to practice the wheel lift and discuss feedback within the set time frame, how and what feedback is provided based on the criteria and how to translate the feedback into future performance. Figure 5.2 shows a potential layout of the area to enable maximum individual participation, as well as opportunity for differentiation to be built into the task with students setting their own obstacles or choosing to perform the technique to the side of them.

The criteria identified for the checklist could include:

- Pedal to build speed;
- Set in ready position;
- Just before the obstacle, push one pedal stroke hard with your power foot to drive the bike forward;
- Through the pedal drive, transfer weight back to rear of saddle and lift front wheel with arms still in attack position;
- Clear front wheel of object; and
- Ensure that the head shouldn't rise significantly, and land back in ready position to repeat for next obstacle.

A picture could be included on the criteria sheet, with key positional points to support the observation. During the task, the coach would continue to move around, observe and interact

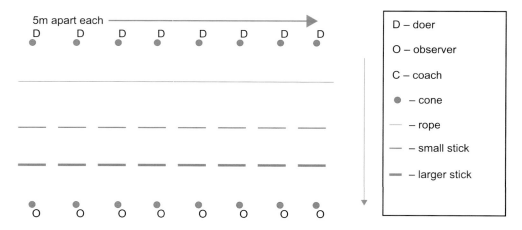

FIGURE 5.2 Possible layout for front wheel lift practice using Reciprocal Coaching Style.

with the participant observers as necessary to ensure feedback alignment and ongoing interaction to support progression and success. This can predominantly be achieved by asking questions of the observer.

Example 4—Over Arm Serve—Volleyball

The Reciprocal Style could be used to great effect when teaching any movement where the cues or body of knowledge can be identified. To maximise feedback, ensure that all players know what is needed for success, and improve error detection (Goldberger & SueSee, 2020), the Reciprocal Style is of great value. For example, in volleyball, the coach may wish to plan an episode to maximise practice of an overarm serve (no jump) and may also hope to develop error detection skills amongst the team so that they can aid their teammates. An example of a Reciprocal Style task sheet is supplied later (Figure 5.3). The coach would plan this task sheet in the pre-impact stage. In the impact set the coach would explain the task sheet, the two distinct roles the players would play, the role the coach would play, and the social skills needed for giving appropriate feedback. After this is done and the opportunity for questions is provided, the players may be asked to choose a partner, or the coach can do this themselves. The players would then be asked to select a place where they can work through the episode and perform both the role of the 'doer' and the 'observer'. The coach would move around the area, speaking only to the observer and asking them to identify things the 'doer' was performing well or needed corrective feedback on. If the coach gives feedback to the doer, they have returned to characteristics of Practice Style and made the 'observer' redundant.

Example 5—Tennis

An example will now be provided to illustrate the shifting of decisions between our previous tennis example in Chapter 4 using Practice Style (Task Coaching) to the shifting of decisions between Practice Style and Reciprocal (Peer) Coaching. The decision 'transfer occurs in the post-impact set of decisions' (Mosston & Ashworth, 2008, p. 271). In this case, a player assesses another player's performance (i.e., a practice partner). This is achieved through performance criteria, which in the example we provide is for the backhand volley. The performance criteria are provided by the coach. In this example, we will use the Forehand Groundstroke (Table 5.1). The performance criteria (or a task card that illustrates and describes the task) is provided to the partner. The partner then observes the performance of the other player and offers assessment based on the criteria provided by the coach. After one player has completed the task, they then alternate roles. Reciprocal Style Coaching is not limited to providing an avenue for offering feedback, as it also presents opportunities for 'social development as the partners systematically "help" each other within a constructive relationship to learn the task at hand. Giving and accepting feedback are important social skills that can be learned and practiced' (Mosston & Ashworth, 2008, p. 271). In Reciprocal Style Coaching, a 'new dimension evolves that goes beyond the mere performance of the physical tasks, such as social interaction, giving, receiving, and trying out ideas, correcting, and succeeding' (Mosston & Ashworth, 2008, p. 136). In the example of tennis we provide here, each player takes turns observing a player performing a skill based on a coach-prepared task card. Players alternate roles as the 'doer' and 'observer' as they 'check-off' the skill requirements of the task in doing so, socially interact with one another.

OVER ARM SERVE:

There will be 2 roles **for** you to play in the following activity.

One role is the **DOER**, and the other role is the **OBSERVER**.

OBSERVERS ROLE: Read the criteria

Observe the DOER

Give feedback based on the criteria,

and information to improve.

DOER ROLE: Know the criteria

Do your best to perform the skill correctly,

Listen to feedback from the OBSERVER

and respond appropriately.

COACH'S ROLE: **Speaks only to OBSERVER**

Criteria	Most of the time 16<	Sometimes 10-15	Inconsistent 10>
Feet are about shoulder width apart with one foot slightly in front of the other.			
Knees are slightly bent.			
Weight is on the back foot, and ball is held out in front at eye level.			
Elbow is facing straight ahead, and palm is up.			
Ball toss is straight up.			
Weight moves to front foot			
Elbow straightens.			
Ball is contacted at 1 o'clock with cupped hand.			
Hand is hard and follow through.			

The person I was observing was: ....

The feedback I gave was:

FIGURE 5.3 An example of a Reciprocal Style task sheet.

TABLE 5.1 Performance Criteria checklist for the Forehand Groundstroke.

Order	Skill Criteria	Always	Sometimes	Rarely
a.	Assume a ready position			
b.	Ensure that non-hit hand supports the throat of the racquet			
c.	Turn side on to coming ball			
d.	Beginning of a circular motion			
e.	Racquet follows a low to high swing path			
f.	Contact is made in front and to the side of the body			
g.	Follow through as a natural extension of the swing			
h.	Racquet finishes over the opposite shoulder			

What did your partner do well?

What your partner can improve?

Table 5.1 is an example of a performance criteria checklist of the backhand volley, which may be applied in a Reciprocal Style Coaching episode between two players in a coaching session.

Conclusion

It is our experience that sport coaches often put injured players in peer coaching roles during training. Reciprocal Coaching (Peer Coaching) is about learning to give and receive feedback from peers. It is a style that can be used for the purpose of enhancing player communication and relationship skills. Research in coaching and physical education have shown an improvement in motor skills learning with only half the number of practice trials (Wulf et al., 2010; Goldberger & SueSee, 2020). If the objective of a coach is to empower a team leadership group with on-field 'in the moment' coaching, then the Reciprocal Coaching (Peer Coaching) style is a good one to use at training by placing leadership group players in the role of providing feedback on individual and group game performance during tactical timeouts in a match simulation or game form practice task. This acts to familiarise players with receiving feedback or being led in discussions by the leadership group players. In physical education literature, there are numerous studies considering peer teaching; however, there appear to be very few studies into the effects of Reciprocal Coaching (Peer Coaching) in sport settings, providing opportunities for research initiatives to add to our understanding of the benefits, limitations and potential constraints on player learning when in a reciprocal (peer) coaching role.

References

Atkins, M. R., Johnson, D. M., Force, E. C., & Petrie, T. A. (2015). Peers, parents, and coaches, oh my! The relation of the motivational climate to boys' intention to continue in sport. *Psychology of Sport and Exercise*, *16*, 170–180.

Engelmann, J. M. (2016). Peer assessment of clinical skills and professional behaviors among undergraduate athletic training students. *Athletic Training Education Journal*, *11*(2), 95–102.

Goldberger, M., & SueSee, B. (2020). Effects of the reciprocal teaching style on skill acquisition, verbal interaction and ability to analyse in fifth grade children in physical education. In B. SueSee, M. Hewitt, & S. Pill (Eds.), *The Spectrum of teaching styles in physical education* (pp. 116–127). Routledge.

Holt, J., Kinchin, G., & Clarke, G. (2012). Effects of peer-assessed feedback, goal setting and a group contingency on performance and learning by 10–12-year-old academy soccer players. *Physical Education & Sport Pedagogy, 17*(3), 231–250.

Legrain, P., D'Arripe-Longueville, F., & Gernigon, C. (2003). Peer tutoring in a sport setting: Are there any benefits for tutors? *The Sport Psychologist, 17*, 77–94.

Marty, M. C., Henning, J. M., & Willse, J. T. (2010). Accuracy and reliability of peer assessment of athletic training psychomotor laboratory skills. *Journal of Athletic Training, 45*(6), 609–614.

Merian, D. Z., & Snyder, E. M. (2015). Peer coaching in American intercollegiate athletics: An investigation of team dynamics, confidence and student-athlete learning. *International Journal of Evidence Based Coaching and Mentoring, 13*(2), 81–100.

Mosston, M., & Ashworth, S. (2008). *Teaching physical education* (1st online ed.). https://spectrumofteachingstyles.org/assets/files/book/Teaching_Physical_Edu_1st_Online.pdf

Nadeau, L., Richard, J.-F., & Godbout, P. (2008). The validity and reliability of a performance assessment procedure in ice hockey. *Physical Education and Sport Pedagogy, 13*(1), 65–83.

Pill, S. (2016). *Learning in, through and about movement in secondary physical education: A practical resource to support strengths based and inquiry perspectives into Australian curriculum: Health and physical education and middle years International Baccalaureate physical education*. ACHPER(SA).

Richard, J.-F., Godbout, P., Tousignant, M., & Gréhaigne, J.-F. (1999). The try-out of A team sport assessment procedure in elementary and junior high school physical education classes. *Journal of Teaching in Physical Education, 18*, 336–356.

Wulf, G., Shea, C., & Lewthwaite, R. (2010). Motor skill learning and performance: A review of influential factors. *Medical Education, 44*, 75–84.

6
COACHING BY INDIVIDUAL PROGRAMMING (SELF-CHECK)

Style D

Shane Pill, Brendan SueSee, Joss Rankin and Mitch Hewitt

Coaching by Individual Programming (Self-Check) is fundamentally about the player/s engagement in self-assessment. The role of the player is to check their performance against criteria prepared by the coach. A coach may use this style where the aim is to develop the player's self-awareness about proficiency of performance, or to help the player move towards being a more self-regulated learner (Mosston & Ashworth, 2008). Feedback on performance has shifted from a peer in Style C to the individual player to self-check when a coach uses this coaching style.

A coach's verbal behaviour must reflect the intent of this style of coaching by ascertaining the players have the capability to self-check, by listening to the player talk about their performance and avoiding the temptation to direct and tell, by leading the player to discrepancies in their description and assessment, and by helping the player identify discrepancies they cannot identify (Mosston & Ashworth, 2008). Style D is well suited to the coach asking questions in preference to offering statements and directions to help the player develop their ability to reflect on their performance against the criteria provided by the coach. Applying a range of probing and clarifying questions in the analysis will prompt the player's ability to analyse critically. When using this style, the role of the coach is not necessarily to offer direct feedback on performance, rather, to preferentially offer feedback by way of inquiry as an aim of this style of coaching is to help the player become less dependent on the coach for correction and direction (Mosston, 1981).

Coaching by Individual Programming (Self-Check) is a step towards the development of autonomy-supportive coaching opportunities. Autonomy-supportive coaching is characterised by the coach providing choice within boundaries, a rationale for tasks, asking players for input, providing opportunities for players to take initiative, providing non-controlling competency feedback, focusing on self-referenced evaluative criteria, and avoiding coercive statements with players (Occhino et al., 2014). However, it is not as simple as saying that autonomy-supportive coaching styles are necessarily better than a more controlling coaching style, such as Styles A, B and C of The Spectrum. The Spectrum theory is clear in that it is a non-versus perspective on styles as each style has its time and place in assisting player learning. We acknowledge that autonomy-supportive, and what might be described as more

DOI: 10.4324/9781003041443-7

controlling coaching styles, are each related to players motivational responses (Ambrose & Anderson-Butcher, 2015) and learning needs. It is well accepted that determinants of a coach's effectiveness are the behaviour, temperament, education and experience of the coach, and the capability of the coach to bring these meaningfully to the context of the player to effect change in player outcomes. This includes the coach understanding how the needs of players as learners change as they develop from child to adult, from novice to expert (Côté & Gilbert, 2009). Self-controlled practice that allows a player to obtain information when desired or needed, and that can provide them with the opportunity to ask for feedback after successful practice attempts, is desirable for players seeking self-determination (Wulf, Shea & Lewthwaite, 2010).

It is important to note that from a Spectrum of Coaching Styles perspective Coaching by Individual Programming (Self-Check) remains within the reproduction cluster of styles. It is necessary for coaches to understand that there is the potential for players to unrealistically self-evaluate, and unrealistic positive self-evaluation can negatively affect the player performance development. It may be necessary for players to have a realistic view of their performance provided by a coach in order to set goals and behaviours to progress (Hofseth et al., 2017).

Coaching for heightened player self-awareness may assist players to counter potential negative effects of performance pressure that comes from induced self-consciousness that occurs relative to expectations of performance at high levels of practice (Beilock & Carr, 2004). There is evidence that the effectiveness of skill learning can be enhanced when a learner is given some control over the practice conditions. For example, the learner deciding when they want, or do not want, to receive feedback has been shown to lead to more effective learning than predetermined feedback schedules (Wulf et al., 2010). Some researchers have suggested Style D is appropriate to achieve self-regulatory skills and to establish a mastery-oriented climate. Research has shown mastery climates encourage a positive attitude toward learning, effort (Ames, 1992; Corno & Rohrkemper, 1985; Nicholls, 1989), exercise and sports (Christodoulidis, Papaioannou & Digelidis, 2001). It also contributes to the belief that effort and ability bring about success and satisfaction (Treasure, 1997; Treasure & Roberts, 2001) and that success is achieved through intrinsic interest, effort, and cooperation (Walling & Duda, 1995). Finally, it directs the learner to focus on effort (Walling & Duda, 1995) and maintenance of effort during classes (Christodoulidis et al., 2001). A coach wishing to promote self-regulatory skills and establish a mastery-focused climate should consider Style D (Papaioannou et al., 2012).

Examples of Coaching by Individual Programming (Self-Check)

Example 1—Outdoor Pursuits (Kayaking)

The Individual Programming (Self-Check) coaching style could be used for a participant attempting to refine the technique of an Eskimo roll that is used as a 'self-rescue' to right a kayak that has capsized with the paddler still inside. There are a clear set of actions to perform this technique correctly; however, self-perception of performance can often differ from actual performance due to a range of factors such as disorientation upside down under water, fear and anxiety and required speed of execution. The Individual Programming Style would then be useful for a participant who has developed a level of comfort practising the roll but is finding it difficult to consistently right the boat from a capsized position. The coach would provide the criteria (that has been created during the pre-impact set) to the participant as follows and, in this example, set a camera up to capture the participant's performance:

- Set paddle parallel to your boat with dominant hand in front and wrists rolled forward;
- Once boat is capsized, bring chest towards bow of the boat, lifting paddle to the surface of the water;
- Sweep paddle across the surface of the water in a 'C' motion, engage the paddle blade with the surface of the water;
- Continuing from the previous motion, flick your hips to right the boat whilst drawing down onto the water with the paddle; and
- As you are righting the boat, the boat and your hips should rise first, followed by torso, shoulders and finally your head.

The impact set enables the participant to attempt several practices agreed upon by the coach and participant before the participant reviews the footage during the post-impact set. This example is provided as the order of the body emerging from the water is critical. Raising the head early to inhale oxygen causes the hips to drop and the boat to flip back upside down; however, participants often perceive that their heads remained down during the action. By viewing the footage captured, the participant can assess their performance against the set criteria and determine areas for refinement and establish a plan or action with the coach. The coach can engage in questioning to prompt verbalisation and reasoning from the participant, promoting a sense of self-control over performance and improvement for the participant.

Example 2—Baseball/Softball

The Individual Programming coaching style could be used for a player taking live batting practice. In the pre-impact set the coach would have decided the objective for players to work on was 'live hitting' and error identification through self-assessment (self-check). During the impact set the coach would explain what would be occurring, the objectives (hitting and self-check), and the criteria, which could be written on a whiteboard. The pitcher may be told to just throw fastballs to the inside, middle and outside of the plate. The criteria given to the hitter could be as follows:

- Take a comfortable, balanced stance;
- Gently rock and step towards the pitcher;
- Turn back knee towards the ball;
- Ensure that hands are straight to the inside part of the ball;
- Keep head down through impact (shoulder to shoulder);
- Hit the bottom half of the ball; and
- Follow through out towards the pitcher.

At the completion of the specified number of swings (the post-impact set), the coach can ask the batter what they did well and what they need to work on from the criteria provided earlier. If the batter identified the outside pitch as a point of weakness, and something they needed to work on, the next round may only be outside pitches. The coach may engage in a discussion to check how the player has reached that conclusion and what they think the technical reason is. Through this process, the coach is creating an environment which is allowing the player to practice the skill of self-reflection and error identification so that that they move towards more independence (or freedom) with their decision-making. This is important in terms of the continued development of the player in terms of them not relying on the coach as much, but equally, as many sports (tennis) do not allow the coach to coach from the stands.

Example 3—The Set: Volleyball

Just like the Reciprocal Style Coaching—Style C, if the subject matter or sub-routine cues can be identified, then they can be used for a Style D coaching episode. The volleyball set provides another example of how it can be used, this time with a task sheet. Using a task sheet ensures that the criteria or cues cannot be forgotten as easy as when they are verbally given to the athlete without a task sheet. Whilst the Individual Programming coaching style can be done without a task sheet, the coach should be aware that the cues may be forgotten, or the cognitive load may be as such that they may not be able to deal with performance, as well as critiquing their own performance, hence why a task sheet (card) or writing the cues on a whiteboard may be of assistance. An example is provided in Table 6.1.

To coach this episode, the coach may have decided that the players need to work on their setting and self-correction of errors (pre-impact set). Using Style D would be a method of coaching that meets these objectives. During the impact set, the coach would demonstrate the content or cues for the set and then explain the behaviour expectations, in this case collecting a ball and finding a place in the gym where the players can set against the wall. The coach may also suggest that the players pair up, and using a recording device (such as a mobile

TABLE 6.1 Self-Check task sheet for the set.

Name: Date:		**Instructions:** Perform the set against the wall and assess your technique against the criteria provided later. Provide feedback/and suggestions on how to improve the performance.
HAVE I	YES/NO MARK WITH × OR ✓	Feedback/FIX BY
Got my feet about shoulder width apart and weight evenly balanced . . .?		
Got my shoulders facing the direction I am setting . . .?		
Contacted the ball with my fingertips in a diamond formation . . .?		
Contacted the ball in front of my forehead and evenly (about 11 o'clock) . . .?		
Straightened my legs and extended my arms . . .?		

phone), player B could record player A. During the post-impact set, Player A would then be able to use the recorded footage and stop it at appropriate places to check their performance against the criteria.

Example 4—Tennis

The application of Coaching by Individual Programming (Self-Check) is a highly effective coaching style, where the objective of the experience is to develop self-awareness in connection to the proficiency of a player's performance, in addition to promoting a greater awareness of self-regulation. In this style, the role of the coach is to compose all subject matter, criteria, and logistical decisions. The role of the players is to work 'independently and to check their own performance against the criteria prepared by the teacher' (Mosston & Ashworth, 2008, p. 141). Within a tennis coaching context, Coaching by Individual Programming (Self-Check) may be enacted in tennis by the following example.

In the pre-impact phase, the coach determines the desired learning content for the session. The example in Table 6.2 relates to the player having the capacity to 'Set up an attack using width' during a competitive rally situation. The specific outcomes relating to this coaching scenario is linked to a tactical objective (i.e., setting up an attack using width). However, the coach, in this session, may also wish to implement Coaching by Individual Programming (Self-Check) for players to assess a series of technical elements of an identified tennis stroke—such as the skill criteria for a backhand groundstroke. So, as evident, this coaching style can be utilised to assess both technical and tactical elements of a player's game. Regardless of the pre-impact content designed by the coach, during the impact phase of the coaching session—the player is provided with a 'checklist'. Table 6.2 relates to the aforementioned tactical challenge of 'Setting up an attack using width'. At the completion of each competitive rally, the player indicates the outcome, as outlined on the Self Checklist. In other words, has the player's performance (during the impact set of the experience) achieved the content outlined by the coach in the pre-impact set.

TABLE 6.2 Self-Check task sheet—setting up an attack using width self-check.

Player name: _____

Game element:
1. Setting up an attack using <u>width.</u>

Activity description:
The player is challenged, during a competitive rally, to position their respective shots into the wide areas of their opponent's court with the related outcome of winning the point.

Hitting a wide forehand that results in winning the point	Hitting a wide backhand that results in winning the point
Total	Total
What I did well on my forehand?	What I did well on my backhand?

This style is particularly ideally aligned to coaches who covert the use of questions and inquiries that are designed to prompt the player's thoughts surrounding their performance. Additionally, this style of coaching is well suited for players (and coaches) to engage in reviewing and critiquing a tennis match by viewing vision of the contest. In this way, coaches can pose well-articulated questions to the players in connection to their performance in conjunction with players forming their own reflections regarding their respective performance in achieving the tactical challenges presented in the pre-impact phase of the coaching experience.

Conclusion

We agree with Wikely and Bullock (2006) that coaching, as an educational relationship, 'needs to move between an interaction that facilitates access to new information and one that encourages self-determination' depending on the need of the player's learning (p. 22). It is our experience as coaches that Coaching by Individual Programming (Self-Check) is relatively common in elite junior and senior sport programmes. For example, Shane, recalling his experience coaching at a semi-professional Australian football (AFL) club, explains that those players from U16 through to the top-level 'league' team were expected to watch vision of games and self-check their performance against their performance benchmarks and development criteria before meeting with their 'line coach' to discuss game performance. In this process, it was important for the coach to listen to the player talk about their performance and avoid the temptation to direct and tell while helping the player identify discrepancies or gaps in understanding between their reflection and the performance criteria (Mosston & Ashworth, 2008).

References

Ambrose, A. J., & Anderson-Butcher, D. (2015). Exploring the independent and interactive effects of autonomy-supportive and controlling coaching behaviors on adolescent athletes' motivation for sport. *Sport, Exercise, and Performance Psychology*, *4*(3), 206–218.

Ames, C. (1992). Classroom: Goals, structures, and student motivation. *Journal of Educational Psychology*, *84*, 409–414.

Beilock, S. L., & Carr, T. H. (2004). From novice to expert performance: Memory, attention, and the control of complex sensori-motor skills. In A. M. Williams & N. J. Hodges (Eds.), *Skill acquisition in sport: Research, theory and practice* (pp. 309–327). Routledge.

Christodoulidis, T., Papaioannou, A., & Digelidis, N. (2001). Motivational climate and attitudes towards exercise in Greek senior high school: A year-long intervention. *European Journal of Sport Science*, *1*(4), 144–152.

Corno, L., & Rohrkemper, M. (1985). The intrinsic motivation to learn in the classroom. In C. Ames & R. Ames (Eds.), *Research on motivation in education* (Vol. 2, pp. 53–90). Academic Press.

Côté, J., & Gilbert, W. (2009). An integrative definition of coaching effectiveness and expertise. *International Journal of Sports Science & Coaching*, *4*(3), 307–323.

Hofseth, E., Toering, T., Jordet, G., & Ivarsson, A. (2017). Self-evaluation of skills and performance level in youth elite soccer: Are positive self-evaluations always positive? *Sport, Exercise, and Performance Psychology*, *6*(4), 370–383.

Mosston, M. (1981). *Teaching physical education* (2nd ed.). Merrill.

Mosston, M., & Ashworth, S. (2008). *Teaching physical education* (1st online ed.). https://spectrumofteachingstyles.org/assets/files/book/Teaching_Physical_Edu_1st_Online.pdf

Nicholls, J. G. (1989). *The competitive ethos and democratic education*. Harvard University Press.

Occhino, J. L., Mallett, C. J., Rynne, S. B., & Carlisle, K. N. (2014). Autonomy-supportive pedagogical approach to sports coaching: Research, challenges and opportunities. *International Journal of Sports Science & Coaching*, *9*(2), 401–415.

Papaioannou, A., Theodosiou, A., Pashali, M., & Digelidis, N. (2012). Advancing task involvement, intrinsic motivation and metacognitive regulation in physical education classes: The self-check style of teaching makes a difference. *Advances in Physical Education*, *2*(3), 110–118.

Treasure, D. C. (1997). Perceptions of the motivational climate and elementary school children's cognitive and affective response. *Journal of Sport & Exercise Psychology*, *19*, 278–290.

Treasure, D. C., & Roberts, G. C. (2001). Student's perceptions of the motivational climate, achievement beliefs and satisfaction in physical education. *Research Quarterly for Exercise and Sport*, *72*, 165–175.

Walling, M. D., & Duda, J. L. (1995). Goals and their associations with beliefs about success in and perceptions of the purposes of physical education. *Journal of Teaching in Physical Education*, *14*, 140–156.

Wikely, F., & Bullock, K. (2006). Coaching as an educational relationship. In R. Jones (Ed.), *The sports coach as educator: Re-conceptualising sports coaching* (pp. 14–24). Routledge.

Wulf, G., Shea, C., & Lewthwaite, R. (2010). Motor skill learning and performance: A review of influential factors. *Medical Education*, *44*, 75–84.

7
SMALL GROUP COACHING (INCLUSION)
Style E

Shane Pill, Brendan SueSee, Joss Rankin and Mitch Hewitt

Mosston (1966) originally called this style 'use of the small group' (p. 93). It became evident, however, that the style required more than small numbers in groups. The style called for a specific designation of the role of each member in the group, for example, players, observers, and recorders. In a physical education setting, the emphasis was on inclusion as members of the group had a role in addition to that of player that they could perform, and therefore, if not strong in the playing aspect of the task, the individual may be able to perform strongly in one of the other two roles. Therefore, the setting is more inclusive than if there is only one role the individual was being judged on (player) and one criterion for success (being a good player). Physical education teachers may see parallels to the way the use of small groups was described by Mosston (1966) and cooperative learning models and the sport education model (Siedentop, 1994). In the sport coaching context, when coaches focus on different roles within groups, which require a range of skills, such as interaction and communication (and not just psychomotor skills), more players are catered to as more opportunities exist to contribute. For example, use of the Sport Education model aims to create an environment where 'each team member takes on a role that contributes to the team (such as, player + coach), or the class environment through membership of a committee (such as, player + event manager)' (Pill & Williams, 2017, p. 12) and the social support from peers requires the cultivation of supportive rather than competitive behaviours (Pill & Williams, 2017). With adult sport teams, we have experienced this environment created by coaches for pre-season camp 'during our playing days' expressly for the purpose of cultivating positive group dynamics while developing player capacity for self- and peer-regulated role responsibility.

Although originally describing this style as 'The Use of a Small Group', later Mosston described Style E as the Inclusion Style (Mosston, 1966, 1981). The nature of there being multiple performance criteria in the one task remained but was expanded to include the idea of multiple challenge points within the 'player' role of the one task. The metaphor of the 'slanty rope' was used by Mosston (1981) to explain the notion of the variable degree of difficulty necessary to cater for all stages of player learning in a group environment. The metaphor is this: imagine the challenge is to jump over a rope a metre off the ground. If you ask all players to jump the rope at this height, it assumes every player is at an equitable challenge

DOI: 10.4324/9781003041443-8

point. In other words, there is a single standard for the achievement of the outcome of jumping the height of the rope. If the objective is exclusion, or, to sort the players who can jump over this height and who cannot, then a single standard matches the task objective. This is the premise of a high jump competition, where the bar is set at the same height for all competitors. If, however, the aim of the task is inclusion, then adjustments must be made to the height of the rope to cater for the range of readiness of all the players. The solution is to slant the rope so those not yet ready to jump over 1 metre have a lower standard matched to their level of readiness, and those who can jump more than 1 metre have the rope at a height that matches their capability (Mosston, 1981). Extending the concept into small group coaching, there would not be one practice group with all the players jumping over one rope set at the same height or multiple small-numbered groups all jumping the same height; there may be three or more small groups practising jumping over the rope, each group with the bar at a height to cater for the players' various challenge points. Research has found that the Inclusion Style is effective in developing skill performance for 'average' level performers (Beckett, 1991; Goldberger & Gerney, 1986; Goldberger, Gerney & Chamberlain, 1982) and impacts positively on students' goal orientation and motivation (Salvara et al., 2006; Kirby et al., 2015). Others (Goudas et al., 1995; Zeng et al., 2009) have reported that females of upper elementary and college-age preferred Inclusion Style as it provided them with greater control and decision-making over the task, in addition to experiencing less anxiety. Chatzipanteli (2018) suggested that Inclusion Style additionally encouraged players to apply metacognitive strategies, such as monitoring, self-evaluation and reflection.

Challenge Point

A concept for coaches to consider when using Small Group Coaching (Inclusion): Style E is the Challenge Point Framework (Guadagnoli & Lee, 2004). This framework is premised on the benefits of 'appropriate' failure when the objective is learning. Three considerations underpin the Challenge Point Framework: (1) Learning cannot occur in the absence of information; (2) learning will be stymied if there is too little or too much information; and (3) an optimal amount of information depends on the skill level of the individual and degree of difficulty of the task. Furthermore, the degree of difficulty can be divided into two considerations: the nominal task difficulty and the functional task difficulty. The nominal difficulty is constant regardless of who and under what conditions the task is performed. For example, a beach volleyball game played in 24°C heat with a south-westerly wind blowing at 10 knots is the same for all players on the court. Functional difficulty is the challenge relative to capability of the individual player. For example, novice volleyball players would encounter a higher functional task difficulty in a game of beach volleyball played in 24°C heat with a south-westerly wind blowing at 10 knots than an Olympic beach volleyball player (Guadagnoli & Lee, 2004). From this example, the Challenge Point Framework would suggest that a functional task challenge for a novice player would be too low for an expert performer, and the reverse for a neophyte. The conditions under which a player practices will make the task more or less challenging and depending on the conditions the coach sets in the task design. Therefore, the level of challenge will either be optimal for learning or sub-optimal for the player. Optimal learning is obtained by adjusting the degree of difficulty with regard to the capability of the player.

Desirable Difficulty

If the objective is learning for the players to be better at something in the future than presently, then the challenge point setting is not about making the task 'easy' or 'comfortable' for the player. It is about 'task difficulty'. 'Task difficulty' that challenges the player is more desirable if the objective is long-term learning. This coaching behaviour leads to the idea that tasks need to be 'effortful' to focus or engage player attention. A coach can aim to establish in the motivation mindset of the player an understanding called 'desirably difficult'. This mindset is one where the player understands the value of the challenge, that the level of difficulty may lead to inconsistent performance or even short-term failure, to achieve long-term improvement (Yan, Guadagnoli & Haycocks, 2020).

When a task, or an element within a task, is too difficult for a player, it is referred to as a 'rate limiter'. A 'rate limiter' is a phenomenon that discourages the progression of learning (Ford & Williams, 2013). A strength deficiency following an injury affecting the throwing ability of a cricketer during fielding practice would be considered a 'rate limiter'. A 'rate limiter' may also be an element of the task design which places the player outside of a 'desirable difficulty' mindset and into a situation of performance anxiety due to a mindset that the challenge is beyond their respective ability. Alternatively, the player may not reach a 'desirable difficulty' mindset due to the challenge point of the practice task being too simple. As a result, they develop the mindset of boredom and then do not provide full effort or commitment to the task.

The coach's role in the small group is not to tell the player whether their choice is appropriate. If the coach simply chose to directly instruct the player, then the style would revert to Practice Style—as the coach is making the decision about the appropriateness of the practice and not the player. The coach's role when intentionally using an Inclusion Coaching Style is to discuss with the player the reason for their choice pertaining to the level of difficulty and then collaborate with the player to develop the skill of choosing the most appropriate challenge point based on reasoned decision-making.

Inclusion Style coaching in tennis has been described as 'athlete-centred' as it encourages players to begin to explore their movement potential and problem-solve to meet movement challenges (Hewitt et al., 2018). Inclusion Style coaching has been associated with a mastery climate (Morgan, 2017). Mastery climates have been shown to enhance player motivation to learn in young and elite players (Curran et al., 2015; Leo et al., 2009; Pensgaard & Robert, 2002).

Examples of Small Group Coaching (Inclusion): Style E

Example 1—Baseball

Small Group Coaching in Baseball could be used for batting. In the pre-impact set the coach could create three levels (or more) of challenge. Level one could be hitting off a tee, level two live hitting with the pitcher telling the hitter where the pitch will be thrown (inside, middle or outside of the plate) and Level three live hitting. The impact set requires the players to choose the level at which they will practice (the challenge point). At the completion of the practice episode (post-impact set) the coach would have a conversation with the player about reasons they (the player) believed that this was the most appropriate challenge point and whether they should practice again at this point or move to a new challenge point. It is important to remember that the coach's role is not to make the decision about the appropriate level or challenge point, but to ask questions to guide the learner back to the criteria for success and the level that the player is most capable of performing. This can be a challenge at first for many coaches; however, if the journey towards independent and self-regulated learners is what is desired, then coaching episodes where the player has the opportunity to practice selecting an appropriate level of practice assists this objective.

Example 2—Outdoor Pursuits (Rock Climbing)

Small Group Coaching (Inclusion) Style can often be observed in outdoor adventure settings. Groups are required to fulfil a range of roles to complete a task that may have multiple entry points for successfully achieving an outcome. Rock climbing is an example that draws upon the original conception of the style in enabling a range of roles as well as the evolution that requires participant decision-making to determine the level of difficulty in which they complete the outcomes associated with the act of climbing. This may include applying a range of climbing techniques and challenge individually perceived limitations in completing the activity.

In an indoor top-rope rock-climbing setting, climbing routes are set using different coloured holds to indicate a route to take to the top of a wall, and the routes are allocated a grade to indicate the difficulty of completing that climb. For instance, on one wall, serviced by one rope to climb with, there may be a series of black plastic holds to the top of the wall that has been graded at 18, a series of green holds graded at 14, a series of purple holds graded at 11, and a route described as using all available holds graded at 6. The Australian and New Zealand grading system for climbing difficulty simply uses numbers; the higher the number, the more difficult the climb is. The challenge remains for participants to attempt to apply a range of climbing techniques and push the boundary of what they believed they were capable of; however, participants can select the difficulty of climb based on the holds they use to meet their own challenge point. This enables the coach to observe the appropriateness of the choice and engage in conversation with the climber to assist (through questioning) them to determine if adjustments are needed or progression is possible. Although the coach has designed the experience during the pre-impact set, participants are able to make a range of decisions about how they apply themselves and to which climb during the impact set, and during the post-impact set, facilitate the evaluation of effectiveness of performance to influence future action.

In an outdoor top-rope rock-climbing setting, participants often can fulfil a number of roles including the climber, belayer or back-up belayer, all requiring their own set of techniques necessary for group members to be able to safely and successfully climb and be lowered to the ground. There is also, as with indoor climbing, the opportunity to attempt different grades, as well as different styles of climbing. By setting up multiple options, climbers can engage in a conversation about the difficulty they wish to attempt to climb, as well as consider a climb requiring a different style of climbing to further challenge their climbing ability.

Example 3—Bowling (Cricket)

The Small Group Style of coaching could be applied to a beginner cricket episode to meet many objectives. Let us presume that a coach has a team of beginners (or second season) players with a variety of abilities in bowling (pre-impact set). If the coach insists on one level of challenge (bowling off a full run-up with correct delivery stride), it may be that the challenge

TABLE 7.1 Three challenge points for bowling.

Challenge level	Content	Success criteria
Challenge point 1	Practice delivery stride cues (see Chapter 3 example) and bowl ball.	Ball bounces once before partner fields it. Partner can field ball without moving more than one step in any direction for the bowler to score a point.
Challenge point 2	Three-step run up and bowl	Ball bounces once before partner fields it. Partner can field ball without moving more than one step in any direction for the bowler to score a point.
Challenge point 3	Bowl off usual run-up	Ball bounces once before partner fields it. Partner can field ball without moving more than one step in any direction for the bowler to score a point.

point is set at a level where some will experience success and some will experience failure. The Small Group Style—E is used for creating an episode with multiple challenge points so that all are more likely to experience some success at practice and improve. For example, three challenge points for bowling are set in Table 7.1. During the impact set, the coach would demonstrate and explain the three challenge points. Each player is asked to choose a challenge point at which to practice. Each player will be in a pair and will bowl to their partner (e.g.) x 20. During (or at the completion of) the episode the coach would ask the players, 'Do you think you have chosen an appropriate level of challenge to practice at (post-impact set)?' When using this coaching style, it is not the coach's job to tell the player if their level is appropriate or not. It is the player's role to learn to make decisions about appropriate levels of practice and adjustment if necessary.

Providing 'success criteria' can help the player know if they should move their challenge point or stay practising at their original chosen level. This can be helpful in cricket when beginners are bowling in a game, and they may not be experiencing success. The player may decide halfway through an over that a full run-up is not working, and they may decide to bowl off a three-step run-up. If a Small Group Style episode has occurred during training and the coach encourages the players to make similar decisions during a game (if they present themselves), then the players may have the confidence to make such decisions. Style E episodes create opportunities for players to think about their performance and make changes to achieve success. If this occurs, the player has shown independence in their decision-making about their own performance by choosing a level that they can participate at and focusing on what they can do rather than what they cannot do.

Example 4—Tennis

Effective coaches have, as previously outlined, a capacity to 'tailor their content and instruction to the specific learning readiness and interests of their students by integrating concepts and implementing teaching strategies that are responsive to the student's diverse needs' (Lyle & Cushion, 2010, p. 52). A tennis example that illustrates Small Group Coaching (Inclusion) could be applied to a game called 'Rally Like the Pros'. In this tennis game, players have been provided with the problem of 'How might you conduct a consistent rally with your partner?' Applying the principles of Small Group Coaching (Inclusion), the coach provides a series of prescribed stages of challenges for players to engage in. The pedagogical practice referred to as game modification, which can occur by modifying the challenge point during point play, becomes highly relevant in this style. For instance, the coach may suggest in the presented problem of attempting to conduct a consistent rally to provide players with a series of choices to conduct the rally. As an example, whereas, in the common form of tennis the ball is only permitted to bounce once in the court, players may be offered the decision of allowing the ball to bounce once or twice to play the ball, which is ultimately determined on each player's individual challenge point. Similarly, the coach may decide to provide additional challenge points that relate to the player's choice—which essentially presents as the key pedagogical tenet of Small Group Coaching (Inclusion). These might include:

1. Players have the option of first 'tapping' the ball with the racquet to first control the ball, with or without permitting the 'tapped' ball to bounce (for additional control), before returning the ball to their opponent;
2. In a similar example of applying Small Group Coaching Inclusion: Style E, players may decide to select a lower compression ball—which flight time is slower—in order to increase time to establish a balanced body position before returning the ball over the net to the opponent; and
3. In one final example, the elimination of tennis racquets in favour of throwing and catching the ball during the game presents yet an additional entry-level challenge point choice for some players who may not necessarily possess the physical skills to perform the task. This form of simplification permits maximum participation and empowers the player to select an appropriate challenge point to maintain play at 'their' chosen level.

Conclusion

The role of the coach when adopting Small Group Coaching (Inclusion) is most evident in the pre-impact set of decision-making that relates to the player's roles and/or entry challenge point (i.e., level of performance) for the task (Mosston & Ashworth, 2008). The most inclusive execution of this style, with respect to task challenge point, would occur when the coach has discussed with the player the suitable challenge point entry for the task, or to allow the player to view the multiple options, self-assess and then select an appropriate entry point. The role of the coach is to observe the players and, when appropriate, engage in conversation in connection to the player's performance at the given challenge point in which they are playing, in addition to whether they are practising at the optimal challenge point for that player (Mosston & Ashworth, 2008). If coaches desire players who are able to individually make decisions to select an appropriate level of practice, reflect on their practice and make changes, if necessary, Small Group Coaching (Inclusion) provides opportunities for these skills to be practised.

References

Beckett, K. (1991). The effects of two teaching styles on college students' achievement of selected physical education outcomes. *Journal of Teaching in Physical Education*, 10, 153–169.

Chatzipanteli, A. (2018). Inclusion teaching style and metacognition in physical education classes. *Education Journal*, *1*(1), 51–59.
Curran, T., Hill, A. P., Hall, H. K., & Jowett, G. E. (2015). Relationships between the coach-created motivational climate and athlete engagement in youth sport. *Journal of Sport and Exercise Psychology*, *37*(2), 193–198.
Ford, P. R., & Williams, A. M. (2013). The acquisition of skill and expertise: The role of practice and other activities. In A. M. Williams (Ed.), *Science and soccer: Developing elite performers* (pp. 122–138). Routledge.
Goldberger, M., & Gerney, P. (1986). The effects of direct teaching styles on motor skill acquisition of fifth grade children. *Research Quarterly for Exercise and Sport*, *57*, 215–219.
Goldberger, M., Gerney, P., & Chamberlain, J. (1982). The effects of three styles of teaching on the psychomotor performance of fifth grade children. *Research Quarterly for Exercise and Sport*, *53*(2), 116–124.
Goudas, M., Biddle, S., Fox, K., & Underwood, M. (1995). It ain't what you do, it's the way that you do it! Teaching style affects children's motivation in track and field. *The Sport Psychologist*, *9*, 254–264.
Guadagnoli, M. A., & Lee, T. D. (2004). Challenge point: A framework for conceptualizing the effects of various practice conditions in motor learning. *Journal of Motor Behavior*, *36*(2), 212–224.
Hewitt, M., Edwards, K., Reid, M., & Pill, S. (2018). Applying the game sense approach and Mosston and Ashworth's inclusion style-E to promote athlete-centred tennis coaching with junior novice players. In S. Pill (Ed.), *Perspectives on athlete-centred coaching* (pp. 193–205). Routledge.
Kirby, S., Byra, M., Readdy, S., & Wallhead, T. (2015). Effects of spectrum teaching styles on college students' psychological needs satisfaction and self-determined motivation. *European Physical Education Review*, *21*(4), 521–540.
Leo, F. M., Sánchez, P. A., Sánchez, D., Amado, D., & Calvo, T. C. (2009). Influence of the motivational climate created by coach in the sport commitment in youth basketball players. *Revista de Psicología del Deporte*, *18*(suppl.), 375–378.
Lyle, J., & Cushion, C. (2010). *Sports coaching: Professionalisation and practice*. Churchill Livingston Elsevier.
Morgan, K. (2017). Reconceptualizing motivational climate in physical education and sport coaching: An interdisciplinary perspective, *Quest*, *69*(1), 95–112.
Mosston, M. (1966). *Teaching physical education*. Merrill.
Mosston, M. (1981). *Teaching physical education* (2nd ed.). Merrill.
Mosston, M., & Ashworth, S. (2008). *Teaching physical education* (1st online ed.). https://spectrumofteachingstyles.org/assets/files/book/Teaching_Physical_Edu_1st_Online.pdf
Pensgaard, A. M., & Roberts, G. C. (2002). Elite athletes' experiences of the motivational climate: The coach matters. *Scandinavian Journal of Medicine and Science in Sports*, *12*, 54–59.
Pill, S., & Williams, J. (2017). Pursing physical education outcomes through sports education. *Active + Healthy Journal Promoting Informed Practice*, *24*, 11–14.
Salvara, M. I., Jess, M., Abbott, A., & Jozsef, B. (2006). A preliminary study to investigate the influence of different teaching styles on pupils' goal orientations in physical education. *European Physical Education Review*, *12*(1), 51–74.
Siedentop, D. (1994). *Sport education: Quality PE through positive sport experiences*. Human Kinetics.
Yan, V. X., Guadagnoli, M. A., & Haycocks, N. (2020). Appropriate failure to create effective learning: Optimizing challenge. In N. J. Hodges & A. M. Williams (Eds.), *Skill acquisition in sport: Research, theory and practice* (3rd ed., pp. 313–329). Routledge.
Zeng, H. Z., Leung, R. W., Liu, W., & Bian, W. (2009). Learning outcomes taught by three teaching styles in college fundamental volleyball classes. *Clinical Kinesiology*, *63*(1), 1–6.

8
COACHING BY GUIDED DISCOVERY
Style F

Shane Pill, Brendan SueSee, Joss Rankin and Mitch Hewitt

Coaching by Guided Discovery Style F is characterised by the logical and sequential design of questions that lead the player/s to a coach's pre-determined response. The role of the coach is to design the question sequence, and the role of the player/s is to discover the answer—a concept, an idea, a principle of play, a tactic or a strategy (Mosston & Ashworth, 2008). Note here, we refer to tactics as the individual player response to the requirements of the movement and to strategies as pre-determined ideas about how to play moments or phases of play (phases: offence, transition to defence, defence, transition to attack, starts and restarts).

When Coaching by Guided Discovery, each question posed by the coach requires a single correct answer. The cumulative effect of the sequence of questions is a converging process towards the target answer along a predominantly pre-determined 'pathway'. If the player/s already know the answer, then it is not discovery; it is retrieval practice of known knowledge. Retrieval practice is valuable if the coach's objective of the episode is consolidation of knowledge and understanding, or to context the development of new knowledge or understanding by firstly recalling what is already known and understood so the connection to the new learning is clear to the player/s. SueSee, Pill and Hewitt (2020) suggested that in the field of physical education, guided discovery is often claimed to be used when using a constraints-led approach, or a Tactical Model, such as Teaching Games for Understanding (TGfU) or a Game Sense approach; however, in some cases, these episodes are retrieval practice due to the player's previous knowledge with no 'discovery' of new knowledge.

Using questions with players is a common coaching practice and consistent with athlete-centred coaching. From a learning perspective, sport pedagogy researchers have found that the well-considered use of questions is an effective form of pedagogy for focusing attention on key concepts and cues, for recall of understanding, clarifying understanding, problem-solving, and the development of decision-making skills (O'Connor et al., 2021). Episodes with players that consist of randomly generated 'on the spot' questions, review questions, exploratory questions, and divergent questions are not examples of guided discovery. When planning for guided discovery, the coach should anticipate the ideal response to each question as each question asked by the coach is based on the response given to the previous question. Ideally, the first question 'sets the scene' for discovery by creating dissonance in

DOI: 10.4324/9781003041443-9

which the player searches for the answer. Each question asked from there moves the player 'a step' towards the last response, which is stating the discovered concept, idea, principle of play, tactic, or a strategy, or demonstrating the answer through movement (Mosston & Ashworth, 2008). These 'steps' can often be important for establishing context or purpose for the 'final' pre-determined answer or response. Unlike Styles A–E, when Coaching by Guided Discovery a coach never tells the answer because the idea is to keep the player in cognitive dissonance to promote inquiry until the dissonance ceases to exist as the discovery is made (Mosston, 1966). Opportunities arise for using Guided Discovery when a player does not know the answer or solution to a problem (cognitive dissonance). The coach has two possible choices in such a situation. First, they can tell the player the answer or, second, they can guide the player to the correct, single response using Guided Discovery. The coach may be tempted to tell the player the answer as they believe this would be faster, and in some cases it may be. However, if the 'telling' option is chosen, a learning episode is created, which does require the player to possess the skill or confidence to search for the solution or solve the problem.

An important skill of the coach, when applying Coaching by Guided Discovery, is to listen to the players' responses to interpret the significance or completeness of the response in order to know whether to re-frame the question to get a more complete or meaningful response, or to move on to the next question. If the player does not know the answer to the question, Mosston and Ashworth (2008) suggested that the cognitive 'jump' or step the coach is asking the player to make is too overwhelming, and therefore, another question is appropriate requiring a smaller 'cognitive step' or 'jump'. Guided discovery is often associated with game-based coaching (Breed & Spittle, 2011; den Duyn, 1997; Hewitt, 2015; Kinnerk et al., 2018; Pill, 2012a). In addition to being used in a game-based approach as a positive pedagogy for sport coaching (Light & Harvey, 2017), the use of questioning to guide players' learning is central to an athlete-centred approach (Kidman, 2001; Potrac & Cassidy, 2006; Pill, 2018). An athlete-centred approach is a philosophy of coaching aimed at developing player responsibility and ownership for their behaviour as people and as a player.

The difficulty and complexity in generating questions and executing a sequential questioning strategy, like Guided Discovery, is recognised as a potential barrier to coaches fully adopting coaching approaches where facilitating learning by questioning is emphasised, such as the variants of game-based coaching (Harvey & Light, 2015; Pill, 2016a, 2016b). To achieve variants of game-based coaching approaches where inquiry by the coach using questioning strategies with players is a distinctive pedagogical characteristic of the approach requires a proficient understanding of the sport by the coach. Therefore, it has been suggested that to enact game-based coaching well is only possible by coaches who are pedagogical and content experts in their sport—it is only test pilots who can fly it (Launder, 2001). In a physical education context, Howarth (2005) argued that to teach games for understanding requires knowledge about the game and knowledge about how to make learning experiences which require appropriate cognitive demands on the learners to be active in the development of their cognitive understanding. These demands are created through the questioning skills, which, if lacking, can frustrate, impede, or suppress the use of questioning players as a learning option, even for those coaches or teachers with considerable knowledge of the game. However, we agree with Kirk (2016) that it is not only 'test pilots' who can fly with this style of coaching, but many coaches and volunteer community coaches without an education background require assistance to be able to perform this style effectively with confidence.

It is important for us to note that guided discovery explanations in skill acquisition and motor learning literature are not necessarily the same as Coaching by Guided Discovery that we explain in this chapter. For example, in Smeeton et al.'s (2005) investigation of the effectiveness of explicit instruction, guided discovery and discovery learning, the guided discovery group were provided direct instruction in the form of 'look at' statements whereas the explicit instruction group were provided 'look at . . . see how . . .', and the discovery group no information cues at all.

Examples of Coaching by Guided Discovery Style F

Example 1—Outdoor Pursuits (Kayaking)

In kayaking, correct body position in the boat is critical for efficiency of the paddle stroke and conservation of energy. It can be straightforward for a kayaking coach to show and tell participants how to position their body most efficiently to perform paddle strokes; however, it is common to see participants slump in their seats, lean back in the boat and rely on their arms to paddle as they are not experienced with understanding what fluent and efficient paddling feels like. The correct, upright body position is not necessarily 'natural' and as such requires some conscious and deliberate attention to execute.

One example of applying Guided Discovery in kayaking can be considered in the refining of correct paddling position regardless of the range of strokes that may be executed by paddlers, such as forward, reverse, sweep or rudder. The coach could describe a short journey that travels to and from, and weaves through an area of mangroves. The general outline has deliberately been created by the coach during the pre-impact set to allow opportunity for 'discovery' during practice. The journey would allow participants ample time to explore, observe the area, interact with the environment and, for the purpose of this task, apply a range of paddle strokes that challenges the position that they put themselves in, to correctly apply paddle strokes and avoid fatigue.

The impact set, represented by the journey in this example, allows the coach to work with paddlers as they make observations specifically based on paddler body position and the impact on stroke technique execution. Correct position requires paddlers to sit upright with head over hips, maintenance of the 'paddlers box', torso rotation to initiate and execute strokes and knees and feet 'locked' (to allow greater efficiency in torso rotation). A common observation with novice paddlers is that as they begin to feel fatigued or simply search for a 'comfortable position' in the boat, they slump or lean backwards, restricting torso rotation and requiring heavy reliance on arms to pull the paddle through the water. This limits the range of paddle strokes that can be applied and reduces stroke efficiency, increasing paddler fatigue. If the coach were to observe this and tell the paddler to sit upright, they may do so for a short period of time, and as often happens, return to their slumped position as sitting in a kayak upright often feels 'unnatural'. To help the paddler understand 'what' they are feeling as they tire and 'why' correct body position is important, they may guide them to a possible solution. Following is an example of a conversation that represents a possible post-impact set.

COACH (LIZ): Jake, it looks like your arms are getting a bit tired.
PARTICIPANT PADDLER (JAKE): They are so tired; I don't think I'll be able to paddle all day if it's like this.

COACH (LIZ): I'm sure you will but there is something you can do to help give your arms a bit of a rest, do you have an idea what that might be?
PARTICIPANT PADDLER (JAKE): I could stop paddling but then I wouldn't get anywhere.
COACH (LIZ): (laughs) That's one idea but you are right, we would have to go on without you which we can't do. Your arms represent a group of muscles that you are using now, can you think of other groups of muscles that might be able to help?
PARTICIPANT PADDLER (JAKE): Well, it's not like my legs can do anything, what about my abs?
COACH (LIZ): That's an interesting point you make. Your abdominal muscles can be important in doing some of the work to support your arms, but let's think about how we can get them working. What happens if you put your feet back on those pedals in your boat?
PARTICIPANT PADDLER (JAKE): Oh, that makes me sit up
COACH (LIZ): Ok, so if you stay in that position, paddle with me and talk through how you might be able to use your abs as you've suggested.
PARTICIPANT PADDLER (JAKE): Oh yeah, if I sit up, I can twist at my abs and do the longer strokes like you showed us.
COACH (LIZ): And how are your legs helping?
PARTICIPANT PADDLER (JAKE): Well, I'm pushing against the pedals to help me rotate in my strokes and I don't feel like I'm pulling the paddle with my arms so much.
COACH (LIZ): That's great, and I can see you are keeping your elbows at 90 degrees to keep in that 'paddlers box position'. So, if you feel your arms getting a bit tired, what might you focus on to see if you can make an improvement?
PARTICIPANT PADDLER (JAKE): Check that my feet are on the pedals, I'm sitting upright and rotating my body rather than pulling the paddle through the water.
COACH (LIZ): Excellent work Jake, so keep focussing on that as we paddle, even with the other strokes you might use.
PARTICIPANT PADDLER (JAKE): Cheers Liz.
INSTRUCTOR (LIZ): No worries Jake, you're doing well.

In this example, Jake has independently made the discovery about why correct body position is important and how it helps him to paddle more efficiently and effectively. As this is occurring during the task, Liz can have similar conversations with other paddlers as it becomes relevant while they are exploring, allowing each of these paddlers to work through their own process of discovery, guided by Liz.

Example 2—Baseball

In baseball Guided Discovery could be used if a batter was having difficulty with a pitcher's fastball. The batter seems to be behind or late with their swing and not able to make a change to cope or catch up. The coach observes for a few at-bats (or in practice) before deciding that the player is not making the change. It would be simple to tell the player a solution; however, the coach decides to guide the player to a possible solution (pre-impact set). During the Impact set the conversation might follow this sequence of questioning:

COACH: Hey Farouk—you seemed to be getting jammed a bit by that inside fastball?
PLAYER: Yeah coach—but what can I do?
COACH: Good question. What can you do?

PLAYER: Well, I can't ask the pitcher to throw slower.
COACH: No, you can't, but how can you give yourself more time to see the ball?
PLAYER: If the pitcher was further away?
COACH: Correct! Can you move the pitcher further away?
PLAYER: No—he has to stand on the plate to pitch.
COACH: That's true, but there are two people in this situation—who else can move?
PLAYER: Me? Where can I move?
COACH: Can you move in the box?
PLAYER: Yes, I can move up in the box or back in the box.
COACH: Which direction would put you further away from the pitcher?
PLAYER: Back in the box. Ahh ha . . . . so I will have more time to see the fast ball?
COACH: Correct! So, what will you do next at bat?
PLAYER: I will move deep in the box! Thanks coach. I'll give it a go.

Example 3—Cricket (Bowling)

When bowling in cricket, the bowler may be trying to place the ball at a certain spot on the pitch. Like all sports that include the delivery of a ball to be struck by the 'opponent', the bowler may at times have accuracy of ball placement issues. The coach could apply a Guided Discovery episode to assist the player in discovering the answer or solution to the problem. For instance, the bowler is observed to be bowling the ball full (i.e., the ball is not bouncing 'on a good length' but 'over-pitched' before it gets to the batter) and a little wide of what is considered a 'good line' (pre-impact set). The following is an example (impact-set) of how the dialogue may play out in a Guided Discovery episode:

COACH: That's the third ball which was a little wide and a little full. What do you think you may need to do?
PLAYER: I'm not really sure!
COACH: OK—let's deal with one thing at a time. Where would the ball bounce if I let it go really early, or up high in my action?
PLAYER: I don't know?
COACH: OK—where would the ball go if I let it go really late in my action?
PLAYER: On the pitch! Probably short.
COACH: Correct! So, letting it go early is the opposite of late, so if I let it go early where might it go?
PLAYER: Up high or full?
COACH: Correct. So, since your last three balls were all full, what does that mean?
PLAYER: That I am letting it go too early.
COACH: Maybe. What's the solution though if you want the ball to bounce on a better length?
PLAYER: Let it go later!
COACH: Correct. Let's give that a go and see if it improves your length.

In this episode the player (with the assistance of the coach) has discovered the principle which affects where the ball bounces on the pitch and what they must do to adjust to achieve a desired outcome.

Example 4—Tennis

The key defining characteristic of Coaching by Guided Discovery is a series of well-sequenced questions specifically designed to lead the player to a single and predetermined outcome or response. In this style one might use the metaphor of 'climbing stairs', with each step representing a separate question, which then leads to another question that complements and extends the player's understanding of the end concept. In the tennis example given in the following, the authors demonstrate a logical set of questions that ultimately leads the player to discover a concept, principle, relationship or rule that was not previously known. Table 2.3 illustrates the pedagogical pathway—applied by the coach—and appropriate application of questions to achieve the predetermined concept. In this example—the end concept that the coach wishes the player to engage with and understand relates to 'How to hit a forehand in a crosscourt direction'.

The sequence of questions in Table 8.1 is specifically designed to lead the player to understand and apply the key concept of hitting the ball in a crosscourt direction during a rally. It is evident, in this example, that the coach pursues a line of questioning related to the technical aspects of achieving the outcome. If the coach chooses, a similar sequence of questions could be implemented to explore and discover a relevant tactical concept. The dialogue between the coach and player highlights that the questions are not just recall questions to assess or consolidate player knowledge at the end of the coaching episode.

A Note on Developing Player Understanding Through Game Play Analysis

The use of questioning by the coach is a teaching strategy used to engage player attention, to check for understanding, and to promote thinking and learning. Different types of questions promote different thinking patterns (Gréhaigne & Godbout, 2020). Matching questioning to player readiness and need is a key strategy in framing coaching sessions as a learning context and the sport coach as educator. Questions which require remembering or recall, comprehension, and clarification of understanding potentially serve an educative role. If the coach's intention is to check comprehension of an already introduced game concept, then questions to prompt player recall are

TABLE 8.1 A sample of predetermined questions related to hitting a forehand groundstroke in a crosscourt direction.

Target Concept: To hit a forehand groundstroke in a crosscourt direction during a rally.
Question 1: What are the different positions that you can place the ball in the court during a rally?
Question 2: To score a point, during this game, you can only hit the ball into this part of the court (crosscourt) to score a point. How will you attempt to achieve this outcome?
Question 3: How did you technically attempt to hit the ball into a crosscourt direction during a rally?
Question 4: Where were your racquet strings pointing when you were attempting to hit the ball in a crosscourt direction during a rally?
Question 5: Where did you attempt to contact the ball with your racquet (i.e., early or late) when trying to direct the ball in a crosscourt direction?

aligned with the coach's intention (O'Connor et al., 2021). However, as explained in this chapter, Coaching by Guided Discovery is a specific sequence of purposeful questioning that is a combination of recall questions, which eventually lead to a discovery of a principle or solution.

Harvey, Cope and Jones (2016) indicated that coaches have difficulty with the purposeful application of questioning. With this experience in mind, Pill (2012b) suggested a matrix for planning questions based on Laban's movement analysis framework to help coaches pre-plan their questioning strategy prior to practice sessions. There are many ways of thinking about a questioning strategy. Questions may be thought of as *skinny or closed* when requiring little thinking and perhaps only recall; *fat or open* when requiring application, evaluation, analysis, or creativity; *high consensus*, where individuals would provide the same or similar response; *low consensus*, which would encourage a diverse range of responses; *review* to specifically recall information; and *true* for questions that prompt an evaluation (Kagan, 2005; Harvey & Light, 2015). Siedentop and Tannehill (2000) suggested questions can be placed in four categories based on the cognitive behaviour that the question encourages: recall questions associated with declarative (conceptual, propositional, or descriptive) knowledge; convergent questions requiring reasoning to apply a solution at the right time; divergent questions to develop new and creative solutions to a problem; and value questions that call for opinion, choice, or the expression of an attitude.

Harvey et al. (2016) summarised three questioning strategies that might be used in a game-centred coaching approach: debate of ideas, reflective toss, and the GROW model. The debate of ideas (Deriaz, Poussin & Gréhaigne, 1998) is a questioning strategy in which play is paused and a pre-selected problem, measure or situation is analysed based on coach observation and player experiences during play. It is our experience that this type of inquiry strategy is often used by coaches in team sport settings during 'tactical time-outs'. A debate of ideas is different to the 'freeze play' (Worthington, 1974) pedagogy, which involves players stopping where they are in play to create a 'living blackboard' through which to analyse a moment in play with a coach. The reflective toss is a question on gameplay experience that the coach uses to 'toss' responsibility for learning to a player as it requires a statement from the player (Harvey & Light, 2015). The GROW model consists of four steps: establish the goal of the activity, examine reality compared to the goal, survey players for obstacles and options, and then establish a way forward.

In the context of developing athletic training professionals, Barnum et al. (2009) discussed the use of 'strategic questioning' as an active learning process aimed at connecting previous learning with new learning. Strategic questioning was defined as 'the conscious adaptation of the timing, sequencing and phrasing of questions in order to facilitate student processing of information at increasingly complex cognitive processing levels' (p. 24). The pedagogical sequence consisted of three types of questions: 'What?', 'So what?', 'Now what?'. We have shown in this chapter that Coaching by Guided Discovery is a sophisticated questioning strategy requiring that a coach know how the sequence of questions develops with purpose. It has specific pre-impact, impact, and post-impact considerations. Notwithstanding any merits of the questioning strategies described earlier or ways of classifying the types of questions, a coach may plan or consider in the moment to use, in a Spectrum of Coaching Styles guided discovery has specific meaning.

Conclusion

Undoubtedly, this is a challenging style to perform well as the coach must resist the temptation to tell the player the answer if the player does not know—and it is equally challenging to know what the player does not know unless there is some form of pre-assessment. Identifying the 'coachable' moment is also difficult for some coaches, especially if they perceive that just telling the player the answer is faster and they can move on to work with another player. This may well be the need in some situations, however, in the long term; if coaches want players who are independent thinkers and problem solvers (such as is suggested as an outcome of Tactical Models for sport coaching such as the Game Sense approach), then a dominant teaching style of telling and directing players to the answers will not lead to players developing this ability because of their experience of coaching.

In effect, Coaching by Guided Discovery is intended to develop 'understanding' rather than simply 'knowing' or 'recalling'. From a cognitive epistemology, players must be placed in episodes where cognitive dissonance occurs, and then guided or supported in their problem solving or search for the answer. From an ecological epistemology, players are being guided in their exploration and identification of affordances in the playing environment by the question sequence the coach uses.

References

Barnum, M. G., Guyer, S., Levy, L. S., Willeford, S., Sexton, P., Gardner, G., & Fincher, A. L. (2009). Questioning and feedback in athletic training clinical education. *Athletic Training Education Journal*, *4*(1), 23–27.

Breed, R., & Spittle, M. (2011). *Developing game sense through tactical learning*. Cambridge.

den Duyn, N. (1997). *Game sense: Developing thinking players workbook*. Australian Sports Commission.

Deriaz, D., Poussin, B., & Gréhaigne, J.-F. (1998). Le débat d' idées (The debate of ideas). *Éducation Physique et Sport*, *273*, 80–82.

Gréhaigne, J.-F., & Godbout, P. (2020). Debate of ideas and understanding with regard to tactical learning in team sports. *Journal of Teaching in Physical Education*. doi: 10.1123/jtpe.2019–0269

Harvey, S., Cope, E., & Jones, R. (2016). Developing questioning in game-centered approaches. *Journal of Physical Education, Recreation & Dance*, *87*(3), 28–35.

Harvey, S., & Light, R. (2015). Questioning for learning in game-based approaches to teaching and coaching. *Asia-Pacific Journal of Health, Sport and Physical Education*, *6*(2), 175–190.

Hewitt, M. (2015). *Teaching styles of Australian tennis coaches: An exploration of practices and insights using Mosston and Ashworth's Spectrum of teaching styles*. PhD thesis. School of Linguistics, Adult and Specialist Education, Faculty of Business, Education, Law and Arts, The University of Southern Queensland.

Howarth, K. (2005). Introducing the teaching games for understanding model in teacher education programs. In L. Griffin & J. Butler (Eds.), *Teaching games for understanding: Theory, research and practice* (pp. 91–105). Human Kinetics.

Kagan, S. (2005). Rethinking thinking: Does Bloom's taxonomy align with brain science? *Kagan Online Magazine*, *8*(3). www.KaganOnline.com

Kidman, L. (2001). *Developing decision makers: An empowerment approach to coaching*. Innovative Print Solutions.

Kinnerk, P., Harvey, S., MacDonncha, C., & Lyons, M. (2018). A review of the game-based approaches to coaching literature in competitive team sport settings. *Quest*, *70*(4), 401–418.

Kirk, D. (2016). 'Is TGfU a model only test pilots can fly?': Teacher-coach development in game-centred approaches. *Research Quarterly for Exercise and Sport*, *87*(suppl), S4–S5.

Launder, A. G. (2001). *Play practice: The games approach to teaching and coaching sports*. Human Kinetics.

Light, R., & Harvey, S. (2017). Positive pedagogy for sport coaching. *Sport, Education and Society*, *17*(2), 271–287.

Mosston, M. (1966). *Teaching physical education*. Merrill.

Mosston, M., & Ashworth, S. (2008). *Teaching physical education* (1st online ed.). https://spectrumofteachingstyles.org/assets/files/book/Teaching_Physical_Edu_1st_Online.pdf

O'Connor, D., Larkin, P., Robertson, S., & Goodyear, P. (2021). The art of the question: The structure of questions posed by youth soccer coaches during training. *Physical Education and Sport Pedagogy*. https://doi.org/10.1080/17408989.2021.1877270

Pill, S. (2012a). Teaching game sense in soccer. *Journal of Physical Education, Recreation and Dance*, *83*(3), 42–52.

Pill, S. (2012b). *Play with purpose: Developing game sense in AFL footballers*. ACHPER Publications.

Pill, S. (2016a). Making learning visible: The pedagogy of questioning in a game sense approach. In J. Bruce & C. North (Eds.), *2015 Game Sense for Teachers and Coaches Conference: Proceedings* (pp. 143–155), Christchurch, November 19–20.

Pill, S. (2016b). Implementing game sense coaching approach in Australian football through action research. *Ágora Para La Ef Y El Deporte | Agora for PE and Sport*, *18*(1), 1–19.

Pill, S. (Ed.). (2018). *Perspectives on athlete-centred coaching*. Routledge.

Potrac, P., & Cassidy, T. (2006). The coach as a 'more capable other'. In R. Jones (Ed.), *The sports coach as educator: Re-conceptualising sports coaching* (pp. 39–50). Routledge.

Siedentop, D., & Tannehill (2000). *Developing teaching skills in physical education* (4th ed.). Mayfield Publishing Company.

Smeeton, N. J., Williams., A. M., Hodges, N. J.m & Ward, P. (2005). Relative effectiveness of various instructional approaches in developing anticipation skill. *Journal of Experimental Psychology: Applied*, *11*(2), 98–110.

SueSee, B., Pill, S., & Hewitt, M. (2020). Reconciling approaches: Mosston and Ashworth's Spectrum of teaching styles as a tool to examine the complexity of any teaching (or coaching) approach. In B. SueSee, M. Hewitt, & S. Pill (Eds.), *The Spectrum of teaching styles in physical education* (pp. 73–84). Routledge.

Worthington, E. (1974). *Teaching soccer skill*. Lepus Books.

9
COACHING BY PROBLEM SOLVING (CONVERGENT DISCOVERY)
Style G

Shane Pill, Brendan SueSee, Joss Rankin and Mitch Hewitt

In the previous chapter, Guided Discovery was described as a tightly sequenced series of questions by the coach that led to an anticipated discovery. When Coaching by Problem Solving (Convergent Discovery), the coach's role is to make the decision about the concept to be discovered. The coach designs a problem or question that requires the players to come up with the questions and their own sequence to converge on an answer. The decision about 'designing problems' is at the heart of this coaching style. To do this well requires good insight into the specific elements of the activity, the structure of the activity, and the sequence of progressions (Mosston, 1981). In the impact set, players make decisions about the steps to take and the questions to ask to solve the problem. In the post-impact set, the players check their reasoning and verify their answers or solutions with the coach. Unlike Guided Discovery, the learning objective is known to the players when Coaching by Problem Solving, as it is part of setting the problem (Mosston & Ashworth, 2008).

Convergent thinking is the ability to find the ideal solution to the problem. It represents a style of thinking that allows coaches to develop with players solutions to clearly defined problems. Empirical findings support the idea that convergent thinking is related to cognitive persistence (Zhang, Sjoerds & Hommel, 2020). Cognitive persistence is the willingness and ability to sustain and self-regulate effort and attention to improve performance. Convergent thinking is often associated with game intelligence and game-based coaching approaches (Memmert, 2015). This is because game-based coaching approaches have a long history of positioning the coach as designers of game forms that present specific 'problems' to players so that the players can explore solutions pertinent to the demands (the problem) of the moment (Pill, 2014). Worthington (1974) described deliberate design of game forms as practice tasks using coach knowledge of where moments would occur because the game design was set for these moments to occur. When the moment occurred, Worthington described the coach employing a 'freeze replay' where 'the players must stop precisely where they are at the time the coach demands that they stop' (p. 172) to create a 'living tactical board' (p. 172) to discuss the game problem. We believe this type of approach is well suited to a Coaching by Problem Solving (Convergent Discovery) episode as players see themselves in the problem rather than trying to make abstract conceptualisations.

DOI: 10.4324/9781003041443-10

Problem-Based Learning

Game-based coaching approaches have been described as examples of problem-based learning (Pill, 2016; Turner. 2014). Problem-based learning is very different from other types of inquiry. Problem-based learning is initiated by a real-world challenge, such as specific match day scenario in a sport coaching context. Players apply their knowledge and understanding to the problem through critical reasoning to determine an answer to the problem that was presented. Therefore, Coaching by Problem Solving presented as a problem-based learning task requires a coach to guide the learning process by allowing the player/s self-directed practice interspersed with discussion with the coach to refine understanding. A problem-based task in a sport setting could look like: (1) Coach identifies and clarifies the scenario. (2) Coach defines the problem. (3) Player/s brainstorm explanations and movement solutions using existing knowledge. (4) Players try out explanations as potential solutions. (6) Player/s formulate further learning needs. (7) Player/s share findings and discuss potential further learning needs with the coach. Return to Steps 4–6 or go to 7. Present results to the coach (Pill, 2016). Hubball and Robertson (2004) suggested that adopting problem-based learning has the potential to enhance youth team and player development, but the coach must be prepared to treat their team or training squad as a community of learners. The concept of a community of learners is based on a belief in equally shared participation in the endeavour of learning and may require a cultural shift of expectation by coaches, players and, in some instances, parents.

Setting the Degree of Difficulty

Adult expert problem representations are likely more advanced than youth and novices regardless of age. Experts can therefore generate more extensive, tactical and event profiled descriptions of their decisions compared to novices (McPherson & Kernodle, 2003). This is important to remember when setting the degree of difficulty of the problem-solving challenge when designing games and practice tasks as problem-solving contexts.

Examples of Coaching by Problem Solving (Convergent Discovery) Style G

Example 1—Baseball

Coaching by Style G lends itself to many sports and baseball is no different. Scenarios or problems arise with every hitter as the team (but primarily the pitcher and catcher) try to get the hitter out or, at the very least, do not give the hitter the pitch that they love to hit. In this example, the coach decided that they want to create a practice episode where the pitcher and catcher attempt to 'solve the problem' or pitch to a specific hitter with specific strengths or weaknesses (pre-impact set). The following scenario could be given to the pitcher (right-handed) and catcher for them to solve (impact set). A right-handed hitter with extremely fast hands comes to the plate and stands deep in the box with a slightly open stance. The hitter also pulls the ball and gets a lot of hits to centre-left field. After the scenario is presented, the catcher is asked what he would do to make it difficult for the hitter? The catcher will identify the depth the hitter stands in the box and that he may also have a slightly open stance meaning that they do not like to hit pitches that are away, such as a tailing fastball, fastball away, a slider or a curve ball. Based on this, the catcher will not call for an inside fast ball and will call for those pitches to try to get the hitter to hit pitches which he does not like (pitches to the outside of the plate). The catcher may also be asked as a follow-up question or problem (by the coach): 'I would also move the outfield around to their left (the catcher's right)—why?' The catcher then explains the reasoning. It is the reasoning and dialogue between the coach and player/s that occurs during the post-impact set. Teaching players to use 'if-then-because' statements or thinking has been suggested by some (Pill & SueSee, 2017) as a helpful way to scaffold for players' thinking to help them develop problem-solving skills and verbalise the link between their thinking and actions. As with previous discovery coaching episodes, we note that if the player/s are asked a question or set a problem that they know the answer to, they are not discovering, they are recalling known information and the style has decision structures more closely resembling Practice Style.

Example 2—Netball: Getting Away From the Defender

When coaching beginners at netball, it is our experience that players may not be aware of principles which help them get away from a defender. The concept of changing direction with speed is often not known to the player and thus presents an opportunity to be discovered by the players through the Convergent Discovery process. During the impact set, the coach would provide the objective: players to discover the principle of the influence of speed on defending and explain a practice episode for this to occur. The coach sets a scenario by telling the players that they are going to conduct an experiment to discover the answer to the question, 'What helps us get rid of a good defender?' In Figure 9.1, an attacker (X) and a defender (D) are placed on a marker (M) to begin. The attacker travels towards the marker in front of the coach and then splits (chooses to go left or right) either right or left to that marker to receive a pass from the coach.

The 'experiment' is done three ways. The first way involves the attacker and defender being told that they can only travel at walking speed. The second way requires players to 'jog' slowly, and the third way involves being allowed to 'sprint'-run as fast as they can. The attacker takes note of how successful they are, or are not, at evading the defender using each of the three ways. In this scenario, there is one correct answer—the faster the player changes direction (and the faster the defender is travelling at the moment of change), the harder it is for the defender to get good position on their opponent. The challenge for the coach is

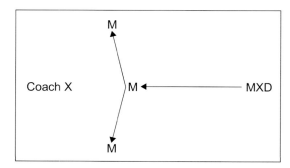

FIGURE 9.1 Positioning of attacker (X), defender (D), markers (M) and coach for Convergent Discovery episode. Arrows show direction the attacker moves before splitting left or right.

'inviting' the players to question the experience and converge on the answer. The feedback given during the discussion or at the end is the post-impact set.

Example 3—Group Adventure Initiative Activities to Enhance Outdoor Pursuits

Outdoor and adventure education lends itself to problem-based learning because the 'problem' faced often has elements of unpredictability that require participants to apply a set of principles to a situation to overcome the challenge. For example, an individual can practice a specific climbing technique such as laybacking on a purposely built artificial rock-climbing wall; however, mastering this wall does not guarantee the climber will be able to complete all laybacking problems presented on a range of walls or cliffs. This practice will undoubtedly help the climber approach a layback problem, but the difficulty of the climb and success of the climber will also be determined by a range of variables presented by the people involved, conditions presented by the environment and the equipment available. This need for problem-based learning also applies to the thinking required to effectively work within teams in these environments, particularly because outdoor pursuits are often conducted over a period of days or even weeks with the same group of people, making the ability to work effectively with others a critical factor for success.

Group adventure and initiative tasks are a form of problem-based learning that can be applied to emphasise the impact of elements of group functioning such as communication, roles and responsibilities and group structures as some examples. These tasks require members of a team to work as a group or several subgroups to achieve a set outcome. The coach of the task will present to the group the problem, the rules that must be followed to complete the task and the desired outcome, all of which has been pre-determined by the coach during the pre-impact set. The coach may then act as a source of clarification while the group works through a series of possible solutions, with the intent to complete the task in the most efficient way possible or one best solution. This is in line with the decision-making of Style G—whilst there may be many solutions the coach is seeking for one solution or answer that the group can come up with, and not to produce many answers as is the case with the next style (Style H) on The Spectrum, explained in Chapter 10. These tasks enable to group to trial a range of solutions, ask questions as they arise throughout the task and reflect on the process undertaken by themselves and the group. The decision-making and problem-solving process during the task afford the participants a range of opportunities to investigate and make decisions during the impact set. Although the problem and the end goal have both been pre-defined by the leader, a dominant focus for observation and reflection, such as the impact of applying a range of task and maintenance roles on the success of the group, also require participants to engage in questioning and reasoning as they evaluate effectiveness and most appropriate strategy during the post-impact set.

Example 4—Tennis

The following example in connection to tennis is designed to elicit a new and single response which may be related to a technical, tactical or movement response from the player. The challenge, which the coach determines in the pre-impact set, is unknown to the player, who must then, during the implementation or 'doing' phase of the anatomy of this style, discover a single correct answer to the problem. In comparison to the next style identified on The

Spectrum—Divergent Discovery-H, where a multitude of appropriate responses are available for the player to discover, Coaching by Problem Solving (Convergent Discovery): Style G only seeks one accurate and precise answer. In this example, the coach proposes to the player how to produce a slice serve that is designed to deviate through the air after contact is made with the ball and the racquet resulting in a 'sliding' effect once the ball contacts the ground. From a tactical perspective, a slice serve is considered highly effective due to its ability to move away from the opponent (either in a left or right direction) once it hits the ground. This potentially possesses additional challenges for the opponent, as the ball is not travelling in a 'straight' or direct trajectory (which presents as more of a predictable response and shot selection). The slice serve may not only force additional and pressured movement but also increase the chance of the opponent not making contact in the desired area of the racquet face (i.e., the middle of the racquet or the 'sweet spot'), which has the potential for a 'miss-hit' that increases an opportunity to apply an offensive play from the server. This additional movement from the opponent, because of the slice serve, applies pressure to the opponent and places the receiver in an uncomfortable and unbalanced position. In this strategy, the receiver may then receive a ball that has reduced pace, placement and control that might result in an unforced error or 'weak' return that ultimately permits an attacking play for the server on the return.

To achieve the aforementioned outcomes, the coach in the pre-impact set poses a single question for the player to negotiate:

1. How do you produce slice spin on your serve?

Through practice (in the impact set), the players are required to explore a range of possible responses (in this case technically) to achieve a desired and single outcome. In this experience, the player is challenged to instigate, reason question, and determine a degree of logic to sequentially make a connection that results in the discovery of the single and anticipated answer. Via this process, the player primarily leads the application of questions to the coach who plays a reduced role in this learning scenario. The player must negotiate a range of ways to grip the racquet to produce the desired 'slice spin' on the serve. For the benefit of our readers, the single response to the coach's original question is for the player to discover the 'continental grip'. This grip is a key technical application for producing slice on the serve to pursue a potentially 'winning' strategy, or at the very least, position the server in a position of tactical advantage.

Conclusion

Selecting Coaching by Problem Solving (Convergent Discovery) is based on the premise that there is a correct response, whether it is in the form of an answer, a movement response, or a tactical solution. The goal is to have the player/s produce the questions and to have the player/s undertake the 'search' for the answer or solution. The pedagogical role of the coach is to design the problem and/or context, to present the problem and its situation to the player/s, verify understandings and expectations before the players begin the exploration, and to provide feedback to the player/s by way of checking their reasoning and verifying their answers or solutions. As problems continually and frequently arise in sport, Coaching by Problem Solving is a style which can be used to prepare player/s by shifting the decisions to them to solve problems which they do not know the answer to.

References

Hubball, H., & Robertson, S. (2004). Using problem-based learning to enhance team and player development in youth soccer. *Journal of Physical Education, Recreation & Dance, 75*(4), 38–43.

McPherson, S. L., & Kernodle, M. W. (2003). Tactics, the neglected attributes of expertise: Problem representations and performance skills in tennis. In J. L. Starkes & K. A. Ericsson (Eds.), *Expert performance in sports: Advances in research on sport expertise* (pp. 137–168). Human Kinetics.

Memmert, D. (2015). *Teaching tactical creativity in sport: Research and practice*. Routledge.

Mosston, M. (1981). *Teaching physical education* (2nd ed.). Merrill.

Mosston, M., & Ashworth, S. (2008). *Teaching physical education* (1st online ed.). https://spectrumofteachingstyles.org/assets/files/book/Teaching_Physical_Edu_1st_Online.pdf

Pill, S. (2014). Informing game sense pedagogy with constraints led theory for coaching in Australian football. *Sports Coaching Review, 3*(1), 46–62.

Pill, S. (2016). Making learning visible: The pedagogy of questioning in a game sense approach. In J. Bruce & C. North (Eds.), *2015 Game Sense for Teachers and Coaches Conference: Proceedings* (pp. 143–155), Christchurch, November 19–20.

Pill, S., & SueSee, B. (2017). Including critical thinking and problem solving in physical education. *Journal of Physical Education, Recreation & Dance, 88*(9), 43–49.

Turner, A. (2014). Novice coaches negotiating teaching games for understanding. *University of Sydney Papers in Human Movement, Health and Coach Education Special Game Sense Edition,* 67–89.

Worthington, E. (1974). *Teaching soccer skill*. Lepus Books.

Zhang, W., Sjoerds, Z., & Hommel, B. (2020). Metacontrol of human creativity: The neurocognitive mechanisms of convergent and divergent thinking. *NeuroImage, 210,* 116572.

10
COACHING FOR CREATIVITY (DIVERGENT DISCOVERY)

Style H

Shane Pill, Brendan SueSee, Joss Rankin and Mitch Hewitt

The purpose of Coaching for Creativity (Divergent Discovery) is for players to discover or generate multiple possibilities that satisfy a question or situation. Until this point in our exploration of coaching styles, the coach has made the majority of decisions regarding 'the answer', and the role of the player/s has been to either replicate and perform or discover the target response or the player/s ability. As with previous styles, in a Coaching for Creativity episode, the coach makes all the decisions in planning (pre-impact set). In the impact-set where the task is initiated, the coach presents the question or problem and the player/s make the decisions about the production of answers. However, as the coach is seeking to stimulate divergent discovery thinking by the player/s, the coach is not seeking known solitary answer or response. Unlike the previous styles, in using this style the players are being asked to discover and produce options within the subject matter (Mosston, 1981; Mosston & Ashworth, 2008). Divergent discovery thinking requires the player to create multiple responses previously unknown to them. During the post-impact set, where the reflection occurs, the coach assists with the development and refinement of ideas using well-considered questions that serve as a source of verification of ideas if required (Mosston & Ashworth, 2008).

Divergent thinking represents a style of thinking for idea generation where more than one solution is workable. Divergent thinking is often applied to 'open' problems and challenges where creative solutions are sought (Benedek et al., 2014). Empirical findings suggest that divergent thinking is related to cognitive flexibility (Zhang, Sjoerds & Hommel, 2020). Daniel Memmert has been at the forefront of the exploration of the concept of tactical creativity and the encouragement of thinking abilities. Memmert has distinguished between tactical intelligence as convergent thinking and tactical creativity as divergent thinking. He defined tactical creativity 'as the generation of surprising, seldom and original solutions in specific tactical situations in team and racket sports' (Memmert, 2015, p. 24). Memmert suggested that coaches are encouraged to integrate tasks aiming for the development of divergent tactical thinking as early as possible in player development, as the effect of these activities are most influential in childhood.

DOI: 10.4324/9781003041443-11

Memmert proposed the 6-D theoretical framework for the Tactical Creativity Approach. The order of the 6-Ds are:

- Deliberate Play: relatively uninstructed and possibly unstructured games;
- 1-Dimension Games: games that offer tactical understanding through a volume of continuously repeating comparable tactical groupings;
- Diversification: a request to come up with new ideas and solutions for different situations;
- Deliberate Coaching: instruction options to manipulate player attention and focus;
- Deliberate Motivation: consideration of instructions that cause particular motivational moods that foster the generation of creative solutions; and
- Deliberate Practice: task centred practice in more advanced games to apply and explore solutions.

(Memmert, 2014, 2015)

The creativity-based differences in decision-making in football were shown to be underpinned by differences in players' visual search strategy. In a study by Roca, Ford and Memmert (2018), the most creative players employed a broader attentional focus, shorter fixation periods, and attention towards more informative locations compared with least-creative players. Most creative players detected teammates in advantageous positions earlier in attacking play scenarios. A differential learning approach seems to enhance learning of creative behaviour. This is where variability and 'noise' (distractions and disturbances) are used to stress the performance of novel movement solutions, accompanied by the encouragement of players to make errors, in order to encourage adaptation and transferable movement skills (Santos et al., 2018).

An over reliance on practice activities that narrow the player's focus of attention to the task and reduce the demand for attentional flexibility can be detrimental to the development of game-related decision-making ability (Furley, Memmert & Heller, 2010) and the development of tactical creativity. A continuously narrow focus of attention on technical task requirements in practice form activities that have no or minimal information relatedness to performance in the context of gameplay can have the long-term consequence of inattentional blindness (Memmert, 2015). Inattentional blindness is where the player's focus of attention results in missing relevant game-related information. For example, practice tasks that continually require repetition of essentially the same passing option 'off the line' do not teach players to scan the environment for passing options from which a choice has to be made. An overuse of task instructions with very specific behaviours to replicate a narrow attention can result in players not developing awareness about other game opportunities that open up during play (Memmert, 2011) and thus coach a failure of awareness (Memmert & Furley, 2007). Because of the representational nature of the focus of practice activities used in a game-based coaching approach, such as the Game Sense approach, players have the potential to be coached in these game form tasks to use a wide focus of attention and become adapted to placing attention more broadly than on a singular task (Pill, 2016). Therefore, the language the coach articulates is very important in the intention to Coach for Creativity (Divergent Discovery). From a cognitive perspective, the language directs the player to the necessary cognitive operation—creativity and not the recalling of known answers. From an ecological perspective, it might be seen to encourage player behavioural flexibility emerging from the search for different movement solutions to the same task outcome. Either way of 'seeing the world', if the coach is seeking multiple solutions, then practice tasks need to be designed to allow for this.

Examples of Coaching for Creativity (Divergent Discovery)

Example 1—Baseball

Coaching beginning players on how to prioritise moving the lead runner around the bases (pre-impact set) provides one of many opportunities for the use of Divergent Discovery coaching. During the impact set, the coach could set up a baseball field with all the players in their appropriate positions and a right-handed pitcher throwing. A runner would be placed at first base and no one is out. The coach could create a 'batting team' of two or three players and set the scenario or problem as 'None out, runner at first. Create three ways to move the lead runner around the bases'. The 'batting team' can throw the ball as a 'hit' so that the ball placement is more accurate, and at this stage, the coach is focusing on the cognitive development or solution creating aspect, more than the psychomotor aspect. The 'batting team' may throw the ball into 'right field', throw a ground ball behind the runner (hit and run), bunt down the first baseline or bunt down the third baseline as possible examples. There are of course numerous other solutions that may be generated in this scenario; however, not are all equal or appropriate. The feedback and discussions which followed would occur in the post-impact set. Once these solutions have been created and discussed, the coach could select three of the solutions produced by the players (or more) and ask the 'batting team' to try each one out ten times to gauge their effectiveness—thus cycling back to the previous chapters coaching style, Convergent Discovery Style.

Example 2—Netball

The game of netball can be classified as an invasion game (Thorpe, Bunker & Almond, 1986) and thus need concepts such as possession, invasion and scoring as a teaching aspect. The Divergent Discovery Style can be used to create episodes which provide the athletes with opportunities to discover or create tactics. Once players have developed the ability to pass and catch with reasonable consistency, they can be set the following problem by the coach. The impact-set begins with the coach suggesting:

> Your task, with your attacking partners, is to create three or more principles/strategies to increase your chances of scoring a point. When playing the game below, implement the strategies created. Planning the strategy first and then implementing it is acceptable.
>
> Rules/Constraints: The playing area is a third of the netball court (e.g., defensive third, (Figure 10.1). There are 3 attackers and 1 defender. Attackers are trying to score a point by the ball travelling from one sideline to the other. A point is scored if they can pass the ball to one of their players who is standing over the sideline opposite to where they began. Play begins with attacker 1 standing on the sideline and passing the ball into the court. Usual netball rules of no running with the ball and the defender being 3 feet/1 metre from the person with the ball.

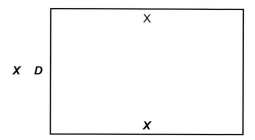

FIGURE 10.1 Third of a netball court. X = attacker, D = defender.

This Divergent Discovery scenario would work with players who do not already know the strategies. If they know the strategies, then they are recalling them, and this, therefore, would be considered a Practice Style episode. SueSee, Pill and Hewitt (2020) suggested that there are always challenges when using groups when attempting to implement discovery episodes—for two reasons. First, not all players arrive at the challenge or problem with comparable knowledge. Therefore, if someone knows the answer to the problem, they are not solving the problem; they are recalling a known strategy. Second, when one player discovers the solution to the problem and informs the other players, the discovery process has ended. Or as Mosston and Ashworth (2008) suggested, 'the other learners who hear (or see) the response become the receivers. They can no longer discover it. For these students, the discovery process has been aborted' (p. 221). A solution to this problem is to ask each player to write their strategy on a post-it notes first without talking and then to share. Sometimes the strategies will be the same, but at least the players will have created their own strategy if they have followed the coach's instructions. The players can then trial the strategy. The feedback and discussions which occur between the players and coach would occur during the post-impact set and would revolve around the coach asking questions to verify the solutions created by the players.

Example 3—Outdoor Pursuits (Rock Climbing)

Adventure education has long been closely aligned with the delivery of outdoor education programmes and outdoor pursuits alike. Although the definition of adventure is disputed and has evolved within a variety of social contexts, adventurous outdoor pursuits are often thought of as having an element of an unknown component to explore or encounter a significant element of new learning (Beames, Mackie & Atencio, 2019). The application of a Divergent Discovery coaching style inherently encourages participants to explore a range of possible solutions when encountering this unknown, unpredictable or unplanned learning that is synonymous with these ideas of adventure. When considering the application of a Divergent Discovery coaching style within adventurous outdoor pursuits, two examples in different contexts immediately come to mind:

1. A relatively experienced rock-climber in a top rope setting making the transition to learning to traditionally lead climb under supervision and

2. Making the transition from simply participating in the activities of an expedition to planning, preparing, conducting, and evaluating a 'self-directed' expedition.

In the first example a rock-climber who has experienced top rope rock climbing will have most likely engaged with the Divergent Discovery Style of coaching as they apply a range of learnt and discovered climbing techniques to ascend the cliff face that their rope has been set up on. In this setting there may be a range of possible ways to reach the top of the climb; however, it is not uncommon for a climber to receive information (beta) from a belayer or other group members about how to move their body and complete the climb. It is also quite possible for the climber to simply suggest that they are unable to continue and simply be lowered down in a top rope setting. In making the transition to traditional lead climbing, the participant must now make a range of decisions to keep themselves safe and determine what they will view as success or the solution that they establish. Once the participant has worked with the required equipment under supervision and demonstrated a level of understanding and safe application, the coach may initiate the pre-impact set by presenting the participant with the challenge to apply safe placement, rope management and climbing techniques to reach the top of a section of cliff. The decision about the challenge or problem has been made by the coach and would include the choice of an appropriate location for the skill level of the participant. Once the challenge has been set, the participant has a range of decision to now make during the impact set in learning. They must determine an appropriate route to take, identify the procedures for leading the climb, apply a range of climbing techniques they deem most appropriate and choose what pieces of equipment to place based on their capability, perception of safety and emotional state. The range of possible solutions to the initial challenge is what represents the opportunity for creativity or 'divergence' in producing a solution to the 'problem'. Once the climbing has been safely completed, both the participant and coach will share their thoughts and reasoning regarding the decisions that have been made during the impact set. The evaluative process that unfolds with the intention of informing future action represents the post-impact set of the learning. With this example then provided, you may wish to consider how the second example outlined earlier presents the opportunity for creativity through exploration and design by applying a Divergent Production Style of teaching within the context of adventure education.

Example 4—Tennis

As indicated earlier in this chapter, the key tenet of Coaching for Creativity (Divergent Discovery) strives to position a particular focus on a player's cognitive capacity and to create a plethora of possible solutions to a question that the coach presents during a coaching session that ultimately leads to a series of unknown and new experiences (Mosston & Ashworth, 2008). This commonly occurs in the impact or implementation phase of the overall anatomy of this coaching experience. A practical example of Coaching for Creativity (Divergent Discovery) may be seen in the game of 'Net Attack'. In this game, players are provided by the coach with the divergent question: 'How might you set up opportunities, during gameplay, to win the point from the net position?'. As illustrated prior, this question is posed during the pre-impact or planning phase of the coaching session. During the impact or implementation phase of the coaching experience, players are then challenged to sample, explore and experiment with the multiple solutions related to the coach's question. In connection to attacking the net, we are aware that there exists a variety of possible responses (i.e., divergent responses—not just one) in connection to responding to the coach's question. Some of the possible responses that players may discover during this game include:

1. If my opponent returns a ball that lands in a short position in the court, I have the opportunity to move forward—towards the net—and attempt an offensive pattern of play (positioning my opponent under pressure) to ultimately win the point from the net;
2. My aggressive or well-placed serve places my opponent under pressure and in a defensive position, so I move toward the net to take advantage of a 'weak' return and win the point from the net; and
3. My opponent's serve (either slow or without placing me under pressure) presents as an opportunity for me to attack the net with an approach shot that may result in winning the point from the net because of a 'weak' return from my opponent.

Conclusion

Coaching for Creativity (Divergent Discovery) is an 'open ended' process in that the content of a practice task is open ended because there is the possibility of multiple solutions, whether that be movement solutions or questions the players wish to explore. The process of Coaching for Creativity is therefore dynamic. When used in a group situation, it is important that when Coaching for Creativity the coach provides an opportunity for all players to suggest a solution, the opportunity for any player's solution to be attempted and that the coach fosters a supportive and inclusive group climate where there is tolerance for solutions, and of the players that suggest them, that don't work or are less optimal than other ideas. Therefore, when Coaching for Creativity with groups and teams of players, the coach must consider the affective domain of learning lest the joy that can be inherent in the process of discovery turn to stress in anticipation of an unsupportive group response to an individual's idea. Finally, we would like to add that even though many episodes of Coaching for Creativity may occur with one player telling the other players the answers (and thus aborting the discovery process for others), there are still positives from this. Often other players will question the solution suggested, and valuable discussion will follow as one player is required to justify their newly generated ideas. Whilst the cognitive process of discovery and creativity may have been reduced for some, other valued experiences may result.

References

Beames, S., Mackie, C., & Atencio, M. (2019). *Adventure and society*. London, UK: Palgrave Macmillan.
Benedek, M., Jauk, E., Fink, A., Koschutnig, K., Reishofer, G., Ebner, F., & Neubauer, A. C. (2014). To create or to recall? Neural mechanisms underlying the generation of creative new ideas. *NeuroImage, 88*, 125–133.
Furley, P., Memmert, D., & Heller, C. (2010). The dark side of visual awareness in sport: Inattentional blindness in a real-world basketball task. *Attention Perception & Psychophysics, 72*, 1327–1337.
Memmert, D. (2011). Sports and creativity. In M. A. Runco & S. R. Pritzker (Eds.), *Encyclopaedia of creativity* (2nd ed., pp. 373–378). Academic Press.
Memmert, D. (2014). Tactical creativity in team sports. *Research in Physical Education, Sport and Health, 3*(1), 13–18.
Memmert, D. (2015). *Teaching tactical creativity in sport: Research and practice*. Routledge.
Memmert, D., & Furley, P. (2007). 'I spy with my little eye!' Breadth of attention, inattentional blindness, and tactical decision making in team sports. *Journal of Sport & Exercise Psychology, 29*, 365–381.

Mosston, M. (1981). *Teaching physical education* (2nd ed.). Merrill.
Mosston, M., & Ashworth, S. (2008). *Teaching physical education* (1st online ed.). https://spectrumofteachingstyles.org/assets/files/book/Teaching_Physical_Edu_1st_Online.pdf
Pill, S. (2016). Game sense coaching: Developing thinking players. In M. Drummond & S. Pill (Eds.), *Advances in Australian football: A sociological and applied science exploration of the game* (pp. 42–49). ACHPER Publications.
Roca, A., Ford, P. R., & Memmert, D. (2018). Creative decision making and visual search behavior in skilled soccer players. *PLOS ONE*, July 10, 2018. https://doi.org/10.1371/journal.pone.0199381
Santos, S., Coutinho, D., Goncalves, B., Schöllhorn, W., Sampaio, J., & Leite, N. (2018). Differential learning as a key training approach to improve creative and tactical behavior in soccer. *Research Quarterly for Exercise and Sport*, *89*(1), 11–24.
SueSee, B., Pill, S., & Hewitt, M. (2020). Reconciling approaches: Mosston and Ashworth's Spectrum of teaching styles as a tool to examine the complexity of any teaching (or coaching) approach. In B. SueSee, M. Hewitt, & S. Pill (Eds.), *The Spectrum of teaching styles in physical education* (pp. 73–84). Routledge.
Thorpe, R., Bunker, D., & Almond, L. (Eds.). (1986). *Rethinking games teaching*. Loughborough: University of Technology.
Zhang, W., Sjoerds, Z., & Hommel, B. (2020). Metacontrol of human creativity: The neurocognitive mechanisms of convergent and divergent thinking. *NeuroImage*, *210*, 116572. www.sciencedirect.com/science/article/pii/S1053811920300598

11

PLAYER DESIGNED—COACH SUPPORTED

Style I

Shane Pill, Brendan SueSee, Joss Rankin and Mitch Hewitt

This style (along with Styles J and K) is different from the previous styles, in that they are a series of episodes and will not be achieved, in most cases, in one coaching session. The Player-Designed—Coach Supported style requires 'learners to think, plan, and design in a variety of episodes representing an array of different teaching—learning styles' (Mosston & Ashworth, 2008, p. 280). If the players have not experienced the range of styles, and thus developed their skills to make decisions about their learning, then they will have very little ability to draw on knowledge of decision-making concerning teaching styles and learning needs. If this situation was to occur, and a coach attempted to implement a Style I episode with a player who had no experience with the range of styles, it would be most likely that the player would choose a series of Practice Style Episodes: or as Mosston and Ashworth (2008) suggested, 'if they have not previously experienced such deliberately planned episodes in different teaching—learning styles, they will be inadequately prepared for this experience' (p. 280). In using a Player Designed—Coach Supported coaching style, the coaching episode is characterised by the player engaging in a systematic process of examination and exploration of an issue or question designed by the coach. In this experience, the player's independence as a learner becomes pronounced. The coach only designates the subject matter area and interacts as the player requests. The player designs the questions and/or problem and then seeks the solution. Unlike all previous coaching styles that might be contained in a single practice session, this style of coaching (and those that follow) requires a series of sessions to achieve the learning outcomes. It is relevant at this point to highlight that a Player Designed—Coach Supported style is not an 'anything goes' perspective in relation to the content of the session (Mosston & Ashworth, 2008).

In the pre-impact set (planning), the coach still makes the decisions about the subject matter, but the player will be required to make decisions about how to investigate the subject matter and create the learning experiences (Mosston & Ashworth, 2008). During the implementation of the impact set (delivery), the coach establishes the learning expectations with the player/s. During the practice tasks, the coach is available, answering and asking questions, and offering feedback as requested. In the post-impact set (reflection), the player/s verify their answers or solutions against the learning expectations established by the coach and communicate outcomes with the coach (Mosston & Ashworth, 2008).

DOI: 10.4324/9781003041443-12

The story of Australian football (AFL) coach David Parkin, in 1995, giving his players more control in regard to their thinking about and for the game and hence more accountability for their performance has been quite impactful on Shane's views on sport coaching and his shift to an athlete-centred coaching perspective (Pill, 2018). 'They [the players] decided how we would play against that particular opposition, sat down and mapped out the method', Parkin said (Caffrey, 2020). A challenge for coaches is to progressively shift the reliance of players on the coach asking the questions to enable players to attend to their performance, to the players being able to reflect and determine solutions and to use the coach as a 'checking mechanism' for their thinking. In this shift, the coach's questions generate player questions and not guided discovery of solutions to the question/s posed by the coach. When players can generate their own questions with an advanced understanding of the game and themselves as a performer in the game, they have reached the stage of being capable of being self-directed learners.

Player Designed—Coach Supported coaching episodes are arguably examples of autonomous supportive environments, derived from the amount of player self-determination. Coatsworth and Conroy's (2009) study with youth swimmers found coach autonomy support predicted competence and relatedness satisfaction in the coach-athlete relationship. Halperin et al. (2017) study in martial arts showed immediate advantages in force production and velocity with experienced athletes, given the choice over the order of punches in a practice task. Alvarez et al. (2009) study with youth footballers suggested that an avenue to develop self-determined motivation is to provide players the opportunity to be autonomous and develop their competence in an environment the player perceives as supportive and respectful of them. Perceived autonomy support from the coach has been shown to be a possible predictor of youth players' intrinsic motivation (Ambrose & Anderson-Butcher, 2007; Jõesaar, Hein & Hagger, 2012) and predictor of intrinsic motivation to accomplish with Paralympic athletes (Banack, Sabiston & Bloom, 2011). Mageau and Vallerand (2003) suggested autonomy-supportive coaching environments are presented by coaches when they provide players:

- A rationale for tasks;
- Choice within boundaries;
- Acknowledgement of player/s ideas and perspectives by (for example) seeking their input into a practice;
- Opportunities to take initiatives;
- Non-controlling feedback;
- Limited tangible rewards and avoidance of controlling statements; and
- Player self-referenced evaluative criteria.

Examples of Player Designed—Coach Supported Coaching

Example 1—Baseball

An example of Style I in baseball is along the same lines as the AFL example suggested earlier in this chapter. During the pre-impact set, the coach suggests to the players the subject matter or task to solve is to develop a match plan to play a team which they lost against in a previous encounter. The objective of the Style I episode could be stated as: 'You must have a strategy (based on evidence) of how to pitch and set the field to every hitter in the upcoming game next week. We must also recognise any limitations in our games and develop personal practice sessions to improve these restrictions'. Quite clearly, this will not be achieved in one practice session. In the impact set, the coach would encourage questions about how they (the player) would do this. For example, a player may ask: 'How do we base the strategy on evidence'? The coach could refer to the opposition's statistics. Regarding the personal weaknesses, the coach may suggest that to identify their limitations the individual players may consult the statistics from the season so far or, in fact, previous seasons. Checking against statistics and identifying ways they frequently got 'out' could assist in identifying weaknesses and things to improve and form the basis of a Style D episode. If the player identified that they frequently got caught out in rightfield, they may assume a weakness with the outside pitch (to a right-handed hitter) and ask a teammate to assist in a Reciprocal Coaching Style episode. The players may have questions regarding the length of time or how frequently they need to practice, or they may even identify their weaknesses and ask the coach to help them devise a practice strategy. Undoubtedly, many coaches will experience, when using Style I for the first time, a 'long silence' as players realise that they are being provided with a significant degree of ownership in connection to decision-making. If the players have not had experience with the previous styles discussed in this book, it may be anticipated that they will not have developed the skills or expectation to make decisions and take responsibility for the direction of their game development (Mosston & Ashworth, 2008). Therefore, to achieve the objectives of Style I, it may require a 'series of episodes over a period of time, including both reproductive and productive experiences, structured by the individual learners . . . ' (Mosston & Ashworth, 2008, p. 276).

Example 2—Cricket

Player designed—Coach Supported Style could be applied to cricket players who may be having problems with a particular shot in the sense that they are consistently getting dismissed whilst playing it. For the sake of this example, we will choose the off drive. The off drive is a shot where the bat is swung vertically and hit to the right-hand side of the batsman (if they are a right hander), usually on the ground. To begin the episode in the pre-impact set, the coach may say to the player, 'The off-drive is the shot you have been dismissed playing the most this season. You need to improve on this shot'. At this point it is easy to think that the coach's job is done, or the coach has not given much help. During the impact set, the learners' role is to identify 'the series of questions that will guide the investigation' (Mosston & Ashworth, 2008, p. 278). If the coach had told them what the steps were, then the player would not have this opportunity. This certainly does not eliminate or relieve the coach during the experience. Importantly, the coach remains a crucial educative 'cog'. The coach is 'available for the requests and questions of the learners: and to:

1. Observe the learner's performance/solutions as they are developing;
2. To observe the process being used by the learner;
3. To offer answers only when directly asked by the learner; and
4. To alert the learner to any discrepancies between the stated intent and action.

(Mosston & Ashworth, 2008, p. 278)

It is anticipated that the player would engage with the coach by asking questions about why they get dismissed on a regular basis on this shot. The coach may then use a Guided Discovery episode to assist the player in deciding how do they know they have a weakness besides getting out? How can you see what your weakness is? This may seem confusing as now we have suggested that the coach has chosen a teaching style during the impact set. Mosston and Ashworth (2008) suggested that the coach (teacher) is not 'passive, removed, or absent from the experience. Rather, it implies that the teacher does not impose comments or directions on students . . . questions, rather than statements, are the primary forms of communicating with the learner when the teacher observes discrepancies or has insights to share' (p. 279).

The player may decide that a Self-Check episode is required to identify the weakness and then compare it to how the shot is supposed to be played. From here the player may decide on a remedial drill and use Practice Style to improve the weakness. From this example, it can be seen how the Player Designed—Coach Supported style may be a series of episodes and not just one episode. During the post-impact set, the players' role is to assess their programme according to the criteria they designed, make adjustments that are necessary and communicate to the coach what they have or have not achieved.

Example 3—Outdoor Pursuits (Bushwalking)

Individuals who enjoy their experiences with outdoor pursuits will often seek to undertake them with greater levels of independence. The transition from participating in these pursuits as a dependant to engaging with a level of self-reliance requires the application of a range of tasks and responsibilities previously undertaken by the leader. Froude and Polley (2008) identify several technical skills that are generic, regardless of the outdoor pursuit or adventure activity undertaken such as trip planning, navigation, weather interpretation and first aid. Bushwalking is one such activity in which individuals may choose to engage with the purpose to explore otherwise inaccessible areas and to experience extended journeys in natural environments.

In South Australia, individuals who have undertaken a range of bushwalking experiences may wish to gain recognition of 'Basic Skills Bushwalking' and furthermore a 'Bushwalking Leadership Certificate' awarded by 'Bushwalking Leadership of South Australia'. To do so, they must undertake an overnight bushwalk, including all aspects of trip planning, preparation and review. In applying a Player Designed Style, the participants supervising assessor would set the participant the challenge of designing an overnight bushwalk that is deemed to be appropriate for their own level of ability. In the pre-impact set the supervisor assessor has established a framework for undertaking the task but enables the participant to make all logistical decisions such as where to go, route taken, camping locations, equipment, and participants. By setting this challenge, the participant would likely recognise that they have a range of decisions to make during the planning and camp phases of the trip being undertaken. In establishing all the tasks and decisions that they will be responsible for, the participant may then choose to conduct their own research in relation to the area, investigate a range of possible options for the trip and engage the supervisor when questions arise due to the range of possible solutions to safely and successfully completing the task.

In the example of undertaking the self-reliant bushwalk, the non-linear nature of the pre-impact, impact and post-impact sets of decisions can be observed (Mosston & Ashworth, 2008). As there are essentially multiple impact sets represented by performance of tasks in planning, preparation walking over multiple days and application of camp craft, individuals will have several opportunities to reflect (example of post-impact decision-making) and make modifications necessary to the changing or unknown conditions (requiring adjustments to planning and revisiting pre-impact set decisions). Such examples provide multiple opportunities for participants to engage in post-impact set decision-making as they undertake ongoing reflective cycles to make sense of their experiences. In this way we might suggest that the potential non-linear nature of decision-making made possible through Self Designed Coaching provides opportunities for participants to undertake experiential learning by carrying out a concrete experience, making reflective observations, drawing conclusions and conceptualising application of these to new experiences or as the current experience evolves and actively experimenting with a range of these new learnings (Kolb, 2014). As such, participants embody their understanding, enhancing the richness of learning (Luckner & Nadler, 1997).

Example 4—Tennis

In this example, it is important to clearly identify the range and distribution of decisions attributed to the coach and player. This is designed to assist both player and coach to negotiate and navigate this style accurately and purposefully—so everyone is clear on their respective role. The distribution of decisions is indicated in Figure 11.1.

In this example, the coach has identified, via viewing the player's matches and/or by statistical analysis, that the player is required to improve their respective ability to engage in extended rallies—prior to determining and considering an attacking 'move' during a rally when playing against a player that represents a 'Counter Puncher' playing style. A Counter Puncher's strength includes:

1. They enjoy engaging in long rallies;
2. Most of their points are played from behind the baseline and consistency is considered their primary 'weapon';
3. 'Counter Punchers' thrive on hitting the ball deep in the court and pushing their opponents to the back of the court (to prevent an attacking move); and
4. Forcing their opponents to make poor decisions, i.e., commencing an attacking strategy from an incorrect ball (for instance, attempting to enforce an offensive strategy when the ball is deep and when the player is under pressure and 'should' be returned in a neutral manner), is considered a 'Counter Puncher's' additional positive playing characteristic.

In this case, the coach has identified and determined the subject manner that require assistance (i.e., pre-impact set). During the impact set—the implementation or the 'doing' phase—the player takes responsibility to attempt to determine the problem and then begin to solve the issue and investigate the broad challenge, situation or issue to then attempt to produce a

Pre-Impact (Planning) ------- Coach
Impact (Implementation) ------- Player
Post-Impact (Feedback & Assessment) ------- Player

FIGURE 11.1 The decision distribution for the coach and player during Player Designed—Coach Supported: Style I.

workable and detailed programme designed to resolve the content focus as identified by the coach. At this point, the coach has already determined the general subject logistical decisions for the player. The role of the player is now to make decisions about how to investigate the general subject matter (as aforementioned) and to produce questions that lead to a specific focus within the topic, which result in identifying the processes and procedures that will ultimately serve to discover the solutions/movements/strategies and to designate the performance criteria. The player, at this point, may implement a series of episodic learning options, including, Self-Check Style, Reciprocal Style or Guided Discovery Style to assist in solving the problem.

In connection to the post-impact set, the obligation of the player is to attend to their designed programme (i.e., as outlined in the implementation or 'doing' stage of their decisions) and aligned to the performance criteria they designed during this stage, to implement modifications that are necessary. Importantly, these adjustments require in-depth and meaningful communication with the coach to determine if they have been achieved or not.

Conclusion

The Player Designed—Coach Supported Style is the first of three styles which require the player, for the first time, to create subject matter. The past styles (A–H) have required them to use the cognitive process of either memory or discovery. A second characteristic of these three styles (I–K), which highlights their difference compared to other styles, is their inability to be delivered in one episode. Despite the lack of empirical evidence at this stage, the merits of using The Player Designed—Coach Supported Style would be based on the objective and desire of the player (and coach) for the player to make more decisions regarding their learning and coaching, thus becoming more responsible for the creation of coaching episodes which led to the achievement of the desired objectives. Finally, the Player Designed—Coach Supported Style is a form of self-directed learning (Knowles, 1975) that has shown to be related to academic performance, creativity, life satisfaction, future aspiration and lifelong learning (Chatoupis, 2018; Edmondson, Boyer & Artis, 2012; Greveson & Spencer, 2005; Miflin, Campbell & Price, 2000).

References

Alvarez, A., Balaguer, M., Castillo, I., & Duda, J. (2009). Coach autonomy support and quality of sport engagement in young soccer players. *The Spanish Journal of Psychology, 12*(1), 138–148.

Ambrose, A. J., & Anderson-Butcher, D. (2007). Autonomy-supportive coaching and self-determined motivation in high school and college athletes: A test of self-determination theory. *Psychology of Sport and Exercise, 8*(5), 654–670.

Banack, H. R., Sabiston, C. M., & Bloom, G. A. (2011). Coach autonomy support, basic need satisfaction, and intrinsic motivation of Paralympic athletes. *Research Quarterly for Exercise and Sport, 82*(4), 722–730.

Caffrey, O. (2020). Parkin's 1995 Blues an unstoppable force. *The Canberra Times*, April 19, 2020. www.canberratimes.com.au/story/6727578/parkins-1995-blues-an-unstoppable-force/

Chatoupis, C. (2018). Implementing the learner designed individual program style in physical education. *Strategies, 31*(2), 19–25.

Coatsworth, J. D., & Conroy, D. E. (2009). The effects of autonomy-supportive coaching, need satisfaction and self-perceptions on initiative and identity in youth swimmers. *Developmental Psychology, 45*(2), 320–328.

Edmondson, D. R., Boyer, S. L., & Artis, A. B. (2012). Self-directed learning: A meta-analytic review of adult learning constructs. *International Journal of Education Research*, 7(1), 40–48.

Froude, C., & Polley, S. (2008). *Outdoor education: Foundations for tertiary and senior secondary education*. Impact Publishing.

Greveson, G. C., & Spencer, J. A. (2005). Self-directed learning: The importance of concepts and contexts. *Medical Education*, 39, 348–349.

Halperin, I., Chapman, D. W., Martin, D. T., Lewthwaite, R., & Wulf, G. (2017). Choices enhance punching performance of competitive kickboxers. *Psychological Research*, 81, 1051–1058.

Jõesaar, H., Hein, V., & Hagger, M. S. (2012). Youth athletes' perception of autonomy support from the coach, peer motivational climate and intrinsic motivation in sport setting: One-year effects. *Psychology of Sport and Exercise*, 13, 257–262.

Knowles, M. S. (1975). *Self-directed learning: A guide for students and teachers*. Association Press.

Kolb, D. A. (2014). *Experiential learning: Experience as the source of learning and development*. FT Press.

Luckner, J. L., & Nadler, R. S. (1997). *Processing the experience: Strategies to enhance and generalize learning*. Kendall/Hunt Publishing Company.

Mageau, G. A., & Vallerand, R. J. (2003). The coach-athlete relationship: A motivational model. *Journal of Sports Sciences*, 21(11), 883–904.

Miflin, B. M., Campbell, C. B., & Price, D. A. (2000). A conceptual framework to guide the development of self-directed, lifelong learning in problem-based medical curricula. *Medical Education*, 34, 299–306.

Mosston, M., & Ashworth, S. (2008). *Teaching physical education* (1st online ed.). https://spectrumofteachingstyles.org/assets/files/book/Teaching_Physical_Edu_1st_Online.pdf

Pill, S. (Ed.). (2018). *Perspectives on athlete-centred coaching*. Routledge.

12
PLAYER INITIATED—COACH SUPPORTED
Style J

Shane Pill, Brendan SueSee, Joss Rankin and Mitch Hewitt

The defining characteristic of this coaching style is that the player initiates and has responsibility for designing the learning experience. Pre-impact planning shifts to the player, including the coaching styles to be used. The role of the coach is to participate in response to the player's requests, although, when or if discrepancies arise between the players intent and actions, the coach has a responsibility to initiate questions (Mosston & Ashworth, 2008). The coach is a resource available to the player and the player therefore assumes (or should assume) responsibility for their learning. The player delineates expectations including how they will engage with the coach (Mosston & Ashworth, 2008).

Elite players often have a sense of responsibility and drive for self-direction in their learning.

> Players like Ponting, McGrath and Warne had a tremendous sense of ownership about their training, which shone through in their overall performances [. . .] I am adamant that those who steer away from placing all their faith in others to tell them what to do and accept a generous portion of personal responsibility in their cricket, will get a break on the pack.
>
> (Mike Hussey, 2015, p. 29: Australian representation—79 Test Matches, 185 One Day Internationals, 38 T20I)

We could not find much research on Player Initiated—Coach Supported coaching style. Much of the research on sport coaching seems to be conducted on the assumption that the coach is significant in player technical and tactical learning and their psychological wellbeing. Consequently, the research focus is on identification of coaching characteristics, behaviours and competences, and validating and proof of concept of theoretical models of coaching. Similarly, as the player chooses Style J, it presents challenges for researchers who wish to study the effects of this style as it cannot be chosen by a researcher to be implemented on an athlete. There have been a couple of interesting studies reporting the effectiveness on learning of player public posting combined with self-recording monitored by coach (Critchfield & Vargas, 1991; McKenzie & Rushall, 1974) and the posting of self-set goals monitored by coach (Ward & Carnes, 2002). However, in the Ward and Carnes (2002) research, players 'received

DOI: 10.4324/9781003041443-13

feedback and error correction of their performance' (p. 3), which is more in line with Style B, and not Style J.

One study we did find investigated player-driven video analysis to enhance reflective practice in football (soccer) talent development (Hjort, Henriksen & Elbaek, 2018). In this study, an online video analysis platform was used by players to tag game actions in the analysis process. Following the player-driven video analysis, the players engaged with a coach in a reflective feedback conversation. Video analysis is widespread in academy and high-performance coaching contexts. It may take the form of player movement tracking, event tagging, tactical analysis, statistical analysis, game highlight detection, and game moment reconstructions, to name a few of the applications. Often the video analysis is to support coach decisions on what feedback to provide to the players so the coach can guide the player development. Hjort et al (2018) research found that without education in the process prior to implementation, it can be difficult for some players to know what to focus on when analysing video or how to use their analysis in conversation with a coach. This result is in line with claims we have made earlier in Chapter 11 that if players have not experienced the many decisions required when coached by many styles from The Spectrum, they will struggle when asked to make these types of decisions.

Player Initiated—Coach Supported episodes might also be thought of as the 'consultant coach'. An area of sport where this often gets discussed in media is sport psychology and 'mental skills training' coaches. We are not suggesting this as an example of a Player Initiated—Coach Supported relationship. In Chapter 2 we gave the example of Kenyan Julius Yego, Javelin Gold Medallist at the World Athletics Championships, 2015. After a period of training in Finland prior to the 2012 Olympics, he kept in touch with his Finnish coach by Skype for a period and continued to use self-coaching through YouTube. This use of the coach may be an example of a Player Initiated—Coach Supported relationship.

Examples of Player Initiated—Coach Supported: Style J

Example 1—Baseball

In the pre-impact set the player may come to the coach and tell them that they wish to learn a new position or transition from catcher to centerfield. For the purpose of this chapter, the player says that they wish to assume responsibility for the learning experience or experiences. It is the player's desire and not the coach's. The Player-Initiated Style will usually be a series of episodes (Mosston & Ashworth, 2008) because if the skills could be learnt in one short episode, it is likely that the player has already had a high level of skill. The learner would identify the numerous skills to be learnt as an outfielder (backing up, catching fly balls, fielding a ground ball, hitting cut-off man, etc.) and set about planning learning experiences to develop these skills. They may create their own learning experiences and choose the coaching style/s. For example, they may ask the coach to teach them (using Practice Style) the cues for fielding a ground ball. They may then ask someone to hit the balls and they will practice the skill. The player will decide to ask the coach for feedback after generating their own criteria (Reciprocal Style), or maybe they will not, choosing to identify their own errors or things they are doing well (Self-Check Style). A challenging part for the coach in this situation is to accept that the player will decide when and how the coach is involved and to ask questions if they notice incongruence between the players intent and their actions.

Example 2—Surfing

A novice or beginner surfer could use the Player Initiated—Coach Supported style to learn how to surf. Typical of this style the player is now responsible for independently initiating the behaviour and making 'all the decisions in the pre-impact, including which teaching—learning behaviours will be used in the impact, and create the criteria decisions for the post-impact' (Mosston & Ashworth, 2008, p. 283). Mosston and Ashworth suggested that this teaching style occurs when the player approaches the coach or authority figure and says that they wish to design and be responsible for their own learning. This style is different from the previous style (Style I), in that the learner has decided the subject matter and again it will be a series of episodes decided by the player, who initiates and conducts the teaching-learning episodes. The player will make a 'plan of action, to identify issues and questions, to search for information, to construct knowledge, and to organize all these elements into a meaningful framework—to make all decisions within the anatomy' (Mosston & Ashworth, 2008, p. 284). The role of the coach 'is to accept the reality that the learner is, in fact, ready to make all the decisions in the ensuing series of episodes. The teacher, then, assumes the role of a standby resource—a guide or advisor who is available to the learner' (Mosston & Ashworth, 2008, p. 284).

To help illustrate how this style looks in terms of decision-making, it will be described hypothetically via pre-impact, impact, and post-impact coach-learner decision-making.

Pre-Impact Set

In the pre-impact set, Dennis (the player) has decided he wants to learn how to surf. He approaches Mrs Kerrigan (surfing teacher or person with surfing experience) and states his desire, 'I am going to teach myself to surf'. Mrs Kerrigan asks, would Dennis like her to teach him? Dennis says he wants to teach himself but asks can he get help if he gets stuck. Mrs Kerrigan is fine with this. Dennis begins by watching someone surf and identifying that he needs to learn the following:

1. Surf craft such as paddling, duck diving, how to sit on his board and turning the board around;
2. Paddling into a wave and standing (popping) up; and
3. Turning.

Dennis then asks Mrs Kerrigan if it is sufficient for him to know how to surf, and she says it sounds fine. The coach is not involved in the pre-impact decisions. These planning decisions are shifted to the learner (Mosston & Ashworth, 2008). Dennis also decides to learn in this order.

Impact Set

During the impact set, Dennis begins by paddling, duck diving and turning in a calm body of water (no waves). He has some idea of how to do this from watching other surfers and is essentially copying what he has seen. He has chosen this still water environment as he believes it is what is most appropriate given his stage of learning. Thus, he has decided to try and reproduce a body of knowledge or essentially, he is doing 'individual and private practice of a memory/reproduction task' (Mosston & Ashworth, 2008, p. 94) minus coach feedback. Dennis is therefore involved in a Practice Style episode. Let's assume he achieves some success; however, he wants to be sure he is doing it correctly and so he contacts Mrs Kerrigan and asks her if they could schedule a time where she observes him performing the three skills. Being fiercely independent on this task, he asks, 'If I am doing some things wrong can you not tell me the answers, rather, can you ask me questions to help guide me to the solution'. Here, he is asking her to use Guided Discovery. After this episode is completed, Dennis returns to the waves and activity is again Reciprocal Style to refine the skills, but he asks Mrs Kerrigan to provide feedback as per Coaching by Reciprocal Style, as the player has set the content or objective in the pre-impact set, created the learning episode and criteria in the impact set and is asking for feedback from the other player in the post-impact set.

Post-Impact

When Dennis asked Mrs Kerrigan to use Guided Discovery, it is hoped that she would acknowledge the learner's responses and their discovery of the target as per Coaching by Guided Discovery. If Dennis had performed the task well, and there was nothing for him to improve on or discover, then Mrs Kerrigan would give feedback as per a Coaching by Reciprocal Style episode.

The second series of episodes relates to paddling into a wave and standing up. Let us assume that Dennis, buoyed by his success, is very keen to catch some waves. He asks Mrs Kerrigan to come surfing with him and teach him how to paddle in and stand up. He is essentially requesting to be taught by Style B—Coaching by Task (Practice).

Pre-Impact set

Mrs Kerrigan decided to let Dennis borrow a 'mal' (8-foot board) so that it is very stable for him to ensure success. She decides to also begin by drawing the outline of a board on the sand and having Dennis practice pop-up on a stable platform (the task) before going into the water.

Impact Set

Mrs Kerrigan implements the two episodes, first modelling the content and then providing Dennis with the opportunity to practice.

Post-Impact Set

Dennis receives feedback from Mrs Kerrigan as per Coaching by Task (Practice)—Style B.

The final piece of subject matter, Dennis decides that he will go it alone now. He decides he wants to learn how to turn to the right and left. Being a technically savvy gentleman, he knows he could watch a YouTube clip for tips and learn how to turn. If he did this, he would be using Coaching by Task (Practice) as he would be practising a memory task. That is, he gained the knowledge or saw a model of how to perform the task, was perhaps provided with some cues by the YouTube clip and is attempting to replicate them. The only thing that is missing from this being a Coaching by Task (Practice) is the feedback from the teacher.

Dennis, with no knowledge of turning and a fierce streak of independence, is presented with an opportunity for an episode of Coaching by Problem Solving (Convergent Discovery).

That is, Dennis is looking for one way to turn his board to the right and one way to turn his board to the left. The only point of difference here is that in Convergent Discovery, the coach decides the subject matter; however, in this episode Dennis is the teacher and deciding the problem to solve or discover a solution to the problem of turning his board to the left. Or, to explain differently, this is a sub-episode (of the Player Initiated—Coach Supported Style) where Dennis has chosen to learn this last piece of content through a Player Initiated episode.

These hypothetical examples demonstrate how the Player Initiated—Coach Supported coaching style is a series of episodes which, in this example, sometimes involved a coach (at the request of the player) but in most practice episodes did not.

Example 3—Outdoor Pursuits (Kayaking)

In many outdoor pursuits, there is a point where individuals can competently participate in the chosen activity but may wish to develop more advanced techniques to enable them to extend what they can achieve. This may be represented by a competent snowboarder who wishes to access more difficult terrain or attempt elements within a terrain park, a mountain bike rider wishing to successfully land large drops whilst on a downhill run or navigate a technical rock garden or a surfer seeking to perform an aerial manoeuvre whilst riding a wave. For this example, we will explore the opportunity for a kayaker to engage in Self or Player Initiated Coaching. The example describes a kayaker (John) who is out paddling with a more experienced friend (Lucy), who is a kayaking instructor and has been engaged in teaching and learning by John to act in the role of a 'coach'.

In the lead up to a day paddling with his friend, John has discovered that it is possible to right a kayak that has capsized without the assistance of another paddler or exiting the cockpit of the kayak. John effectively initiates the pre-impact set within a Player Initiated Style by deciding that he would like to learn how to perform a self-rescue technique known as an Eskimo roll. John watches some videos of kayakers performing Eskimo roles; however, as he will soon be kayaking with his friend Lucy, he decides to call her and ask if she will help him learn this technique. Lucy says that she would love to and tells John that it might then be valuable to bring a pair of goggles on their paddling day to help him see underwater whilst practising.

On their day out kayaking, John indicates that he would like to just start off by paddling and having some fun exploring the area as they had originally planned and then before lunch practise some Eskimo rolls in the shallows so that they can just hop out of the water if needed. The conversation and suggestions initiated by John are representative of the range of decisions being made by the learner during the impact set. Once they return to the shallow water before lunch, Lucy asks John if this is when he would like to begin to learn. John suggests that he would like Lucy to show him an Eskimo roll and then have a practice session based on what he sees. Lucy performs her roll and then tells John that there is a lot of components occurring that are difficult to see but also says that as he has initiated the learning, she is happy to be guided by what he feels comfortable with. Once John has a couple of unsuccessful attempts, he asks for some suggestions from Lucy. At this point Lucy asks John a range of questions about underwater orientation, levels of comfort whilst upside down underwater and what it feels like when he is attempting to right the boat. These questions are accompanied by a range of activities that are built out of what John feels he needs support with, such as remaining calm under water, orienting himself in relation to the boat and surface of the water and 'feeling' the action supported by Lucy in shallow water. As John initiates how and when Lucy supports the learning process, recognising that she has the area of expertise, the decision-making in the impact set is initiated by John. Throughout the learning, John has initiated and performed most of the tasks and based on the gaps in his knowledge and technical ability, he recognises how and where Lucy might be able to help him advance and initiates for her to be involved. John has initiated this process and determined what he is aiming to achieve; thus, he is also responsible for making the decisions in the post-impact set, such as determining how successful he was and what he wishes to engage with next in relation to this technique and its further applications.

Example 4—Tennis

To provide an accurate and practical example of Player Initiative—Coach Supported Style, in a tennis example, it is imperative, in the first instance, to understand the defining characteristics of this coaching experience. In this instance, it is the player's choice to determine learning, as opposed to the coach's decisions that dictate the outcome. In this style, the player requests to engage in this coaching initiative and to design a full learning experience which includes making all decisions, including the topic to explore, plan and implement—this also includes criteria for evaluation. The major caveat and implication associated with this coaching interaction is that the coach is suitably qualified in connection to the content. This point is essential, for if the player requires assistance, guidance, content expertise, the coach is available to provide suggestions to further the support of the player. If these elements are apparent, the coach's role is now to accept the player's readiness to make maximum decisions, in the coaching interaction, to be supportive, in addition to participate according to the player's requests. With these theoretical aspects considered—practical perspective—the authors will now provide an example, involving tennis, to illustrate this coaching example.

Like the coaching instance provided in the Kayaking example, there are inevitably situations whereby the player wishes to extend their respective range of skills. In this example, the authors make a direct reference to the serve. In this case, Steven (the player) has identified that to increase the possibility of defeating a particular opponent, an additional 'type' of serve is required to increase success. For the purpose of context, Steven is a competent tennis player, however, only currently possesses two 'types' of serves; that being a wide sliding serve designed to place an opponent on 'full stretch' in the wide areas of the court in addition to a 'T' serve that is positioned down the middle of the service box, designed to force the opponent in the opposite direction (i.e., down the middle of the court—potentially also at 'full stretch'). Steven has realised that a players' ability to produce a range of serves with variety has the capacity to confuse the opponent and produce unpredictability—for instance, the more options Steven can produce on the serve, the more it potentially results in winning additional points (from the serve) as the opponent is unable to prepare for not one or two types of serves, but perhaps three. Steven has identified this phenomenon and decides to create decisions (in the pre-impact phase) to add an additional serve to his current repertoire of serving options. Steven also determines the additional serve he would like to focus on (i.e., he decides in the Impact phase). In this case, it is a 'body serve'. This serve is designed to direct the ball at the opponent's body. So, at this point, Steven has made all the decisions related to the pre-impact and impact phase of the learning experience. From this point, Steven contacts his coach—a more experienced exponent of this type of serve—and discusses the skill—both from a tactical and technical aspect. Steven now commences to practice this new skill with the assistance, and supportive guidance from his coach. During this experience, Steven has created a post-impact set of performance skill criteria to conduct his performance. At this point, the coach has accepted the player's readiness to make the maximum number of decisions and supports Steven's requests in connection to his performance. It is, however, highly relevant, at this point, to indicate that if there exist discrepancies between what the player (Steven) has suggested and subsequentially performing (i.e., intention and action) that the coach serves as an influential resource related to a positive learning experience for effective performance during tennis matches. The initiated player—this style of coaching—will recognise and acknowledge how they utilise the coach (Mosston & Ashworth, 2008).

Conclusion

Many studies demonstrate that self-controlled practice can benefit the effectiveness of motor skill learning. For example, for some players providing the opportunity to self-select their feedback schedule may be more effective for their learning than a prescribed feedback schedule (Wulf, Raupach & Pfeiffer, 2005). The benefits of self-control in motor skill learning appears to be a 'robust phenomenon' (Chiviacowsky & Wulf, 2002, p. 408). However, it is important for coaches to note that the generalisability of results from studies using simple laboratory tasks to the learning of complex motor skills in sport practice environments is not straightforward and cannot always be assumed (Wulf & Shea, 2002).

References

Chiviacowsky, S., & Wulf, G. (2002). Self-controlled feedback: Does it enhance learning because performers get feedback when they need it? *Research Quarterly for Exercise and Sport*, 73(4), 408–415.

Critchfield, T. S., & Vargas, E. A. (1991). Self-recording, instructions, and public self-graphing: Effects on swimming in the absence of coach verbal interaction. *Behavior Modification*, 15, 95–112.

Hjort, A., Henriksen, K., & Elbaek, L. (2018). Player-driven video analysis to enhance reflective soccer practice in talent development. *International Journal of Game-Based Learning*. https://doi.org/10.4018/IJGBL.2018040103

Hussey, M. (2015). *Mike Hussey winning edge: Behind the scenes of elite cricket*. Hardie Grant Books.

McKenzie, T. L., & Rushall, B. S. (1974). Effects of self-recording on attendance and performance in a competitive swimming training environment. *Journal of Applied Behavior Analysis*, 7, 199–206.

Mosston, M., & Ashworth, S. (2008). *Teaching physical education* (1st online ed.). https://spectrumofteachingstyles.org/assets/files/book/Teaching_Physical_Edu_1st_Online.pdf

Ward, P., & Carnes, M. (2002). Effects of posting self-set goals on collegiate football players' skill execution during practice and games. *Journal of Applied Behavior Analysis*, 35, 1–12.

Wulf, G., Raupach, M., & Pfeiffer, F. (2005). Self-controlled observational practice enhances learning. *Research Quarterly for Exercise and Sport*, 76(1), 107–111.

Wulf, G., & Shea, C. H. (2002). Principles derived from the study of simple skills do not generalize to complex skill learning. *Psychonomic Bulletin & Review*, 9, 185–211.

13
PLAYER SELF-COACHING
Style K

Shane Pill, Brendan SueSee, Joss Rankin and Mitch Hewitt

Player Self-Coaching: Style K is another episodic coaching style. That is, it is made up of numerous coaching episodes and cannot be achieved by one style or in one episode. In the Player Self-Coaching Style, the player decides the subject matter or activity and the coaching episodes that they will implement to achieve a desired goal. It also involves an aspect that they do not already know how to perform. In this style, compared to other styles located on The Spectrum, the point of difference is that the coach is not involved in any aspect in this episode. The player has decided to completely pursue private and self-determined practice. The player will make all the decisions in the pre-impact, impact and post-impact sets of the learning experience. In this coaching style, there is no 'external' coach assigning the goal or the topic—the player does this. This is not to say that another person or coach cannot give feedback if requested by the player. Mosston and Ashworth (2008) suggested that 'feedback from outside sources occurs when the individual chooses to take his/her ideas to others; the individual chooses to shift from Self-Teaching to another decision relationship' (p. 291). While this style of coaching may require some attributes that other styles do not, we note that a player who makes all the decisions, all the time may 'not be able to adapt to conditions that bring him/her into contact with other people, social mores, and traditions' (Mosston & Ashworth, 2008, p. 292).

The Player Self-Coaching Style sees the player assume the role of coach and learner. All decisions about the coaching and learning in the episode are assigned to the player. In Chapter 2, where a brief overview of each teaching style was provided, we gave the example of Kenyan Julius Yego, Javelin Gold Medallist at the World Athletics Championships, 2015, using online videos to initially coach himself javelin, practising with sharpened sticks he cut from trees. Footballer Craig Johnston tells the story of how after travelling to try out as an apprentice at Middlesbrough F. C. at 15 years of age, he was told after the first trial game to get packing and go home. Banished from training with the others, he stayed on until he could save for his airfare home to Sydney. During this period, he came to a realisation as to how he could plan his training, design practice tasks to improve his technical ability, implement focused goals, achieve constant repetition and a mistake metric to judge his improvement in order to develop his game to the level of the local players. Two years later, an opportunity arrived to be on the team sheet due to a shortage of players as illness had gone through the squad, and he made an impact, going on to be a highly acclaimed professional footballer (Johnston & Jameson, 1989).

DOI: 10.4324/9781003041443-14

There are many examples of player self-coaching from adolescents to elite players. Nick Farr-Jones is one of Rugby's most celebrated players. In his biography (Fitzsimons, 1993) is the story of schoolboy Farr-Jones playing for the 15s age group team being told by an older lad that while Nick was proficient at passing from right to right, he sprayed the ball wildly when passing from left to right—not desirable for a half-back. The story goes that he was told by this older lad that he would never be any good until he could pass with equal accuracy on both sides. Early the next morning, Nick was observed repetitiously passing the ball from left to right, aiming to hit a thin tree. This was just the beginning. Having heard that golfers sometimes swing with two clubs so that when they play with one it feels light at the tee, Farr-Jones devised a practice task using a house brick to develop his passing before the start of the 16s season the following year. The learning example of Farr-Jones passing to hit the tree is undoubtedly chosen by the player (from the description in the book). The addition of passing the house brick to develop strength and overcome a weakness (based on the modification of another task in another sport) demonstrates how Self-Coaching is not the repetition of a known learning experience, but numerous experiences, and in this case, the creation of something new to the player also.

Ricky Ponting is one of Australia's best-ever test cricket batters. In 2008, he was going through a form slump. To help him address technical issues with his batting that were affecting his performance, he used a big screen TV as he faced deliveries from a bowling machine. Placing the image capture on 5-second delay, he filmed himself facing deliveries from a bowling machine and reviewed each shot immediately after it was played on the screen. 'Sometimes you know yourself what you are doing but to put your finger right on it is a little more difficult', Ponting said. 'With this set-up, you hit one and you give yourself time to have a look at the replay and digest it. It can pick up everything, head position, back lift and whatever it is you want to work on' (DNA India, 2008). This example by Ponting shows how the player using Player Self-Coaching and has chosen to create a coaching episode using Self-Check Style D, to coach himself. It may be suggested that due to Ponting's knowledge of cricket, he was able to make the choice to use Style D. That is, he knew enough about what he was supposed to do; he just needed the ability to see himself do it.

There is little research in this area of sport coaching. One reason for this is due to Self-Coaching being revealed when feedback from others is sought or when the individual decides to talk about it with others, such as when an autobiography is published, or an interview occurs. One study we located was by Bradbury (2000). This study of New Zealand athletes found that the main reasons for player self-coaching were a lack of available and suitably qualified coaches, player incompatibility with available coaches, and financial considerations. In contrast, the examples we provide earlier show highly motivated individuals use their knowledge of the sport as independent, self-regulated learners. Another study, by Hars and Calmels' (2007) of elite gymnasts use of self-observation within practice, indicated that the gymnasts did this for self-assessment within practice with the aim of increased skill performance, suggesting the elite athletes have very particular goals in mind when observing the self on video.

Examples of Player Self-Coaching: Style K

Example 1—Alex Honnold—Rock Climbing

Alex Honnold preparing for climbing El Capitan is one example of the Self-Coaching style that contained many episodes, as opposed to a single episode. When asked 'How did you begin to prepare physically?', Honnold replied:

> The thing about preparing for Freerider was nobody has ever done it before. It isn't like other physical feats where you can pull up a website or read the book of someone who has done it before. I knew that for me to feel comfortable free soloing Freerider I was going to climb it over and over again.
>
> *(Thorp, n.d.)*

This is perhaps a good example as there was no one who had done this before so no one could give knowledge to Honnold about what to do. From the quote just cited, Honnold's choice of coaching styles seems to be heavily reliant on Practice Style and preparing so that everything was predictable. Since Honnold had also not climbed El Capitan before, he also had to create Convergent Discovery episodes (sought a solution to a problem or numerous problems) and then, once satisfied that the problem was solved, reverted to Practice Style to refine the solution. Using Practice Style coaching, he reduced the unknowns (and subsequently increased the knowns) and made the climb more predictable and reduced his stress. This is an example of the player/athlete (Honnold) choosing to self-coach and choosing to use Practice Style coaching where he was both the coach and player.

To explain this coaching episode in specific detail, it will be outlined using the three places the decisions were made. In the pre-impact set, Honnold would have decided, 'I will climb El Capitan free soloing'. He had climbed El Capitan with a rope 50 times, but he wanted to do it without a rope (free soloing). He then needed to decide what it was he needed to do and how he would prepare himself by acquiring the skills to complete the task.

In the impact set he began climbing, usually down El Capitan backwards or from the top. Honnold had decided that he would be using a lot of Practice Style episodes. This is evident when he says:

> I'm on the summit, about to rappel down the face with over a thousand feet of rope to spend the day practicing. Once I found sequences that felt secure and repeatable, I had to memorize them. I had to make sure that they were so deeply ingrained within me that there was no possibility of error. I didn't want to be wondering if I was going the right way or using the best holds. I needed everything to feel automatic.
>
> *(Honnold, 2018)*

In this text Honnold specifically mentions memorising sequences and why he wanted this. His comments reflect why he chose Practice Style. Further to this he also shows how long this Self-Coaching Style episode went for (and again alludes to the justification of Practice Style) when he says 'after two seasons of working specifically toward a potential free solo of El Cap, I finally finished all my preparations. I knew every handhold and foothold on the whole route, and I knew exactly what to do. Basically, I was ready' (Honnold, 2018). These quotes seem to suggest that in Honnold's situation (where uncertainty or coaching styles that required discovery would be deadly and not appropriate), he chose to use many Practice Style episodes to achieve his outcome—excellent, accurate and efficient recall of a known route, handhold and foothold.

The post-impact set (or sets) were numerous. Honnold refers to a diary for reflection so he seems to give himself feedback often. After free soloing Half-Dome (also in Yosemite), he comments, 'that night in my climbing journal, I duly noted my free solo of Half Dome, but I included a frowny face and a comment, "Do better?"' (Honnold, 2018). Besides this showing that he used a journal for recording post-impact feedback, it also shows how he was not happy with not preparing and using a discovery episode during the climb. Honnold (2018) says, 'I was disappointed in my performance, because I knew that I had gotten away with something. I didn't want to be a lucky climber. I wanted to be a great climber'. In this situation, Honnold seems to believe that deliberate practice and recalling what to do at the appropriate time is what is needed. Given that mistakes at 3000 feet would mean death, it is hard to argue with his conclusions. Rarely are most sporting situations performed with such high stakes as the example included here.

Example 2—Sally Pearson—Hurdler

Sally Pearson's London Olympic Gold medal is sometimes presented as an example of Self-Coaching as she had no official coach. Twelve months before the London Olympics, she had decided to coach herself. She says:

> It took me hours and hours and hours on the first day to write a program out and decide what was best for me and what I could and couldn't do, being an older athlete and having these injury troubles, Pearson said.
>
> She put together a small group that would be called 'Team Pearson'.
>
> It included a couple of close friends, her mum Anne, two training partners, a biomechanist, physiotherapist, manager Robert Joske, long-time race agent Maurie Plant and, of course, Kieran.
>
> *(Gullan, 2017)*

From this information alone, it is difficult to know who did what. However, it is presumed that if Pearson accessed these people when she wanted and made all the decisions in line with the Self-Coaching Style (and did not ask these individuals to coach her or devise coaching sessions), then she may have been using a Self-Coaching style. Alternatively, if the team members were asked by Pearson to coach her or create a coaching episode, the style would revert to The Player-Initiated Style mentioned in the previous chapter and not Self-Coaching as there are clearly people assuming the decisions made by a regular 'coach'.

Example 3—Outdoor Pursuits (Surfing)

The origins of adventure are synonymous with mystical quests and dangerous exploration that brought with it wealth and status or, unfortunately, peril (Beames, Mackie & Atencio, 2019). Although the concept of adventure has evolved over time, with significant influence from cultural norms, accessing outdoor adventure has often been limited for those from disadvantage or with disability (Beames et al., 2019). In more recent times, there has been a recognition that the benefits experienced through adventurous pursuits should not be reserved for the privileged or fully able bodied. Examples such as those described by Anderson et al. (1997) and Warner, Martin and Szolosi (2020) identify the significance of outdoor adventures specifically for people with a disability. Deciding to engage in outdoor adventure sports with a physical disability can however come with a set of challenges often not previously experienced in the same ways by many others to provide insight or act as a coach who understands the specific context presented.

Derek Rabelo is a professional surfer who is also blind. Born with glaucoma, Derek was surrounded by a family with a passion for surfing, but it was initially thought that due to his disability he may never have the opportunity to surf (Dumas, 2015). Although Derek now seeks the input of a coach to surf professionally, he originally engaged in Self-Coaching to learn to surf. As it was believed that Derek would be unable to surf, at the age of 17 he had to independently decide that he wanted to learn how. Derek's initial experiences were inspired by stories of surfing and the sound of the ocean; however, it was he who entered the water and began to embody his experiences of paddling on a board and catching waves rather than being coached how to do so. Derek engaged in all decision-making in pre-impact, impact and post-impact sets as he needed to decide that he would like to try to surf and then find a way to surf that was completely new to him and those around him. In an interview investigating his passion for surfing, Derek said, 'I cannot see it as you do, but I can feel and hear it better than you', giving an insight into the way that he experienced surfing so differently than those with sight, who often talk about watching the set to choose the right wave.

In Derek's example he began learning to surf by applying a Self-Coaching Style out of necessity as there was disbelief that he would ever be able to surf and no prior example to build from. Several other examples with similarities to Derek's story exist in that a need to learn to do something differently has been presented, and individuals have found a way to overcome their specific challenges. One such example is that of Jesse Dufton. Jesse is a rock climber, who at the age of 30, had to relearn how to rock-climb without sight due to a rare genetic condition that degenerated his vision. Both of these examples recognise the application of episodic coaching, in which both Derek and Jesse reach out to coaches and enter learning using various coaching styles, but components of the learning have originally been completely independent, self-driven and born from a need for a new way of experiencing and undertaking a specific task.

Example 4—Tennis

The game of tennis in Australia, particularly during the early 1950s and early 1960s, presents as possibly a highly credible, genuine and accurate example of Player Self-Coaching. A widespread trait of many Australian coaches during this era was their commitment to training their players more intensely than their contemporaries. However, this training referred to physical training as opposed to learning how to play the game of tennis. According to Neale Fraser—Australia's longest-serving Davis Cup Captain (24 years) and a member of the Australian Davis Cup team from 1955 to 1963 while Harry Hopman was coach—Hopman was a physical trainer . . . he was rarely a coach (N. Fraser, personal communication, October 20, 2013). Australia's foremost tennis player of the first three decades of the twentieth century, Norman Brookes, received very limited formal coaching instruction. A common experience of some of Australia's greatest players, so many of whom from Brookes, Patterson, Anderson and Crawford to Bromwich, Sedgeman, Hoad, Rosewall, Emerson and Laver, received minimal or no professional coaching in their formative years. Learning the game through individual practice—which we are discussing in this chapter—was a common experience among many tennis players. For example, Australian tennis great, Tony Roche, spent long hours practising hitting tennis balls against the walls of his father's garage, on which he scrawled a series of numbers, each identified with a particular stroke. Roche became adept at keeping the ball in play while using the designated stroke to hit each number in turn (Whitington, 1975). This particular form of Self-Coaching is quite common amongst contemporary players where they are afforded primary responsibility for their own practice in the absence of a coach. The player is responsible for the planning, implementation and feedback (reflection) in connection to this coaching experience. However, should the player, in the example of Tony Roche's experience, seek advice, guidance or assistance from a 'significant other' in connection to their respective performance, then this would be appropriate and available in this coaching experience.

In the Roche example, the player has decided to completely pursue private and self-determined practice. The player has made all the decisions in the Pre-Impact, Impact and Post-Impact sets of the learning experience. There is no 'external' coach assigning the goal or the topic—the player does this. The Roche example is not unique. To this day, sporting biographies often contain examples of players acting independently and with self-direction in their practice, in other words Self-Coaching.

Conclusion

From our reading, it appears difficult to find examples in sport of a Self-Coaching Style in academic literature as most reported as such seem more in line with the decision-making structure described in The Player-Initiated Style. That is, it may be more accurate to say that athletes or players may train alone but are in fact implementing a session that someone else (a coach) has created (either recently or in their past training experiences). Many reasons could be attributed as to why this is the case; however, that is not the aim of this chapter. It is important to consider that the common or usual formula for sporting success has more often than not involved a coach. That is not to say that the Self-Coaching Style is out of reach of players. Some coaches may believe they have players who do not have the self-discipline, skills or knowledge to use Self-Coaching. We would suggest two responses to this belief. First, not all athletes respond best to every coaching style. In part, the need for The Spectrum as no one style can achieve all things for everyone. The second response we would hope a coach would consider is reflecting on the coaching styles which they have used to coach their players. Have they used coaching styles that required their players to develop decision-making, problem solving, solution generating, taking responsibility for feedback for others and themself and reflection? If they have not, then concluding a player is unable to use Self-Coaching would be a fair assumption as they have not been provided with coaching experiences that allowed them to develop the skills to be able to make decisions in line with the Self-Coaching Style.

References

Anderson, L., Schleien, S. J., McAvoy, L., Lais, G., & Seligmann, D. (1997). Creating positive change through an integrated outdoor adventure program. *Therapeutic Recreation Journal*, *31*, 214–229.

Beames, S., Mackie, C., & Atencio, M. (2019). *Adventure and society.* Palgrave Macmillan.

Bradbury, P. E. (2000). Athletes doing it for themselves: Self-coaching experiences of New Zealand Olympians. Unpublished Doctorate of Philosophy thesis. Massey University, Auckland Albany Campus.

DNA India. (2008). *Ponting goes hi-tech to overcome batting slump.* May 9, 2008, 07:12 PM IST. www.dnaindia.com/sports/report-ponting-goes-hi-tech-to-overcome-batting-slump-1163437

Dumas, D. (2015). *Pipeline and aims for the heaven.* www.smh.com.au/national/nsw/blind-brazilian-surfer-derek-rabelo-conquers-pipeline-and-aims-for-the-heavens-20150806-gisp00.html

Fitzsimons, P. (1993). *Nick Farr-Jones: The authorised biography*. Ransom House.
Gullan, S. (2017). *How Sally Pearson coached herself to be one of the best athletes in the world*. www.dailytelegraph.com.au/sport/how-sally-pearson-coached-herself-to-be-the-one-of-the-best-athletes-in-the-world/news-story/3d86f1914c60b758c1dec6481ba6c206
Hars, M., & Calmels, C. (2007). Observation of elite gymnastic performance: Processes and perceived functions of observation. *Psychology of Sport and Exercise, 8*, 337–354.
Honnold, A. (2018). *How I climbed a 3000-foot vertical cliff—without ropes*. www.ted.com/talks/alex_honnold_how_i_climbed_a_3_000_foot_vertical_cliff_without_ropes/transcript
Johnston, C., & Jameson, N. (1989). *Walk alone: The Craig Johnston story*. HarperCollins.
Mosston, M., & Ashworth, S. (2008). *Teaching physical education* (1st online ed.). https://spectrumofteachingstyles.org/assets/files/book/Teaching_Physical_Edu_1st_Online.pdf
Thorp, C. (n.d.). How Alex Honnold got strong and conquered El Cap for 'free solo'. *Men's Journal*. www.mensjournal.com/adventure/how-alex-honnold-got-strong-and-conquered-el-cap-for-free-solo/
Warner, R. P., Martin, B., & Szolosi, A. M. (2020). Exploring the inclusive praxis of outward bound instructors. *Education Sciences, 10*(9), 241. https://doi.org/10.3390/educsci10090241
Whitington, R. S. (1975). *An illustrated history of Australian tennis*. Macmillan.

14
EPISODIC COACHING

Brendan SueSee and Shane Pill

Episodic coaching is the idea that the session plan consists of a series of intentionally designed episodes, each episode with its learning objectives and an aligned coaching style. The session plan may consist of a series of episodes, with each episode using the same coaching style. For example, if a coach created a learning episode that had the objective of throwing at a target, they may use Practice Style with the target to throw at being a practice partner. The second episode could be a game-like activity in pairs where two athletes are to play 'catch'. The players take turns aiming to throw to their partners with a pass caught at chest height being 1 point and at head height 2 points. The players practise not only the skill of throwing at a target but also the skill of being the judge/umpire of the score. Further, players may be told they need to give positive comments about 'why' the throw scored when their practice partner scores a point. This activity uses Practice Style—Style B, but besides developing the skill of throwing and catching (physical channel or domain of learning), it also emphasises on the ethical channel (self-umpiring—fair calls: a social domain of learning) and the social channel by giving a positive constructive comment to the practice partner (a social domain of learning). Whilst the subject matter is slightly different between the initial Practice Style episode and the next, Practice Style is used throughout both episodes as the practice outcome intent is identical—reproduce known skills.

When the objective is substantially different and, more importantly, if the decision-making by the coach and participant is different from the aforementioned example, then different coaching styles will be matched to meet the objectives. For instance, in the previous example the coach may have desired for the participants to not only practice throwing and catching, but the coach may also have wanted the participants to self-correct their performance. If this was the case, a Self-Check episode would be appropriate. This would be used to reinforce a learning objective through repetition.

A session plan may consist of episodes that result in more than one coaching style being intentionally used during the practice session. This would be used as there is more than one learning objective for the practice session. For example, if a coach thought that players were not self-correcting when errors occurred during games, they may decide a series of episodes using the Reciprocal Style or Self-Check style were necessary so that players would learn and practice this skill instead of waiting for the coach to tell them.

DOI: 10.4324/9781003041443-15

To demonstrate episodic coaching, we examine a tactical or 'game-based' model coaching episode to identify the decisions being made between the coach and the player/s. This will allow the coaching episode to be placed on The Spectrum of Coaching Styles. By doing this, we detail important pedagogical concepts and unify pedagogical decision-making that take place when sport coaching.

The coaching episodes mentioned in Table 14.1 are examples of Practice Style as the players are required to reproduce known skills or movements and apply them. It is assumed that the coach would be giving corrective feedback or reinforcing feedback in these situations, perhaps even directing feedback by asking questions of the players. There is thus an opportunity for a Guided Discovery episode if the player is unaware of why a specific technique needs refining or adjustment. The episode that may lend itself to a convergent episode is the activity in Episode 5, where the ball is ricocheting off the net. The coach could ask the players (if they did not already know the answer) to complete 'if-then' questions regarding the ball movement before it hits the net. For example, 'if the ball contacts the net with the widest side, then it is likely to. . . .?'. If the player does not

TABLE 14.1 Australian football (AFL) coaching session plan as a series of teaching episodes.

Australian football (AFL) U18 Pre-season Session Plan
Episode 1   5:30 pm   **Team Meeting**—head coach outlines practice
Episode 2   5:45 pm   **Warm Up** Part 1
Lane work: closed (no defender) progressing to open (passive defence)
Episode 3   6:00 pm   **Warm Up Part 2** Trademarks Practice: Wolf
                                                Ball

Station 1   Spread from stoppages
Station 2   Kicking to space—long kicking
Station 3   Conditioning: Acceleration, Speed and Balance (with footballs)
Station 4   Working in congestion—Handball in 'tight spaces'
Station changeovers/ 15 minutes each station
Episode 4   7.00 pm   **Match Simulation**: Full ground ball movement exiting from
                                                inside defensive 50.
Episode 5   7:20 pm   **Warm Down**—Line/positional groups:
                                Craft Work drills separated into Forwards, Midfield, Defenders.

Forwards: 'Strong hands' in marking. For example, marking a medicine ball instead of a football. Medicine balls being heavy and harder and therefore harder to mark. Medicine balls thrown to a player to mark.
Midfield: Blocking, nudging and wedging an opponent at a contest to get them off balance.

1v1 close contest. Ball is thrown at a coach at a rebound net, and the ricochet off the net is contested. One player is designated to either block, nudge or wedge their opponent to achieve an advantageous position to take the ball into possession and be able to break from the contest while their opponent is off balance.

Defenders: Defensive starting points—intercept marking.
Ball is kicked to a 1v1 marking contest.
The final episode, episode 5, contains movements and skills specific to the three broad positions in Australian Football and therefore the players have been divided accordingly to practice the specific skills relevant to the three positions.

---

know the answer, the episode would require a series of observations for them to reach a conclusion. If they did already know the answer, it is an example of recall or review and thus Practice Style.

Table 14.1 identifies five episodes which will be placed on the Spectrum. Episode 1 is the Team meeting with the coach outlining the content which will be covered in this training session. It is presumed that the objective of telling the players what they will be doing is so that they will, at some point over the next 2 hours, perform these episodes. This episode shares similar characteristics with Practice Style coaching in that the coach is outlining the subject matter. The coach has made these pre-impact decisions about what the team will practice during the session. The player's role is to perform the subject matter/skills as outlined by the coach. Whilst feedback is not provided during episode 1, it will be presented during episodes 2–5. During the session briefing, a coach may ask questions to see if players understand the alignment of the activities to session objectives, player learning outcomes, or at semi-professional/professional level, the alignment of activities to developing the identified 'system of play' for the season.

Episode 2 is the warm-up which consists of lane work. This involves three lines approximately 15–20 metres apart facing each other (Figure 14.1). These three players will pass between each other as they run together left to right.

Initially commencing on the left, the three players at the head of the line begin with a ball and run toward the line directly in front of them (to the right, illustrated the diagram) and handballs the pass (in Australian Football the ball cannot be thrown by hand) to the player at the start of the line across from them and continues running to the end of the line of the player that received the ball. The player now in possession runs to the line where the ball started and passes to the player now at the start of that line and continues running to the end of the line. In this way, the ball and players 'move in their lane' end to end. After a time determined by the coach, three players are nominated to stand in between the lanes (one in between each lane) to provide 'light' defensive pressure on the passing. After another length of time determined by the coach, the activity progresses from running three lanes to a 3v2 'end to end' passing activity. As this is the same warm-up done each week, the players are aware of what is needed and they are working on the skills of running, hand passing and catching. We would suggest that this is another example of Practice Style as the coach has set the subject matter/skills to be recalled or displayed during this episode. The player's job is to recall the skill at the appropriate time and perform it to a specific standard. For example, the players hand pass to the player running with them. The receiving player catches the ball and hand passes to the next person at the front of the opposite line. The players have not been asked to create or discover a new way to do this. They have been shown a way to do this, and it is expected that they will perform the task as described. The coach will provide feedback about how well (accuracy, speed, and intensity, etc.) the skills are being used. Ultimately, the players will be practising a method of hand passing, catching, and running they were familiar with prior to the session. Therefore, the player is practising known knowledge and skills. During or after the activity, the coach commonly offers feedback individually to players or collectively to the group about how the task was performed. This is also in line with the characteristics of the Practice Style of Coaching, where 'the teacher moves from learner to learner, observing both the performance of the task and the decision-making process, then offers feedback and moves on to the next learner' (Mosston & Ashworth, 2008, p. 95).

The lane work adds a 'passive' defender to the activity towards the end, whereby a defender moves in a way that requires the attackers to pass around or over; however, the defender will

Lane work (unopposed = closed). One ball each lane

```
XXXX                    XXXX

XXXX                    XXXX

XXXX                    XXXX
```

Progression- add a defender whose aim is to interfere not tackle or take possession.

Still one ball each lane

D = defender

```
XXXX          D         XXXX

XXXX          D         XXXX

XXXX          D         XXXX
```

Progression 3v2 lane work (one ball) - the aim of the two defenders is to tackle, harass, and take possession if the opportunity presents.

```
  XXXX                      XXXX
         D

  XXXX                      XXXX
         D

  XXXX                      XXXX
```

FIGURE 14.1 Example of 'lane work' activities progressing from a 'closed' task with limited decision-making and no opposition, to progressively more 'open' tasks where players face greater decision-making pressure due to 'full' defensive action by the players in the defensive role.

have been instructed not to perform at full competitive capacity. In this situation, it is easy to conclude that the players may be using problem-solving skills. For the sake of this chapter, we will discuss this from the perspective that solving a problem means not knowing the answer to a problem, and thus the discovery or creation of a new solution. Unless the coaching episode is with novice players, in the situation of having a 'passive' defender the attacking player will run towards the defender and decide to implement a known strategy of evading the defender or passing around, over or under them. It is acknowledged that the attacking player has three options (or more) to choose from; however, they have not been instructed by the coach to find a new way to evade the defender and pass to the other attacker. The attacker is practising the reading of perceptual cues from the defender and reacting accordingly to pass successfully. It is, therefore, not a discovery episode.

Episode 3—Warm-Up Part 2 has four stations, with the players spending 15 minutes at each station (Table 14.2). The placing of these four stations on The Spectrum of Coaching styles will be done in order starting with Station 1—spreading from stoppages.

Station 1—spreading from stoppages. If experienced previously, the players are aware of what needs to be done when the ball is dropped by the coach—obtain possession—decide if your group of 5 is now attacking or defending—spread to space if attacking/mark attackers if defending—hand pass or kick to a team mate on a corner marker/attempt to intercept/tackle if defending. It is presumed in this situation (as the coach has not instructed the players to find a solution to this problem or create five ways to solve this problem) that it is Practice Style Coaching. The players will likely be implementing known skills (hand passing, tackling, running, kicking and marking) to the situation. They will be applying known rules (if I am defending, the closer I am to my opponent the harder it is for them to get possession or if I am behind my opponent the easier it is for them to get the ball) to the situation. This situation could be a style from the production cluster (requiring the production of new knowledge) if two factors were present. First, if the coach directed the players to create a new way to get the ball to the corner without interception, and second, if the players did not know how to do this. If these two factors were present, then this coaching episode could be Convergent Discovery. This situation highlights the importance of the coach knowing the player's cognitive history (or knowledge of the game and skills) when choosing a coaching style. There is little point in asking the player to create something new or solve a problem if the player already knows the answer. Similarly, if there are known movements, skills, principals, or tactics which the coach wants the players to apply, then the players may discover them; however, after this initial discovery Practice Style episodes will follow to increase speed, fluency, accuracy, etc.

TABLE 14.2 Football (soccer) coaching session plan as a series of teaching episodes.

Station 1 Spread from stoppages. This involves the players (team of 5 versus 5) in a small area (20 m by 20 m) trying to run away from the defender and receive a pass or kick from their teammates. Start from a 'loose ball' situation with all players close to the ball. Coach drops the ball, and a team attempts to be the first to the ball. Once in possession of the ball, the team 'spread' from the area to one of the corners of the grid by a chain of continuous possession, while the other team defends and attempts to create a turn-over in possession to them so they can be the team trying to score. Play starts and re-starts from a 'loose ball' situation with all players close to the ball.

Station 2 Kicking to space—long kicking. Players are required to kick a long distance (40–50 m), and their teammates receive the ball (or take a mark) running into space. Kicker picks up the ball from the ground, 'pushes back' from that mark (the position of the ball on the ground) and directs the kick to space so leading player can run onto the ball and mark the ball before it hits the ground or without having to stop and wait for the ball. After the mark, player roles reverse.

Station 3 Conditioning: Acceleration, Speed and Balance (with footballs). This station involves activities designed to improve these components of fitness but requires the player to use a football whilst performing them. For example, a coach feeds a loose ball to a player required to run at the ball, gather it 'cleanly' and then accelerate with the ball.

Station 4 Handball in tight spaces. This would be like Station 1 except in this case the area may be smaller, and the attacking players are attempting to perform as many passes/handballs as possible in a specific time period in a physical environment constrained by size and pressure from defenders.

Station 2—Kicking to space—Long kicking. This involves the players practising the skills of kicking the ball accurately a long distance, trying to 'hit' the receiving player so that they do not have to wait/stand still while marking the ball (catching the ball). If experienced previously, this is another example of a Practice Style Coaching episode. The coach has not instructed the players to create or discover and therefore has not been a deliberate decision by the coach to the players to do these things (discover, create, explore). There is no reason in this practice task that the coach would require discovery or creativity. The coach wants the players to practice these three skills and continue either developing or refining them so that they become more consistent, fast and accurate.

Station 3 requires the coach to feed a 'loose ball' to a player, who is required to run at the ball, gather it 'cleanly' and then accelerate with the ball. In this coaching episode, the player is practising the skills of reading the bounce or roll of the ball, responding to the bounce/roll and use hand–eye coordination to pick up the ball 'cleanly' and accelerate. Once again, the player is being asked by the coach to reproduce known skills and movements and attempt to increase consistency, accuracy and speed through large volumes, and thus the coaching is Practice Style.

Station 4—Handballing in tight spaces requires the attacking players to attempt to perform as many passes (handballs) as possible in a specific time period in a physical environment constrained by size and pressure from defenders. We argue that, like a lot of good practice, the episode is trying to replicate a game situation to provide an opportunity for the players to recognise and respond to cues and pass the ball successfully to a teammate. This is a Practice Style Coaching episode as in these compressed game-like situations, coaches are applying the theory of 'recognition-primed decision-making (RPD) in which experts make rapid, intuitive decisions based on recognizing critical features of dynamic performance situations' (Fadde, 2009, p. 359).

Episode 4 is Match Simulation: Full ground ball movement exiting from inside defensive 50-metre arc on the field. Episode 4 would involve a game-like environment, where everything was identical to the game except perhaps the numbers. Australian Football is 18 versus 18 players; however, this may be 15 versus 15 or less depending on the size of the training squad. In this match simulation, the ball is returned to play by the attacking team usually by a kick from the opponents' goal line. The defender can kick the ball into the field of play or can run it into the field of play but must either bounce the ball before they have travelled 15 metres, or they must kick or hand pass the ball. In this situation, the attacking team is working on getting into space to receive the ball whilst the defending team is attempting to 'mark' the attacking players to reduce options for attacking players to be 'easily' available to gain possession of the ball.

If the coach has said, 'We are trying to get the ball out of our defensive 50 area' then the attacking team will likely use known movements to get into a position to receive a pass, for example, straight-line running away from the defender or running in one direction before changing direction sharply. It is unlikely that the player will decide to create a new movement. They will recall a movement which has either been successful in the past, and they will base this on the defender's abilities. Likewise, the defender will recall strategies that they have learnt in the past and attempt to apply them to the attacker, not to allow them to get into space to receive a pass or kick. Based on this situation (where we are speaking about experienced, high-level players), we would suggest that this coaching episode is largely Practice Style. Another reason we suggest that this is likely Practice Style is based on the instructions of the coach. If the coach has said

'We are trying to get the ball out of our defensive 50 area', then there have been no instructions to create five new ways to get the ball out of our 50". The basic premise of the Spectrum is that 'every act of deliberate teaching [coaching] is a consequence of a prior decision' (Mosston & Ashworth, 2008, p. 8). If there were instructions to create five new ways, then there is a chance that this may be Divergent Discovery Coaching.

Opportunities may arise in this coaching episode, which requires the players to try something new. In this case it may be argued that this was a Convergent Discovery coaching episode as one new response was produced. However, the Spectrum's concept of deliberate coaching (teaching) makes placing this coaching style a little tricky as the coach did not ask for new ways, and, therefore, the coach cannot claim it was due to their instructions or the coaching episode they created. This by no means negates the fact that the player did produce something new; we are merely arguing that the coach has not directed or necessarily intended the player to do so.

If we do imagine the episode described earlier is applied to inexperienced players and the coach's instructions are now 'find two or more ways get into space to receive a pass which you have not tried or used before' then this, we suggest, is a Divergent Discovery coaching episode as the *coach is deliberately instructing the players to produce a movement not used or known previously*, thus producing new knowledge. Similarly, if the players were finding it difficult to move the ball, the coach could stop the match simulation and use Guided Discovery to help the players that are challenged to conclude what is causing the problem. The coach could then set a task (based on the problem identified during the Guided Discovery episode) for the team to solve. If the task required more than one solution, then it could be concluded that the Divergent Discovery style had been used.

In this next section, football (or soccer as it is known in some countries) will be used to illustrate use of The Spectrum of Coaching Styles (Table 14.3). If in Episode 1 (the meeting) the coach is telling the players what the work to be completed in the following five sessions is, we would suggest that this is done with the expectation that the players will perform the work outlined as described. In this scenario the style is Command Style coaching. There will be a time between the expectations presented by the coach and the physical performance of the tasks; however, it will occur as directed.

TABLE 14.3 Coaching session plan as a series of teaching episodes.

Football (Soccer) Senior Team In-season Session Plan		
Episode 1-	5:30 pm	**Team Meeting**-head coach outlines practice
Episode 2-	5:45 pm	**Warm-Up** Dynamic mobility and running Closed (no defender) progressing to open (passive defence) drills
Episode 3-	6:00 pm	**Game Play**: Small sided football 5v5 with a focus on individual possession and passing
Episode 4-	6.20 pm	**Game Training** -Team possession focus
Episode 5-	6.45 pm	**Match Simulation**-Game plan implementation
Episode 6-	7:15 pm	**Warm Down**
Skills groups: goalkeeping, forwards, midfield, defenders		

Episode 2 consists of three broad learning experiences. The dynamic warm-up is likely known movements, which have been chosen to prepare the muscles and which will be used in the session. We would suggest that the players have not been asked to create or discover anything but to either recall the movements which they have done previously, or the ones that the person leading the warm-up is asking them to do. The next part of the warm-up involves closed running, which would entail running with the ball and progressing to a passive defender. In both these cases, whilst the skill practice context becomes slightly more open and 'game-like', we would suggest that this is still Practice Style as the players know what is required, and they have likely been asked to dribble the ball from this cone to the other cone with the intent of practising the skill and warming up the relevant muscles. The introduction of the passive defender requires the player dribbling to go around the defender, but again this is probably a recall of known skills to solve a known problem. The players have not been asked, 'Find a way to maintain possession of the ball and get around the passive defender, using a way which you have not before'. This would be inappropriate in this situation given that the objective could be stated as 'In the shortest possible time, warm-up the relevant muscles for the training session and practice skills focusing on speed and accuracy'. Styles from the production cluster would not be relevant in meeting this objective for this level of player as the muscles are known and the skills are known. Discovery would be time consuming, inefficient and the question must be asked, would players get to this level and be unaware of the muscles to warm-up and the skills to use?

Episode 3 requires the players to play small-sided games of 5 versus 5 whilst Team A tries to maintain possession while Team B tries to intercept the ball or prevent possession. This episode could be coached using numerous styles. First, it is suggested that as the players are senior players, then they are quite experienced and are aware of all the skills needed to maintain possession (well-weighted passes, accurate passes, good first touches, good body position and shape when receiving and running to space). The coach will instruct them to 'Maintain possession of the football for as long as possible'. The coach has not instructed them to use creativity or discovery to solve a problem. In this case it would be Practice Style coaching. Let us suggest that at some point in this episode, a player does not appear to know why they are not receiving the ball and they appear frustrated. The coach may use Guided Discovery questions to assist the player in discovering why they are not getting the ball or the solution to this problem. The coach may ask:

COACH: You are not getting the ball Con, why is this happening?
CON: I don't know—is it because the defender is too good?
COACH: How could you get away from the defender?
CON: I don't know. I'm not fast.
COACH: Maybe, but how can you trick the defender into going one way?
CON: Run in that direction.
COACH: Yes, but he will catch you eventually as you said he is fast. What can you do once you get him going in one direction?
CON: Change direction?
COACH: Okay—give it a go and see what happens.

The player (Con) would try out his solution, and if successful, uses it—thus reverting from Guided Discovery to Practice Style.

Episode 4—Team possession's focus is full game (11 versus 11), with (as the name suggests) a focus on maintaining possession. We suggest the coach will have given instructions along the lines of 'We are playing 11 v 11. We are focusing on maintaining possession. Five continuous passes will equal one point. Think about what you need to do to maintain possession'. For some readers, this task may be viewed as a Constraints-Led Approach (CLA). This is suggested as in the situation given, information transactions between the performer/s and their environment direct the motor behaviour. The motor behaviour emerges and is dynamic as it is shaped by the interaction between the performer (the organism), the environment and the task. This movement coupling (Anson, Elliott & Davids, 2005) occurs due to the interaction between the three categories of constraints, as they 'tune' a functional relationship between movement and information in the specific situated momentary dynamics of the environment. Motor behaviour is therefore considered to emerge from the interaction of the constraints (SueSee, Pill & Hewitt, 2020). If this episode is viewed through The Spectrum lens, it is suggested that the terminology or instructions being used is broad or non-specific about the cognitive processes the coach wish the player/s to use and the subject matter in the form of the motor pattern required to perform the task. For example, the coach has not asked the player/s to reproduce any subject matter (i.e., 'Pass or dribble the ball like this') but to 'Maintain possession of the ball. Five passes in a row gets one point'. These instructions would suggest that this is the subject matter, and any method of maintaining the ball within the rules of the game are acceptable. Similarly, with regards to the defenders, there were no instructions given at all suggesting familiarity with the task, and thus memory will be used. The instructions do not suggest using any technique specifically (the foot is presumed) so it is unlikely the athletes will attempt to discover or create a new way of moving the ball whilst maintaining possession as they have not been instructed to do so. We suggest the player/s will be practising a method of passing or moving the ball which they knew before the session. The player/s are still making the decision, that is, to reproduce subject matter deciding on pace, rhythm, number of passes, as they would in Practice Style. During the 11 versus 11 game play, we believe that the coach may stop the game at 'coachable moments' to offer feedback about the task or maybe to ask open-ended questions. If providing feedback, this would be Practice Style as 'the teacher moves from learner to learner, observing both the performance of the task and the decision-making process, then offers feedback and moves on to the next learner' (Mosston & Ashworth, 2008, p. 99). However, if the coach asked open-ended questions, we would argue that it could be Practice Style with review questions. That is, the coach stops the game and asks, 'Why did Dale get the ball?' To answer this question the player thinks about what has just happened and will retrieve the answer from memory—thus using memory as the cognitive operation to answer the question. If the player does not know the answer to the question, an opportunity for Guided Discovery to be used occurs. This type of situation demonstrates the intricacies of coaching and the decisions which the coach needs to make. In this situation, the coach may identify this opportunity and decides to use Guided Discovery. The Spectrum defines Guided Discovery as 'the logical and sequential design of questions that lead a person to discover a predetermined response' (Mosston & Ashworth, 2008, p. 212).

When the coach asks a specific sequence of questions in a structured process, the player correspondingly responds until that player has discovered the only correct answer for each of the questions asked by the coach. Some have suggested that there is confusion in such scenarios when it is assumed that Guided Discovery is being used for all players (SueSee et al., 2020). For example, in a game of 11 versus 11, all players are not starting from the same point of knowledge with regards to maintaining possession. Therefore, an open-ended question to one athlete may involve recalling the answer, whilst to another it will require discovery. Another aspect to consider regarding the coaching style being used hinges around the processing speed of the 22 players when thinking and responding to the questions asked by the coach. For the 22 players to be able to discover the exact same predetermined response (and at the same time), the athletes' processing speeds would all need to be identical (an unrealistic assumption) so that when the coach asked the questions associated with using a Guided Discovery Style, the same response occurred. Using The Spectrum to view this episode suggests it is the one player who is engaged in answering the question/s and is thus the one producing, or discovering, new knowledge (Mosston & Ashworth, 2008). With regards to the other player(s) (who are listening to the coach's questions and athletes' responses), they may learn by reproducing the new knowledge that was produced by the players' response, and the overall coaching style for these athletes remain Practice Style. Alfieri et al. (2011) suggested that 'unassisted discovery-learning tasks involving hands-on activities, even with large group discussions do not guarantee that learners will understand the task or that they will come into contact with the to-be-learned material' (p. 2).

Episode 5 (Match simulation) and 6 (Warm Down) are other examples of Practice Style for the same reasons as suggested earlier. If the athletes are being told to 'play a game' with no other instructions, then they will be replicating skills and strategies which they know. If the athletes are asked questions (whether open ended or not) after an event has occurred (thus requiring recall), then it is Practice style—Review. As was explained in the previous paragraph, the athletes are being asked to reflect on something that has happened and then asked for the solution to this problem or question. They either know the answer, or they do not. For the episode to be from the production cluster of styles, it would require the coach to set a problem or question which required the athlete to be producing knowledge new to themselves. Mosston and Ashworth argued, 'The discovery process, unlike memory, engages learners in production of information that was previously unknown to them' (2008, p. 48). Asking a question which requires the athlete to recall known answers or information would not constitute a discovery episode. Conversely, if the coach asks a series of questions which the athlete did not know the answer to and required a search for the answer, then it may be a production cluster episode. Production cluster episodes or styles are those from Guided Discovery—Self-Coaching Style and are grouped as they require the player to produce knowledge new to themselves or the coach. For example, if an athlete did not know why the opponent kept intercepting a ball, the coach may recognise this coachable moment and choose to use Guided Discovery by asking the player a series of questions to lead them to discover the answer. The dialogue may look like the following:

COACH: Mitch–you keep losing possession to Rebecca, do you know why that is happening?
MITCH: She's too good?
COACH: I'm not sure about that. How close are you to Rebecca each time you lose the ball, or she intercepts it?
MITCH: Very close (memory).
COACH: What does the proximity allow her to do?
MITCH: Smothers the ball and gets it (memory).
COACH: So if she's close, she seems to get it? Finish this sentence for me Mitch; 'The closer I am to Rebecca, the more she gets it. Therefore, the further away I am from Rebecca. . . .?

MITCH: The less likely she is to get it? (discovery)
COACH: Maybe—let's give it a go!

This question shows a series of memory questions concluding with a question which asks the player to 'join the dots' and identify a relationship which he does not seem to know. Even at the end the player may not be 100% sure or convinced until they have applied the strategy.

A key point to consider with the asking of open-ended questions to groups of athletes is the presumption that all the athletes are doing Guided Discovery. Guided Discovery is best done one-on-one with an athlete and not as a group as Mosston and Ashworth suggested that when one athlete has 'discovered the answer (anywhere in the sequence) and utters it aloud, the other learners who hear (or see) the response become the receivers. They can no longer discover it. For these students [players], the discovery process has been aborted' (Mosston & Ashworth, 2008, p. 221). Others (SueSee et al., 2020) have noted similar concerns with Guided Discovery when people presume that they are using it with groups. Coaches need to be aware who is doing the discovery (and who may be recalling) so that the episode is managed in such a way that discovery is achieved by the player who the coach has decided needs to discover the answer, and not an episode that has one player telling other players the answer. We argue that this is important as Guided Discovery is a style which is the beginning journey for the player to discover knowledge previously unknown.

There will be times during games that a problem arises which the player does not know the solution or solutions. Episodes of Guided Discovery (and Convergent and Divergent Discovery) will provide opportunities for the player to develop confidence in solving problems, rather than the player thinking they must wait until the coach tells the answer. If coaching players to solve problems independently is one of the goals of the coaching episode, then discovery styles providing opportunities for player problem-solving need to be used.

Baseball (Juniors) In-Season Session Plan—Canopies of Coaching Styles

The concluding section of this chapter will use a Baseball training session to demonstrate episodic coaching as canopies of the coaching styles. This will differ from the previous examples using Soccer and Australian Football as with those sports we identified as Landmark versions of the coaching styles. Landmark styles (A–K) are defined by decisions, which inherently produce specific objectives. The 11 Landmark styles outlined Chapters 3 to 13 are identifiable by establishing who makes which decisions, about what and when. However, when not all of these decisions are made as per the Landmark styles, canopy designs emerge between each of the 11 landmark styles. Hewitt, Pill and SueSee (2020) suggested that 'a canopy design recognises that a learning episode may be predominantly delivered through one coaching style but include elements of another' (p. 168). Canopy designs are labelled with a plus (+) or a minus (−) depending on the set of decisions. If the decisions move the experience towards the next Landmark Style on the continuum, it is assigned a plus (+). Conversely, if the decisions move the experience away from the Landmark Style's set of decisions, it is assigned a minus (−). Little research has been completed on Canopy designs; however, Hewitt (2015) frequently observed tennis coaches using Practice Style with socialisation, or Style B+socialisation. In this section using Baseball, we will demonstrate that a canopy of coaching styles is more common than we may initially think.

Episode 1—Lap of Field, Stretches and Run-Throughs

For this coaching episode, we will presume that a routine has been established over the season, and the players are instructed to reproduce the known warm-up as a group and are expected to stay together. The lap of the oval run and the stretching as a group has the hallmarks of a Practice Coaching Style—'individual and private practice of a memory/reproduction task with private feedback' (Mosston & Ashworth, 2008, p. 94). This episode described is lacking the private feedback typical of a Practice style as the players are some distance away from the coach, and if the coach yells out to the players (e.g., 'hurry up'!) it is obviously not private feedback to a player. This episode demonstrates a canopy—Practice Style minus feedback, or Style B-feedback. Similarly, who is to 'Hurry up'? Everyone or just one or a few? 'Hurry up' does not stipulate if a part of the movement is to 'hurry up' either. Whilst it may be easy to conclude that this use of Practice Style-feedback is poor coaching, the coach's intent could be to develop more player independence with regards to preparing for the game or training. Thus, Practice Style-feedback could be one such style chosen to develop this. Similarly, if the athletes have done the same warm-up over many weeks, then the content or movements are known and need to be replicated. The run-throughs involved groups of four lined up on the right-field foul line and running through towards second base and stopping there. When the other groups of four have run through, the first line of four runs back towards the right field foul line, thus emulating running from first base to second base. The athletes have usually been told to begin running when the lead runner in their group claps. The sets of run-throughs will be things such as high knees, butt-flicks, karaoke, straight steals and delayed steal. We will presume that no other instructions have been given for the warm-up except to 'do our usual warm-up. You know what I expect'.

This type of warm-up we suggest may include aspects of a stereotypical baseball warm-up. As no objective has been given, we will presume that it is to warm-up the players for training or a game. We would suggest that many learning experiences or drills in coaching have come from experience. This is similar to research on physical education (PE) teachers, which suggests that the most experienced style for PE teachers during their schooling was either the Command Style or Practice Style (Cothran et al., 2005; Jaakola & Watt, 2011; Syrmpas, Digelidis & Watt, 2016; Syrmpas et al., 2017). They teach how they were taught, and we would conclude that for many coaches it is similar. In this case, the warm-up is done like this because it has commonly been done like this. Whilst this warm-up prepares the body for baseball because it is done in some unison fashion, it allows the players to be scrutinised by the coach for not keeping up or staying in line with regards to the run-throughs. This is interesting as nowhere in baseball is synchronous running required so the emphasis on doing this is questionable, to say the least. Doing the warm-up in groups may lead to the conclusion that teamwork is developed, but there is no real emphasis on social skills/teamwork so that conclusion may also be questioned. Our point here is not to criticise the warm-up but to show that unless an objective or outcome is set, then it is likely coaching styles may be chosen which do not reflect the outcome. In this episode (the run-throughs) have aspects of synchronicity and going off a cue but no feedback is given beyond 'hurry up' or 'keep up'. It has characteristics of Command Style, but as synchronicity is not required to do the run-throughs, the athletes are not moving in time with precision, and, the athletes are deciding the stop and starting time, it is not Command Style. This episode is Practice Style with socialisation and minus feedback, or Practice plus socialisation, minus feedback. It is a canopy of Practice Style because it is lacking some of the characteristics and has aspects of others added to it.

Episode 2—Throwing to Warm-Up (Long Toss)

After a warm-up, players pair up and proceed to the foul line in left or right field and play catch to warm up. Again, players may be aware of the routine so they stand approximately 5–10 metres apart and begin to play catch. No objective has been set except to say maybe 'Warm up—Play catch'. This episode would most likely be Practice Style as the players are reproducing a known movement and deciding on the quantity, the distance they throw over, the intensity, etc. In some cases, feedback may be given from the coach reinforcing or correcting technique or a comment about accuracy. The players slowly increase the distance.

Episode 3—Ground Balls, Fly Balls and Bull Pen Work

After the players complete the previous episode, the coach moves to specialist fielding positions, breaking the team into infielders, outfielders, and pitchers and catchers.

The infielders are asked to take their positions on the diamond whereby a coach hits a variety of ground balls (line drives, short hops, high hops, to the backhand, forehand and fly balls). The infielders will be given instructions like, 'Ok . . . . throwing to first' and the coach will proceed to hit ground balls as previously described. The coach may tell the players what is coming ('line drives straight at you') or it may be randomised. This episode has all the hallmarks of Practice Style as the infielders are being asked to reproduce a series of known movements. That is, field the ball and throw it to the first baseman. It is not a discovery episode, however, as the players have not been asked to create or discover a new way of doing things. Even if the infielder does not know exactly where the ball will bounce, it is likely that they will still attempt to position themselves behind the ball in a known posture and field the ball (in a previously known way) and throw the ball using a known technique to first base.

Whilst the infielders are practicing fielding ground balls, the outfielders episode will be made up of fielding ground balls (long hop and short hop) and fly balls (running back, running forward), communicating and backing up other outfielders and playing the ball off the fence. These episodes are providing opportunities to execute the skills of running and catching with the ability to read the flight of the ball off a bat. This is called attunement. Perceptual attunement is the learned ability to detect relevant information for a given task that has the potential to influence emergent decision-making behaviours (Araújo, Davids & Hristovski, 2006; Fajen, Riley & Turvey, 2009; Headrick et al., 2012; Weast, Shockley & Riley, 2011). Skilled performers in sport display attunement to specific perceptual variables relating to a task because of extensive amounts of specific task experience and practice (Smith et al., 2001).

These episodes (including the skill of reading a ball off a bat) again represent Practice Style coaching. It could be an opportunity to use a Divergent Discovery episode for a player who does not know a few of the perceptual cues to help predict where the ball may fall. For example, the coach could ask, 'There are three things you can watch to give you a hint about where the ball will go. Watch me hit the balls for the next 20 hits and then you tell me what you have discovered?' This episode is only possible if the player does not know what 'the three things' are.

During Episode 3, bullpen work will be happening for the pitchers and catchers. Bullpen work is the pitcher pitching to the catcher and working on the pitches in terms of speed and location. It may also be used as conditioning. The pitcher would pitch from full wind-up and/or a set position (runners on base). There can be variations where the coach or catcher may call the pitches (fastball, curveball, etc.) the balls and strikes. Once again, this is the reproduction of a known movement and throwing known pitches over a known distance (60 feet and 6 inches or 18.44 metres). This would represent Practice Style Coaching.

Episode 4—Game Play Scenarios With Live Hitting

In this episode the field is occupied with the traditional positions, including the catcher. The coach may play the position of pitcher for more control of the situation. A portion of the team (4–6) will be hitting in 'live' situations. We will suggest that the objective is for defence to practice in game-like scenarios and the hitters to practice in game-like scenarios. Or as some CLA advocates may describe it as implementing relevant constraints in a practice environment in to help players 'search' for successful movement solutions—a 'discovery approach' (Renshaw et al., 2010). This is an easy conclusion to draw based on what we have described. However, when the experience of the players is considered, and the objective stated by the coach, it allows this episode to be examined through The Spectrum lens.

If for example the coach had a scenario where it was none out and a runner on first, the coach may ask the hitter, 'What are you trying to do in this situation?' The player either knows the answer or they do not. If they do not know the answer, then the opportunity arises for a Guided Discovery episode as we outlined earlier in this chapter. If though, the coach knows the players know the answer, then asking the question is seeking a known response and this is Practice Style B with recall. The batter will then look for an outside pitch to hit on the ground to the right side of the diamond to advance the runner in a textbook hit and run. The fielders (1st and 2nd base) may 'squeeze' the space a little in anticipation of cutting off the ball and implementing a double-play. In this case, we would argue that the coach is creating scenarios that will appear in games and allowing the players to replicate (practice) known strategies in game-like environments. The use of questioning is a strategy to get players thinking about what they will do before each pitch. Thus, practicing a physical and cognitive strategy which the coach wants the players to implement in the game.

Conclusion

This chapter has used The Spectrum to examine many coaching episodes and place them on The Spectrum. It has shown how The Spectrum is a valuable tool to interrogate the coaching style used and to allow coaches to see the decisions that they are making and the decisions that they are asking the players to make. When this is done, the coach can identify the coaching style they are using and, perhaps more importantly, if their actions are congruent with the decisions that they want the players to make and the coaching style they have chosen. In other words, are their actions and intentions matching. If they want their player to self-correct, have they created coaching episodes allow this skill to be practiced? If they have not, then it is perhaps foolish to hope that their players have this skill or can use it. Further to this we have shown that often, coaching models, such as Game-based coaching, are a collection of coaching styles and not just one style. Or, as we have described them in this chapter, a collection of episodes. When coaches (and players) become aware of the decisions that they are being asked to make, then coaching styles will be implemented with greater fidelity to the achievement of task objectives and outcomes.

References

Alfieri, L., Brooks, P. J., Aldrich, N. J., & Tenenbaum, H. R. (2011). Does discovery-based instruction enhance learning? *Journal of Educational Psychology*, *103*, 1–18.

Anson, G., Elliott, D., & Davids, K. (2005). Information processing and constraints-based views of skill acquisition: Divergent or complementary? *Motor Control*, *9*, 217–241.

Araújo, D., Davids, K., & Hristovski, R. (2006). The ecological dynamics of decision making in sport. *Psychology of Sport and Exercise*, *7*, 653–676.

Cothran, D. J., Kulinna, P. H., Banville, D., Choi, E., Amade-Escot, C., MacPhail, A., Macdonald, D., & Kirk, D. (2005). A cross-cultural investigation of the use of teaching styles. *Research Quarterly for Exercise and Sport*, *76*, 193–201.

Fadde, P. (2009). Instructional design for advanced learners: Training recognition skills to hasten expertise. *Educational Technology Research & Development*, *57*(3), 359–376.

Fajen, B. R., Riley, M. A., & Turvey, M. T. (2009). Information, affordances, and the control of action in sport. *International Journal of Sport Psychology*, *40*, 79–107.

Headrick, J., Renshaw, I., Pinder, R., & Davids, K. (2012). Attunement to haptic information helps skilled performers select implements for striking a ball in cricket. *Attention, Perception & Psychophysics*, *74*, 1782–1791.

Hewitt, M. (2015). Teaching styles of Australian tennis coaches: An exploration of practices and insights using Mosston and Ashworth's Spectrum of teaching styles. Unpublished Doctor of Philosophy thesis. School of Linguistics, Adult and Specialist Education, The University of Southern Queensland.

Hewitt, M., Pill, S., & SueSee, B. (2020). Future considerations on The Spectrum. In B. SueSee, M. Hewitt & S. Pill (Eds.), *The spectrum of teaching styles in physical education* (pp. 166–177). Routledge.

Jaakola, T., & Watt, A. (2011). Finnish physical education teachers' self-reported use and perceptions of Mosston and Ashworth's teaching styles. *Journal of Teaching in Physical Education*, *30*, 248–262.

Mosston, M., & Ashworth, S. (2008). *Teaching physical education* (1st online ed.). https://spectrumofteachingstyles.org/assets/files/book/Teaching_Physical_Edu_1st_Online.pdf

Renshaw, I., Chow, J.-Y., Davids, K., & Hammond, J. (2010). A constraints-led perspective to understanding skill acquisition and game play: A basis for integration of motor learning theory and physical education praxis? *Physical Education and Sport Pedagogy*, *15*(2), 117–137.

Smith, M. R. H., Flach, J. M., Dittman, S. M., & Stanard, T. (2001). Monocular optical constraints on collision control. *Journal of Experimental Psychology*, *27*(2), 395–410.

SueSee, B., Pill, S., & Hewitt, M. (2020). Reconciling approaches: Mosston and Ashworth's Spectrum of teaching styles as a tool to examine the complexity of any teaching (or coaching) approach. In B. SueSee, M. Hewitt, & S. Pill (Eds.), *The Spectrum of teaching styles in physical education* (pp. 73–84). Routledge.

Syrmpas, I., Digelidis, N., & Watt, A. (2016). An examination of Greek physical educators' implementation and perceptions of Spectrum teaching styles. *European Physical Education Review*, *22*, 201–214.

Syrmpas, I., Digelidis, N., Watt, A., & Vicars, M. (2017). Physical education teachers' experiences and beliefs of production and reproduction teaching approaches. *Teaching and Teacher Education*, *66*, 184–194.

Weast, J. A., Shockley, K., & Riley, M. A. (2011). The influence of athletic experience and kinematic information on skill-relevant affordance perception. *The Quarterly Journal of Experimental Psychology*, *64*(4), 689–706.

15
GAME-BASED AND DIRECT INSTRUCTION COACHING THROUGH A SPECTRUM OF TEACHING STYLES LENS

Brendan SueSee and Shane Pill

Previous chapters have shown how The Spectrum can be used to examine the behaviour of a coach with regards to coach pedagogical decision-making, and thus the coach can identify which coaching style is best 'fit for purpose'. In this chapter we show how The Spectrum allows coaching models to be viewed in terms of decisions being made (by the coach or player) to identify the complexities of the coaching model and to test the model's assumptions. We do this by viewing two game-based coaching approach (GBA) scenarios and place them on The Spectrum to identify the intricacies and complexities of the GBAs. We will do the same with the Direct Instruction approach—a coaching style that is seemingly at the opposite end of a spectrum. However, we will show that in some cases, despite this view, that both these approaches have some characteristics in common. In doing this we are coming from a 'non-versus' perspective. We will not be making value-laden judgements about the GBAs and their tenets or assumptions, merely identifying the pedagogical decision-makers (coach or player) and the place where the decisions are made (pre-impact, impact, post-impact), thus identifying the style (or cluster of styles) it would be on The Spectrum.

The Spectrum Structures

The Spectrum's structure is underpinned by the concept that every deliberate act of teaching is a result of a previous decision (Mosston & Ashworth, 2008). Mosston suggested that these numerous decisions could be made in three places: the pre-impact set, the impact set and the post-impact set. These three places comprise the anatomy of any style. SueSee, Pill and Hewitt (2020) suggested the pre-impact set involves making decisions with regards to the planning of the teacher-learner interaction. The impact set relates to implementation of the decisions that occur during the face-to-face interaction between the teacher and learner. Finally, the post-impact set refers to assessment decisions that may occur at any point during the face-to-face interaction by either the teacher or the learner. By identifying who (i.e., the coach or player-learner) makes which decisions, the 11 coaching styles emerged (Figure 15.1).

Through the identification of the decision-making relationship (which is occurring during the three impact sets), 'any teaching-learning interaction, model, strategy, or educational

DOI: 10.4324/9781003041443-16

Coaching Styles

Coaching by Command (A)

Coaching by Task (Practice) (B)

Reciprocal Coaching (Peer Coaching) (C)

Coaching by Individual Programing (Self-Check) (D)

Small Group Coaching (Inclusion) (E)

Coaching by Guided Discovery (F)

Coaching by Problem Solving (Convergent Discovery) (G)

Coaching for Creativity (Divergent Discovery) (H)

Coaching by Player Designed—Coach Supported (I)

Player Initiated—Coach Supported Coaching (J)

Player Self-Coaching (K)

FIGURE 15.1 A Spectrum of Coaching Styles.

game' (Mosston & Ashworth, 2008, p. 26) can be identified and placed on The Spectrum. Further to this, The Spectrum presents the first five styles (Styles A–E) as the Reproduction Cluster as the coaching episodes require the player to reproduce knowledge previously known to them. The remaining styles (Styles F–K) are known as the Production Cluster, as they require the production of knowledge that is new to the player (going beyond facts and memory) through the operations of either discovery or creativity. The Production and Reproduction clusters do not work in opposition to each other; rather, they are complementary (SueSee et al., 2020). For example, once a player has discovered a tactic or technique from a Production Cluster style coaching episode, they may then move to refining the skill or tactic through a Reproduction coaching style episode. This is an example of The Spectrums 'non-versus' ideology in the sense that one style is not better than another style; rather, styles work together. Mosston and Ashworth (2008) suggested, 'It is the reciprocation and supportive relationship among these functions that contribute to human growth and development—to the process of educating' (p. 75).

The rest of this chapter will place two examples of game-based coaching approaches (GBAs) and one example of direct instruction under The Spectrum lens to demonstrate the numerous styles which are occurring. It is done with a non-versus approach in that we will not be claiming that any approach is better than another. We aim for these examples to highlight the importance of the players game history, the coach's choice of style to meet an outcome or objective, and how episodic coaching is evident.

Game-Based Approaches

GBAs have been positioned for some time as athlete-centred (Pill, 2018) positive pedagogy (Light & Harvey, 2019) for sport coaching, compared to what is labelled 'traditional' highly directive, coach-centred, and technically prescriptive coaching. GBAs come in a variety of versions, all promising something a little nuanced from the others. Some of the more well-known models include Teaching Games for Understanding (TGfU) (Bunker & Thorpe,

1982), a Tactical Games Model (TGM) (Griffin, Oslin & Mitchell, 1997), Tactical-Decision Learning Model (TDLM) (Grehaigne, Wallian & Godbout, 2005), Play with Purpose (Pill, 2007), Play Practice (Launder, 2001), and the Games Sense approach (Australian Sports Commission (ASC), 1996). Without argument, there are differences between these; however, a common feature of all GBAs is:

> playing the game (modified or adapted for the players' abilities) as the central organisational feature of a lesson. The modified games create constraints that emphasize certain game features in order to develop understanding as students solve the problems they are presented with.
>
> *(Breed & Spittle, 2011, p. 7)*

Many have suggested that using GBAs, players technical actions become the visible expression of their thinking and problem-solving abilities, taught by a type of guided inquiry often labelled 'discovery' (Breed & Spittle, 2011; den Duyn, 1997; Launder, 2001; Light, 2014; Pill, 2011a, 2011b, 2013; SueSee & Pill, 2018). Whilst this chapter will show that GBAs are sometimes a discovery style from what in The Spectrum is called the production cluster (the styles fostering player creativity or discovery), there are times when GBAs are other coaching styles or include the use of other coaching styles. The use of a GBA is a series of coaching episodes and describing GBAs as one style, therefore, does not recognise their true complexities (SueSee, Pill & Edwards, 2016; SueSee, Hewitt & Pill, 2020).

Game-Based Approach—Cricket Net Session

Practising batting and bowling is frequently done in a net so that both batters and bowlers can practice without having to waste time retrieving the ball from a long distance away and to achieve a large volume of practice. A game-based version of a net session can be seen in Figure 15.1. There are two people batting, one facing the bowler and the other at the non-strikers end or bowling end. The players would receive the following instructions. You will face 60 balls. You will bat in pairs. You must find a way to hit the ball between the markers and along the ground. If you hit the markers, you lose a point. If you hit between the markers, you get a point, or a half point if the ball hits the fence 'on the full': in other words, the ball is not hit along the ground. Every time the batter hits between the markers, the batting pair rotate the strike (the batter at the non-striker: bowler end becomes the batter). The aim is to accumulate as many points as possible in the 60 deliveries of the batting pair.

In the pre-impact set (Figure 15.2) the coach has made decisions about what the players will be required to do. It may be suggested that the coach has set a problem to be solved (hit the ball between the markers below 1 metre in height). We argue that at this stage, this coaching episode could either be Practice Style, Guided Discovery or Divergent Discovery Style. It does depend on the coach's intent and the players' cognitive history. First, it may be Practice Style as this is what the coach desires—the recalling of skills to hit the ball below a specific height. Second, and perhaps more importantly, it may be Practice Style if the players choose to recall known skills to achieve the desired result. That is, if the players know the answer to solving the problem and choose to use known skills, then it is Practice Style. If this was to be a Divergent Discovery episode (coach asking player to discover or create multiple solutions to an unknown problem), the coach would need to use words directing the player to 'use a way which you have not done

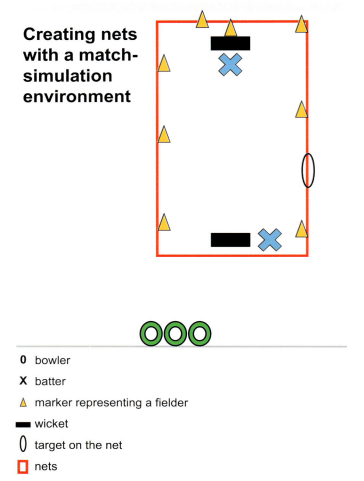

FIGURE 15.2 A game-based version of a net session.

- Pre-Impact: Coach chooses subject matter (hit the ball between the markers below the 1-metre line).
- Impact Set: Players practise hitting a ball the way they have before. That is, they have not been instructed by the coach to 'discover' or 'create' a way to hit the ball which they have not done before.

Players may be stopped during the impact set and asked questions using a Guided Discovery approach to help players identify and solve problems experienced.

- Post-Impact: Coach gives feedback by asking questions and about answers to player questions.

before'. The player would then attempt to solve the problem and consider if they had used a new 'method' to achieve the outcome. If they thought they had used a specific shot before, they would cycle back and try again until they created a new way to achieve the task outcome. Why this episode may be Divergent Discovery and not Convergent Discovery relates to the specific language used by the coach. Convergent Discovery has a single correct answer or solution to be discovered. Whilst the coach has only asked for one way or solution, there are many solutions to this problem, it is just that the coach has only asked the player to produce one solution.

We suggest the episode could include Guided Discovery Style in the impact set. For example, if the player is unable to hit the ball between the markers, the coach may choose to implement a series of questions to guide the player to a desired response or solution. It may be a little like this dialogue:

COACH: You seem to be having trouble contacting the ball?
PLAYER: Yeah absolutely! Especially the off-side (hitting the ball to the right-hand side of the net from a right-handed batsman's perspective).
COACH: Why do you think that is?
PLAYER: Not sure? Can you tell me?
COACH: No way! Let's face a few and conduct an experiment. First ball I want you to look at where your front foot is pointing and positioned in relation to the ball.

Player faces a ball or two and says the following:

PLAYER: I'm stepping towards the bowler and my foot is about 30cm from the ball.
COACH: So where is your weight going?
PLAYER: I guess my weight is going towards the bowler.
COACH: Is that towards the ball?
PLAYER: Kind of, but not exactly to the ball.
COACH: So, you're stepping towards the bowler and your bat is doing what?
PLAYER: I'm trying to hit the ball towards the net on the right.
COACH: When we throw where do we step?
PLAYER: Towards the target! So, I should step in the direction I want to hit the ball?
COACH: I believe so. Why not give it a go and see what happens?

This is an example of an episode where the coach could have told the player the answer (Practice Style) or (as shown here) used the opportunity to allow the player to experience 'the logical and sequential design of questions that lead a person to discover a predetermined response' (Mosston & Ashworth, 2008, p. 212). Some coaches may think that this is inefficient and that the player may change their behaviour 'faster' by telling the player the answer or concept (step towards the ball). It is not the purpose of this book to debate theories of skill acquisition; we only suggest here that if the coach's objective is to develop thinking players who can solve problems individually, then using Guided Discovery provides an opportunity for the player to become familiar with a 'thinking structure' to seek the solution to a problem, in the anticipation that eventually the player/s will learn to how to seek solutions to problems themselves. If this same situation arose in a game, we argue that a coach would not hope for the player to yell out from the pitch, 'Hey what am I doing wrong? Can you tell me?'

In this variation to the practice session, we add an additional challenge by a target on the net. We can encourage the players using the game-based pedagogy of exaggeration to explore when and how to go for the target. For example, using the game condition/constraint: 'If you hit the target, this is worth four runs'.

- Pre-Impact: Coach chooses subject matter (hit the ball between the markers below the 1-metre line and choose 'the right ball' to hit to the target area or the 'right ball' to get into a position to hit at the target on the net).

- Impact Set: Player's practise hitting a ball the way they have before, with the added objective of hitting the target on the net for 'bonus runs'. They have been instructed by the coach to 'discover' or 'create' a way to hit the ball.

Players may be stopped during the impact set and asked questions using a Guided Discovery approach to help students identify problems experienced.

- Post-Impact: Coach gives feedback by asking questions and encourages player questions.

In this coaching episode, the coach has created an opportunity for a discovery episode as the players do not know how to hit the target. They may be aware of the stroke to play to hit the ball to the right side of the net but are not aware of how to get their body in a position to hit the target. Let's presume that the bowler is attempting to bowl at the target of hitting the top of off-stump each time, and the batter is playing a straight bat through this line and therefore unable to hit the target on the net. The coach may ask: 'You are having trouble hitting the target on your right—why is that?'

PLAYER: The bowler is bowling at the stumps, so I have to play a straight bat.
COACH: Where do you need the ball to be to hit the target on the fence?
PLAYER: I need it to be on the off-side or to my right.
COACH: Can you move the ball?
PLAYER: No—of course not!
COACH: Can you move your body, so the ball is in a better position to hit it to the right?
PLAYER: Ahhh . . . yes so I must go to my left (on-side) to give myself room to hit to the right!
COACH: Maybe—why don't you give it a go?

This episode is an example of what could have started as Convergent Discovery style, in that the coach set a problem to be solved—score as many points as possible by hitting through the markers with bonus points for the marker on the net. The player got 'stuck' and was not solving the problem, so the coach decided to implement a Guided Discovery episode and use a series of questions to assist the player in solving the problem.

The use of styles from the production cluster like Guided and Convergent Discovery is to provide the opportunity for the player to use creative processes. The 'specific episodes must be designed for specific cognitive operation such as comparing, contrasting, extrapolating, problem solving, and designing' (Mosston & Ashworth, 2008, p. 18) for players to have the opportunity to practice or experience problem solving.

Direct Instruction

Direct Instruction is sometimes labelled 'traditional' coaching or the historically 'common' coaching approach. It is typically characterised as coach-centred, direct or command instruction, focused on replication of highly prescribed movement models and therefore sometimes also called a technical model of coaching. It is frequently linked to a behaviourist paradigm which is one where the coach directly and explicitly reinforces the operant behaviour they wish to see. This is in contrast to a constructivist paradigm where coaches facilitate individuals to create their own meaning through reflection on action, or an ecological paradigm emphasising to coaches to create environments that provide for the player direct perception of information through an affordance landscape (Light, 2013; Pill, 2020; Woods et al., 2020).

We agree with Cope and Cushion (2020) that direct instruction is often poorly conceptualised in coaching literature. In the extant literature, a command or direct instruction coaching model is frequently compared in a 'versus' perspective to a guided discovery coaching model (often associated with a game-based approach). We will show in the examples that follow that direct instruction as a model of coaching is not a single coaching style. We also show that it is a mischaracterisation of direct instruction to align it directly and solely with a 'drill based' and linear 'part practice' or 'progressive part' practice. Game form activities like play practices, small-sided 'constrained' or modified games, designer games, and match simulations could be coached by direct instruction, not just to teach technical skill perspectives but also to teach tactical perspectives such as principals of play and associated strategies and tactics. Direct instruction could be used in 'whole practice' game representations or in whole-part-whole teaching, such as the play-practice-play sequence typical of game-based coaching models like the Tactical Games model (Pill, 2010).

Direct Instruction—Cricket—Game Play

In this example we use the game of Battlezone (Renshaw et al., 2010). It is a training game for the sport of cricket. Batters are instructed to score as many runs as possible, and they are encouraged to hit the ball along the ground as often as possible (Vickery et al., 2013). Fielders are placed to try and catch the ball or limit running between the wickets. Bowlers aim to limit runs scored or get the batters out. Battlezone is representative of the full game but a scaled game-based experience. For this scenario it will be presumed that the coach has decided to play this game at training. Therefore, in the pre-impact set, the subject matter has been decided by the coach. It is also presumed that the level of coaching is high level juniors who have good skill level. During the impact set the coach will explain the game as such:

> As a batting pair, you will attempt to score as many runs as possible by hitting between the fielders, and on the ground if possible. Bowlers, you attempt to bowl a line to get the batter out, and batters you try and hit the ball where it is bowled. If it is on your right, hit it to the right. If it is on your left, hit it to the left. Remember we also spoke about moving our feet last week—no' 'concrete shoes'. Always step towards the ball. Fielders, you are 'attacking the ball' by coming forward from your starting point.

In this information given (Figure 15.3), the coach is reaffirming the subject matter which they desire to be recalled and performed. If the players are at a high level, they already know what to do; it is a matter of them recalling the skill at the appropriate moment. It is not denied here that recognition of that moment (or recognising the visual cues such as where the bowler lets go of the ball or their hand position) is also an important ability to be developed. What is being suggested is that by the coach telling the players what is to be done—e.g., 'Ball on the right—hit to the right' the coach is prompting a memory or reproduction of thinking with private feedback (Mosston & Ashworth, 2008). This is suggested as the coach is giving the player the subject matter instructions and will then give feedback as to how well this was done to either reinforce the behaviour or modify it (e.g., 'step more towards the ball with your front foot'). The purpose of doing this is for the player to perceive what to do and then

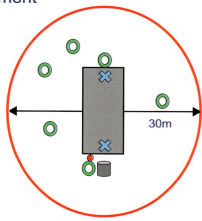

- ◯ – fielder
- ✖ – batter
- ◉ – bowler with ball
- ▮ – bucket filled with cricket balls
- ◯ – fence/boundary

FIGURE 15.3 Battlezone layout.

to do it (perception leading to action). If this is not the case, the question must be asked why the coach is giving this information to the players?

Direct instructions and cues facilitate a player's attentional focus. Attentional focus is the conscious ability of a player to focus their attention to execute a task. A player's attentional focus can be directed internally on their movement process, externally on the outcome or effect of the movement, or on 'nonawareness' where there is no attempt at conscious focus (Benz et al., 2016; Wulf & Weigelt, 1997; Wulf, Höß & Prince, 1998). Analogies and metaphors used as movement cues may provide an external or internal focus of attention. For example, a coach instructing the bowler in delivery stride to 'push the arm high' provides an internal cue, or an external cue by telling the player to 'scrape the sky with your bowling hand', or provides a neutral cue by telling the player to 'get the arm as high as you can'. The intent of the direction is the same in all three instructions; however, the internal cue directs attention to the body (i.e., hand), the external calls attention to the environment (i.e., the sky), while the neutral cue does not focus attention internally or externally (Benz et al., 2016). Many authors have shown that analogies can assist in motor skill acquisition in populations ranging from older adults to young children (e.g., Bobrownicki et al., 2015; Lam, Maxwell & Masters, 2009; Tse et al., 2017a, 2017b; Zacks & Friedman, 2020).

Returning to the Battlezone game, it begins (impact set) as per the coach's instructions with the bowler bowling to the batsman, the batsman attempting to hit the ball to space (and on the ground) and the fielders attacking the ball and fielding it. In none of these situations we have described (and in the context of high-level juniors) are the players required to solve problems or discover or create. The players are not being directed to draw on, create or discover new knowledge but rely on known ways of performing. They are not solving problems (i.e., unknown answers such as 'how do I hit the ball on the ground?') but recalling known movement solutions. The players will attempt to hit the ball between the fielders as per the coach instructions, thus reproducing known skills, or they will try to hit the ball as per the coach's instructions. The fielders will most likely attempt to field the ball in a previously known way, and the bowler will attempt to bowl at the stumps, replicating a movement that they have performed before. We suggest this as that is what the coach has instructed them to do. If they choose to create something new, this is not what the coach has instructed them to do. Every act of coaching involves deliberate decision-making; therefore, the coach has not decided (as evidenced by their instructions) for the player to choose creativity as the dominant operation. We are not arguing that this scenario may not occur; we are arguing (based on Mosston & Ashworth's definition of teaching as deliberate) that the coach has not directed the player to do this and therefore cannot claim that the result is an act of their decision.

In the post-impact set (after each ball), the coach can give feedback, such as 'great job stepping towards the ball and hitting it on the ground'. This language would be typical of direct instruction and a Practice Style because it involves individual practice of a memory/reproduction task with feedback. The type of feedback would be similar, in that it is direct for the bowler and fielders (e.g., 'great job bowling at the stumps'). This example shows how gameplay can be a form of Direct Instruction if the decisions that the player and coach are making are in line with the decisions made during a Practice Style episode.

Another factor of coaching which is sometimes assumed to automatically be a discovery episode is when questioning is used. Both a Constraints-Led Approach (CLA: Davids, Button & Bennett, 2008) and a Game-Based Approach (such as the Game Sense approach: GSA, den Duyn, 1997) are associated with the use of coach questioning of players, often described as Guided Discovery (Breed & Spittle, 2011; Hopper & Kruissenbrink, 2001; Light, 2014; Pill, 2006; SueSee et al., 2016). For example, if the batter was having difficulty with a ball bowled on a right-hander's right side (as they faced the bowler), the coach may ask, 'You seem to be having difficulty making contact, where are you stepping?' If the batter has come to the session with knowledge of what they should do (and thus know the answer), then we would suggest that this is not Guided Discovery; rather, it is a recall episode involving review questions. SueSee et al. (2016) suggested that 'it is not the question on its own which determines whether a player is required to generate new knowledge or recall (review questions) knowledge, it is a combination of the question and the knowledge which the player does or does not possess before the question is asked' (p. 81). We suggest that Guided Discovery episodes are most apparent in one-on-one coach-player interactions as if the other players hear or see a response they can no longer discover and become receivers of the information (Mosston & Ashworth, 2008) or imitators (Metzler, 2011) as the information is not new, and so a discovery process is aborted. When this happens, or the target concept is known by the player, 'the objectives of this behavior are nullified and the question-and-answer experience reverts to a design variation of the Practice style (a review)' (Mosston & Ashworth, 2008, p. 213). Based on the ideas discussed here, questioning by the coach in some cases may also represent an example of Direct Instruction.

This chapter has considered hypothetical GBAs and Direct Instruction practice sessions using The Spectrum of Coaching Styles, highlighting the decisions being made by the coach and players. Through this process, we have shown that broad terminology such as GBAs and Direct Instruction do not adequately describe the teaching-learning decisions being made by the coach and player/s. Similarly, the hypothetical scenarios we have used demonstrate that GBAs can sometimes be versions of Practice Style, and Direct Instruction episodes can be created and coached using Practice Style. We have done this from a non-versus perspective, and we are not claiming that one approach is better than the other, nor that GBAs are failing to achieve what they claim. We seek only to show that coaching is often more nuanced and sometimes more complex than might be presented. We have shown that both GBAs and Direct Instruction have the potential to be more than one coaching style depending on who (coach or player) is making pre-impact, impact, and post-impact teaching-learning decisions.

References

Australian Sports Commission. (1996). *Game sense: Perceptions and actions research report*. Australian Sports Commission.
Benz, A., Winkelman, N., Porter, J., & Nimphius, S. (2016). Coaching instructions and and cues for enhancing sprint performance. *Strength and Conditioning Journal*, *38*(1), 1–11.
Bobrownicki, R., MacPherson, A. C., Coleman, S. G. S., Collins, D., & Sproule, J. (2015). Re-examining the effects of verbal instructional type on early stage motor learning. *Human Movement Science*, *44*, 168–181.
Breed, R., & Spittle, M. (2011). *Developing game sense through tactical learning: A resource for teachers and coaches*. Cambridge University Press.
Bunker, D. J., & Thorpe, R. D. (1982). A model for the teaching of games in secondary schools. *Bulletin of Physical Education*, *18*(1), 5–8.
Cope, E., & Cushion, C. (2020). A move towards reconceptualising direct instruction in sport coaching pedagogy. *Impact: Journal of the Chartered College of Teaching*, September. https://impact.chartered.college/article/a-move-towards-reconceptualising-direct-instruction-sport-coaching-pedagogy/
Davids, K., Button, C., & Bennett, S. (2008). *Dynamics of skill acquisition: A constraints-led approach*. Human Kinetics.
den Duyn, N. (1997). *Game sense: Developing thinking players*. Australian Sports Commission.
Grehaigne, J., Wallian, N., & Godbout, P. (2005). Tactical decision learning model and students' practice. *Physical Education and Sport Pedagogy*, *10*(3), 255–269.
Griffin, L., Oslin, J., & Mitchell, S. (1997). *Teaching sports concepts and skills: A Tactical games approach*. Human Kinetics.
Hopper, T., & Kruisselbrink, D. (2001). Teaching games for understanding: What does it look like and how does it influence student skill acquisition and game performance? http://web.uvic.ca/~thopper/WEB/articles/JTPE/TGFU.htm
Lam, W. K., Maxwell, J. P., & Masters, R. (2009). Analogy learning and the performance of motor skills under pressure. *Journal of Sport Exercise Psychology*, *31*, 337–357.
Launder, A. (2001). *Play practice: The games approach to teaching and coaching sports*. Human Kinetics.
Light, R. (2013). *Game sense: Pedagogy for performance, participation and enjoyment*. Routledge.
Light, R. (2014). Quality teaching beyond games through game sense pedagogy. *University of Sydney Papers in HMHCE—Special Game Sense Edition*, 1–13.
Light, R., & Harvey, S. (2019). *Positive pedagogy for sport coaching*. Routledge.

Metzler, M. (2011). *Instructional models for physical education* (3rd ed.). Routledge.

Mosston, M., & Ashworth, S. (2008). *Teaching physical education* (1st online edition). https://spectrumofteachingstyles.org/assets/files/book/Teaching_Physical_Edu_1st_Online.pdf

Pill, S. (2006). Teaching games for understanding. *Sports Coach*, *29*(2). www.clearinghouseforsport.gov.au/Library/archive/digital_archive/asc_publications/sports_coach/sports_coach_volume_29/29213Pill.pdf

Pill, S. (2007). *Play with purpose*. ACHPER Australia.

Pill, S. (2010). Using tactical games. *Sports Coach*, *31*(1). www.researchgate.net/publication/345130872_Using_tactical_games

Pill, S. (2011a). Teacher engagement with teaching games for understanding: Game sense in physical education. *Journal of Physical Education and Sport*, *11*(2), 115–123.

Pill, S. (2011b). Seizing the moment: Can game sense further inform sport teaching in Australian physical education? *PHENex Journal*, *3*(1), 1–15.

Pill, S. (2013). *Play with purpose: Game sense to sport literacy*. Hindmarsh, SA: ACHPER Publications.

Pill, S. (2018). *Perspectives on athlete-centred coaching*. Routledge.

Pill, S. (2020). Introduction. In S. Pill (Ed.), *Perspectives on game-based coaching* (pp. xvii–xxviii). Routledge.

Renshaw, I., Chappell, G., Fitzgerald, D., Davison, J., & McFadyen, B. (2010). The battle zone: Constraint-led coaching in action. In M. Portus (Ed.), *Proceedings of the 2010 Conference of Science, Medicine and Coaching in Cricket* (pp. 181–184). Cricket Australia, Australia.

SueSee, B., Hewitt, M., & Pill, S. (Eds.). (2020). *The spectrum of teaching styles in physical education*. Routledge.

SueSee, B., & Pill, S. (2018). Game-based teaching and coaching as a toolkit of teaching styles. *Strategies: A Journal for Physical and Sport Educators*, *31*(5), 21–28.

SueSee, B., Pill, S., & Edwards, K. (2016). Reconciling approaches: A game centred approach to sport teaching and Mosston's Spectrum of teaching styles. *European Journal of Physical Education and Sport Science*, *2*(4), 69–96.

SueSee, B., Pill, S., & Hewitt, M. (2020). Reconciling approaches: Mosston and Ashworth's Spectrum of teaching styles as a tool to examine the complexity of any teaching (or coaching) approach. In B. SueSee, M. Hewitt, & S. Pill (Eds.), *The Spectrum of teaching styles in physical education* (pp. 73–84). Routledge.

Tse, A. C. Y., Fong, S. S. M., Wong, T. W. L., & Masters, R. (2017a). Analogy motor learning by young children: A study of rope skipping. *European Journal of Sport Science*, *17*, 152–159.

Tse, A. C. Y., Wong, T. W. L., & Masters, R. S. W. (2017b). Examining motor learning in older adults using analogy instruction. *Psychology of Sport and Exercise*, *28*, 78–84.

Vickery, W., Dascombe, B., Duffield, R., Kellett, A., & Portus, M. (2013). Battlezone: An examination of the physiological responses, movement demands and reproducibility of small-sided cricket games, *Journal of Sports Sciences*, *31*(1), 77–86.

Woods, C., McKeown, I., Rothwell, M., Araújo, D., Robertson, S., & Davids, K. (2020). Sport practitioners as sport ecology designers: How ecological dynamics has progressively changed perceptions of skill 'acquisition' in the sporting habitat. *Frontiers in Psychology*, *11*, 654. doi: 10.3389/fpsyg.2020.00654

Wulf, G., & Weigelt, C. (1997). Instructions about physical principles in learning a complex motor skill: To tell or not to tell. . . . *Research Quarterly for Exercise and Sport*, *68*, 362–367.

Wulf, G., Höß, M., & Prince, W. (1998). Instructions for motor learning: Differential effects of internal versus external focus of attention. *Journal of Motor Behavior*, *30*(2), 169–179.

Zacks, O., & Friedman, J. (2020). Analogies can speed up the motor learning process. *Science Report*, *10*, 6932. www.nature.com/articles/s41598-020-63999-1

16
FROM PHYSICAL EDUCATION TO ALPINE SKI TEACHING AND COACHING

A Figurational Study of The Spectrum

John Williams, John Arnold, James Crompton, Lesley Page and Luke Riddle

The Spectrum has had a long association with Alpine ski coaching within the British context. Indeed, it has endured as the central coaching approach of the British Association of Snowsports Instructors (BASI) for more than 30 years. As the national professional association for ski instructors, BASI was established in 1963. It was set up by skiing and mountain pioneers in Scotland, a few of whom were teachers and lecturers, showing a connection to education at its inauguration. The purpose of this chapter is to examine the use of The Spectrum as a long-term process within BASI. The authors in this chapter employ an autoethnographic approach to provide accounts from Authors 2, 3, 4 and 5 of using The Spectrum which are interpreted using figurational sociology and the extant literature by Author 1, the Chief Investigator (CI). All of us have long-term connection with BASI, with our collective involvement and experiences overlapping across a timeline exceeding three decades. Furthermore, The Spectrum has been constantly employed during our BASI membership.

In this chapter, an autoethnographic approach has been adopted. This form of research differs from traditional qualitative methodologies, where researchers aim to be neutral observers (Grbich, 2013). The word 'autoethnography' can be interpeted as '*auto* (self), *ethno* (culture) and *graphy* writing/presentation (presentation of the self within the culture/s you inhabit)' (Grbich, 2013, p. 120). Investigators who use autoethnography are 'not concerned with an objective truth, but rather with the truth of the experience for them as they experienced it through their body' (Hopper et al., 2008, p. 223). How we used autoethnography was consistent with McMahon and Dinan Thompson (2011), who investigated McMahon's career as an elite swimmer. McMahon used 'self-voice' to describe her memories and experiences, which were then interpreted through the 'academic voices' of both authors.

Author 1 (CI) was provided with memories, as written reflections, of their co-author's use of The Spectrum. Extracts from those memory accounts were chosen by the CI using the following criteria: 1. Those encapsulating use of The Spectrum within BASI as a long-term process, 2. Those describing change within the figuration examined, with the term figuration introduced and explained later. Extracts were also selected using Manen's (1997) framework of lived thoroughness, evocativeness, intensity, tone and epiphany. Lived thoroughness meaning narratives that provide connections and relatability for the reader and

DOI: 10.4324/9781003041443-17

evocativeness being about creating clarity to enable reader reflection. Intensity is selecting words allowing their full value to be used, and tone enables the text to 'speak for itself' to amplify emotional effect and connection. Lastly, epiphany is how text is written to further provoke reader rumination. It is hoped how the memories are presented will stimulate readers to at least reflect on ways the four co-authors have engaged with The Spectrum and perhaps see value and application in their own contexts. Since this paper is entirely concerned with personal memories and perspectives, no ethics permission was sought for this research.

Figurational Sociology and the Extant Literature

Memory extracts were interpreted by the CI using figurational sociology and the extant literature as the academic voice. Figurational sociology was deemed most appropriate in considering The Spectrum as a long-term and evolving social process. Within figurational sociology, the study of such processes is central, as is the concept of the figuration itself, defined by Elias (1978, p. 261) as 'a structure of mutually oriented and dependent people'. The figuration studied here is all the authors, as current BASI members, who are commonly aligned to valuing and teaching The Spectrum. Our figuration, like all figurations, has altered over time, with each of the authors joining at different points. Therefore, figurations are dynamic and also adapt due to the intended and unintended consequences of the actions of those who comprise them (Elias, 1978). A further figurational concept drawn upon is 'habitus', both individual and social habitus. Individual habitus refers to an individual's personality structure or tendency to behave in a given way (Elias, 1994). However, social habitus means the 'social personality structure of people' (Elias, 2009, p. 186), referring to common behaviour, practices or beliefs within particular groups (Elias, 1994). Finally, the figurational notion of social power (Elias, 2013) was also used in the CI's interpretation.

Introduction of The Spectrum to BASI—Author 2 Self-Voice

> *BASI adopted The Spectrum during the early 1990's. However, prior to that I taught it to artificial ski slopes coaches and instructors during coach education courses in the late 1980's. My own knowledge of The Spectrum grew from a presentation by one of Mosston's colleagues at Dunfermline College of Physical Education (PE), Edinburgh in 1981. Senior lecturing staff there enhanced my learning of The Spectrum and encouraged me to apply it to coaching Alpine skiing. In 1990 the first BASI Chief Executive had the foresight and management skills to enable both a technical and a teaching syllabus to be developed. In 1992 the first Trainers' conference was held near Aviemore, Scotland where Trainers were presented with an outline of both syllabi. In the main though most of the training staff saw the skills of the ski instructor to be primarily technical consistent with approaches in PE at the time. Consequently, this kind of approach was reflected in the teaching syllabus. Teaching skills were given scant regard and centred on the EDICT model: Explain, demonstrate, imitate, correct and test.*
>
> *Introducing The Spectrum into the syllabus, whilst maintaining the interest and motivation of the training staff, was a concern for us at the outset. It transpired following Trainer professional learning, that most Trainers appeared to welcome the developments and their interest was maintained. However, other challenges lay ahead. Finding the space and time during training courses to present The Spectrum to instructors, facilitate their learning, practice and assess their competence, were a major concern. Therefore in 30-minute assessment sessions, where peers were being taught, we chose to forego assessing whether any skier development had occurred and instead focused on the instructor's ability to show the appropriate use of a range of the styles in various teaching situations. At the time we acknowledged this was not ideal,*

but with the constraints of the course structure of five days where training and assessment were occurring simultaneously, we chose this option.

A further challenge was in the presentation of The Spectrum in such a way that it maintained the integrity of its underpinning principles and gave instructors an understanding of the developmental, experiential nature of the teaching, or learning dynamic. To a large part this was not achieved unless instructors had some prior experience in using the teaching styles beforehand. We saw excellent examples of this where ski instructors who were also PE teachers or lecturers flourished. The challenge of introducing The Spectrum was compounded, because in the early 1990's outside of the PE sector, it was virtually unknown. In addition, the underpinning principles of The Spectrum, namely, teacher/learner accountability, responsibility and experience, teaching and learning, were at odds with the prevailing teaching and learning models used at the time in PE.

Finally, an interesting challenge lay ahead for us which we did not foresee at the time. This was how the learner perceived the role of the teacher. Most students experienced predominantly subservient learning where the teacher was the 'fountain' of all knowledge and he/she imparted this through explanation and demonstration. Early on when ski instructors introduced the learning styles in their own teaching their students often felt uncomfortable and 'not taught' and 'not learning'. They did not recognise the teaching/learning dynamic, because the sources of knowledge became more experiential, feedback came from themselves and peers and they were confronted with becoming more responsible and accountable for their own learning as a big paradigm shift from the days of EDICT.

Academic Voice (CI)

Author 2 describes how a separate figuration he was part of, at an Edinburgh teacher college, links to the commencement of our figuration. The introduction of The Spectrum to BASI was in the context of coaches and PE professionals having a social habitus that valued EDICT as a direct instructional model. EDICT is also recognised as being highly valued, historically as a dominant discourse in the context of PE by Byra (2006). The strength of this emphasis in PE and sport teaching, typically characterised by linear sequential progression, was such that it was the main pedagogy within the BASI training syllabus at the time. There is some sense in Author 2's account, that the social habitus of BASI Trainers, was nonetheless beginning to change through them becoming accepting of The Spectrum.

The challenges Author 2 mentions, about being time poor in course delivery, are consistent with what Culver, Werthner and Trudel (2019) observed about coach developers having vast amounts of content to deliver in a short time. It is also likely that delivering The Spectrum's 11 teaching styles would amount to what would be considered by many as a large volume of content. Furthermore, it would seem time constraints in course delivery were a tension in maintaining what he describes as 'the integrity of its (The Spectrum) underpinning principles'. Author 2 comments this time pressure meant BASI course candidates without a strong teaching background, in contrast to PE teachers and lecturers, were at a disadvantage in learning about and becoming competent, at an introductory level, in teaching The Spectrum.

Author 2 also comments, particularly through the word 'subservient' about a social power imbalance between the learner and the teacher, with the former traditionally enjoying relatively more social power, this teacher's knowledge being typically taught through direct instructional models. Consequently, the continuum of teaching styles within The Spectrum did not 'fit' with the individual habitus (Elias, 1994) of candidates who upheld and endorsed a restricted direct teaching style. Author 2 states how this lack of connection was extended to clients who similarly valued and expected a direct coaching style.

Using The Spectrum—Author 2 Self-Voice

From a Trainer's perspective sharing knowledge and experience of The Spectrum is very rewarding, especially when students achieve the 'ahh' moment of the full impact of the model on their teaching behaviour. Seeing them shift from teacher-led teaching to learner-led teaching and understanding the shift, is the reward in itself for me. From an instructor's perspective, where the learning episode is sessional, I especially like the learner's response to learning through various styles. Not only does it include more of the group in the dynamic of their own and peers learning but also their enjoyment of the sessions can be greatly enhanced. I enjoy the exchange of roles where the learner begins to shape their own learning as it requires me to move beyond my own teaching and personal agenda and adopt that of my students. Mindfulness has taught me the skills of 'getting myself out of the way' during the teaching/learning dynamic and this has been of great interest to me over the past decade.

An interesting phenomenon is seen whilst teaching higher levels of skier in off-piste all mountain situations. Not exclusively, but often, in this scenario I will use Command and Practice styles regularly because they are the most effective to share information clearly and succinctly which may be of use to the learner in situations which could become a hazard and risk to them. This use of styles impresses upon me how the situational context and not just the intended learning outcomes, influence my choice of style. It also serves to remind me that some aspirant instructors are often of the impression teacher led styles are for beginners and the learner led styles for more advanced practitioners.

Academic Voice (CI)

It seems Author 2 values The Spectrum as part of his individual habitus (Elias, 1994). For example, from the level of satisfaction he expresses as a Trainer in using The Spectrum to facilitate a shift amongst trainee instructors or from the coach making the majority of the decisions to the athlete's making more decisions as they move along The Spectrum. In so doing, it could be argued a more reality adequate (Elias, 1994) construct of teaching is reached. In other words, a more suitable way of teaching beyond the limitations of narrow teacher-centred approaches. As an instructor he suggests the importance of having enough time in using The Spectrum with his clients, through the word 'sessional', implying adequate time is required to allow the use of multiple 'styles' to enable clients to experience enjoyment.

The author's experience and study of mindfulness seem to have continued a modification in his habitus to being a facilitator of teaching rather than a 'fountain of all knowledge'. While a person's habitus is largely formed in their early childhood, it alters throughout life according to the different social experiences they encounter and the different figurations they form (Elias, 1998). The notion more direct styles such as Styles A and B are used where there are safety concerns to students is consistent with Bradford, Hickson and Berg (2020) commenting on the PE context. The suggestion some aspirant instructors consider Styles A–E as being for beginners is perhaps indicative of their habitus and a misunderstanding of The Spectrum.

Using The Spectrum—Author 3 Self-Voice

In BASI courses during the early to mid-2000's and possibly prior, the styles were demonstrated by the Trainers and students were often expected to deliver a lesson using one or more teaching styles other than Command or set a challenge in assessment of using a particular teaching style. The use of a teaching style was used to define an assessment activity. For example, 'Deliver a lesson in the bumps strand, work in the psychological performance thread and use a reciprocal teaching style.' It could be argued this was due to a reluctance of students to be creative by using various teaching styles. Handing responsibility from the teacher to the student can be daunting, particularly for trainee or less experienced instructors. There is often a fear of handing over control, a fear of ambiguity arising as a result, a fear of the process taking too long, or a fear of less perceived value to the paying client (learner).

Over the late 2000's and 2010's, in the advent of a new (still current) *Alpine Manual in 2008, this approach changed. Prior to this edition of the Manual, BASI's approach to ski instructor training involved many teaching concepts but nothing to cohesively bind them together or provide them with form or structure to be deliberately impactful. The 2008 edition included the Task, Information, Evaluation, Development (TIED) Model. TIED gave a clear, cyclic structure to the teaching process from which various teaching tools or concepts, including The Spectrum can be used to add value to each stage. Since then, the emphasis in teaching has been to use The Spectrum in a way relevant to achieving a given lesson's goal.*

For example, a particular session may be most successful using purely a Command Style if the off-piste teaching environment dictates the goal of the session is clarity, brevity and safety. It would be less successful if the goal was to involve the learner in deciding what type of turns they'd like to work on, or if it were to explore lines down a particular slope. A Learner Design or Divergent Discovery Style may be better suited to these scenarios respectively. A particular teaching style may be selected based upon the learner's phase of skill acquisition (Fitts & Posner, 1967), the need to develop either understanding or performance, the desire to build a team or an individual, a preference for where the feedback should come from, or other considerations made about the learner and their goals. The current perspective of teaching styles on BASI courses, is they are one of several teaching tools or concepts instructors have at their disposal to create more successful lessons whilst 'looping' through TIED. Other teaching tools may include goal setting, task presentation, structure of practice, catering for preferred learning styles and climate setting skills. Teaching tools including the teaching styles, are used to add value to lessons, rather than just being done as a 'tick box' exercise.

Academic Voice (CI)

Like Author 2, it would seem Author 3 encountered candidates who were confused about The Spectrum and had a pre-disposition to perhaps overusing the Command Style. This strong preference is indicative of an individual habitus (Elias, 1994) valuing a direct way of teaching, like Author 2's comment about the teacher being a 'fountain of knowledge'. It seems possible, how candidates come to understand teaching contemporarily; for example, their engagement in the training course described is shaped by past experiences that form their individual habitus. Importantly from a figurational standpoint, to adequately understand social phenomena in the present, one must be cognisant of the past (Elias, 1994). In Author 3's account, the need for the Trainer to constrain tasks to encourage candidates to learn and apply the range of styles is some indication of the strength of candidates' individual habitus. The valuing of the Command Style and the teacher as the guardian of knowledge is historically rooted as a long-term process in coach education. The traditional technocratic-led approaches (Maguire, 2013; McKay, Gore & Kirk, 1990) mentioned by Author 2 may well have been what the candidates predominantly encountered in their previous learning. This can then explain the nature of their habitus on the BASI courses.

Author 3's account of the development of the 2008 Manual (British Association of Snowsports Instructors [BASI], 2008) suggests a change in the figuration, from one that included The Spectrum from the 1990s, building on previous historical technocratic approaches to what might be described as a more blended approach purposefully more focused towards the learner. Essentially, TIED (BASI, 2008) enables a cyclical framework to learner development encompassing The Spectrum and other teaching approaches. In serving this value enhancing purpose, TIED perhaps addresses the kinds of criticism levelled at The Spectrum (Hewitt, SueSee & Pill, 2020), albeit in the PE context. These being that The Spectrum is limited and fails to address the full breadth of considerations required in teaching, including design, planning and assessment. There is further change in the figuration in the 2008 Manual and other BASI documents, including the dropping of one of The Spectrum styles (Convergent Discovery), reducing the number of styles to ten. Also, 'Divergent Discovery' is renamed 'Divergent', 'Learner Designed Individual Programme' is called 'Learner Design' and 'Self-Teaching' is changed to 'Self-Teach.' In addition, the identifying letters are removed for each style and the order of styles adjusted, varying across different documents. It is unclear why these changes have occurred, perhaps because of different writer interpretations. Nonetheless, such modification is consistent with endeavours by others in altering The Spectrum for their own contexts. For example, Hewitt et al (2020) reported how the number of styles has been reduced or terminology has been changed by a range of practitioners using The Spectrum.

Using The Spectrum—Author 4 Self-Voice

Since teaching styles were introduced within BASI the capability of a Trainer to assess teaching styles has evolved as their own understanding of The Spectrum has matured. It was common practice for BASI Trainers to assess teaching styles in a one-dimensional manner. For example, Trainers would set up teaching scenarios using a descriptive task. This application of The Spectrum centred the teaching style at the expense of the learning and development of the students. Although this arguably made the assessment of teaching styles an easy task for the Trainer, it missed one of the key points of The Spectrum, the teacher chooses the teaching style in response to the task, environment and skill of the students. This practice started to shift in favour of centring the student when Trainers were given TIED as an experiential learning model to use in training and assessment. This experiential learning model (based on Kolb (1984)) helped Trainers and students understand that the teaching style compliments the learning and therefore creates a richer learning experience.

Currently BASI use teaching styles in a manner allowing more than one style to be used within a session. One of the consequences of putting the students learning at the heart of BASI's experiential learning model is beginner teachers can start to use The Spectrum appropriately and skilled teachers can make use of The Spectrum in a fluid and more complex way. The TIED model provides the teacher with choice over how they use The Spectrum. For example, teachers can choose a teaching style to match the task and learners and continue in this style around the TIED model. Some teachers may be able to use different styles for different learners. For example, in one group the teacher may have some students progress through TIED using Self-check and some moving through TIED using Practice Style. Some teachers may have ability to use different teaching styles at different stages of the TIED model. For example, the teacher may use Command Style to explain the task 'do ten turns between here and that pylon.' When the teacher gathers the information, they may choose to use Self Check, 'how many turns did you do?' In summary, The Spectrum is a tangible tool that strengthens BASI instructors' teaching competence. Without this concrete tool, the instructors' use of TIED would be less successful and BASI would not be producing as competent instructors.

Academic Voice (CI)

The opening sentence of Author 4's account through the word 'evolved' suggests change within the figuration. The example of centring 'the teaching style at the expense of the learning and development of the students' again suggests Trainers, as Author 3 eludes, were previously maintaining too much control of the learning. They were not being student-centred in their own teaching, contrasting with one of the main principles of The Spectrum. As Ashworth (2012 cited in Hewitt et al., 2020, p. 10) noted, 'if teaching is competent and professional all episodes will be student-centred, and all styles do focus on the learners as centre stage learners . . . if the learners' learning is not the focus—then whatever the teacher is doing needs to be re-examined'. That said, it may be Trainers adopted this approach because of the kinds of time pressures described by Author 2. Concerning one of the 'key points' of The Spectrum referred to by Author 4, Mosston and Ashworth (2008) termed this 'mobility ability' meaning the educator can shift between teaching behaviours as required to meet learner needs, content expectations, environmental factors and time constraints. The examples provided about using the TIED model corroborate with observations by Author 3, that the introduction of TIED allowed Trainers and candidates to understand and apply The Spectrum in a more reality adequate or congruent way (Elias, 1994). In other words, TIED enabled them to better fit the model to their specific contexts.

Using The Spectrum—Author 5 Self-Voice

My experience is about attending a five-day BASI Level 4 Teaching Module in January 2007 as a candidate. The first two days included an introduction to The Spectrum. Later in the week we were asked to deliver lessons to our peers on chosen and given topics. We were assessed on our skills and techniques and the evaluation of skills, while also demonstrating the use of different teaching styles. As we progressed through the week, we explored all The Spectrum teaching styles. These were explained in a very 'text-book' manner and seemed very forced and unnatural to how they would be implemented in the 'real world.' The big surprise I found on the course was the performance of the candidates. A vivid memory is how many people ultimately got confused, stuck or lost amongst the artificial delivery of the lessons set as tasks. One day, we had to 'pick out of a hat' a teaching style and technique. I recall as well as being confusing, it felt like were we just 'jumping through hoops' rather than developing our knowledge or making candidates better teachers. Since then, experience has developed my understanding and delivery of ski teaching and while skiing can be very technical, it is not always 'black and white'. Consequently, the use of the different teaching styles, on a daily basis will depend on a range of factors, include learner age, ability and needs/desires, lesson duration, teacher/learner relationship and environmental conditions.

Lesson time and teacher/learner history can affect the ability to use student centred lessons. In Australian ski schools, lessons are often scheduled for short durations, typically for two hours. 'One-off' clients may arrive with the expectation of a successful lesson and as it takes time to form a client relationship, some of The Spectrum styles may have limited effect due to time constraints and limited connection between the teacher and client. If a history exists between teacher/client, it allows for the lessons to be more open and naturally take a client led style, with the teacher guiding the client to acquire the skills for success. Coaching on the other hand, for Alpine and Moguls, calls for a focus on Guided Discovery. The use of different teaching styles, alongside the use of teaching aids, for instance video and timing, can support the athlete in achieving success. It is crucial Instructors have knowledge of the different styles available and how they work. However, more importantly, it is essential they can deliver and adapt each style and to reflect their personality and needs of the client.

Academic Voice (CI)

Unlike Authors 2, 3 and 4, Author 5 writes from the perspective of a candidate importantly attending a course prior to 2008 and the introduction of TIED (BASI, 2008). However, like Author 4, this author recognises that the developmental needs of the learner were not prioritised in the way intended in The Spectrum and candidates were not 'centre stage'. Further, the words ''text-book' manner' and 'seemed very forced and unnatural' suggest a level of discomfort by the Trainer perhaps indicating a lack of knowledge about and/or a dislocation between their preferred teaching approaches and The Spectrum. In other words, The Spectrum may have been at odds with their individual habitus (Elias, 1994). The approach used by the Trainers seems to be more a 'reproduction of knowledge' rather than an attempt to facilitate candidate creativity as the preferred way to introduce The Spectrum (Hewitt et al., 2020).

A common theme in Author 4's account with those of the other authors is confusion amongst candidates. The lack of candidate understanding raised by Author 5 can perhaps partly be attributed to there again not being enough time for Trainers to deliver content in enough depth. Adequate time must be given to enable coaches to experience competence when learning to use The Spectrum in their own coaching. In the context of PE teaching, Byra (2020) suggested that teachers would likely revert back to the styles that typically dominate 'traditional' or the historically common coaching practice, the Command Style and Practice Style (Hewitt, 2020; Hewitt & Edwards, 2013; SueSee et al., 2019; SueSee & Barker, 2019).

From his account, Author 5 did develop competence over time, but from 'trial and error' beyond the course. This post-course development came to embrace other coaching styles. Further, the nature of the ski school teaching environment is commented about by Author 4 and specifically expectations of 'one-off' clients within short lessons. Such expectations may be founded in traditional ideas about learning with the instructor as the 'fountain of all knowledge' discussed earlier.

Summary

We have shown, using figurational sociology and the literature, how The Spectrum has longevity within BASI and has existed as a long-term process for more than three decades. It can be said that overall, The Spectrum is valued by each of us including the CI and forms part of our individual and social habitus. Over time, the figuration examined that includes each author, as current BASI members commonly aligned to valuing and teaching The Spectrum has, in common with all figurations, altered. One example of this modification is the use of TIED to help Trainers and candidates alike better apply The Spectrum and other teaching approaches. Notably, TIED was implemented in 2011, importantly after Author 5 completed the course. We suggest an area for further consideration is to explore if TIED has improved how The Spectrum is interpreted and applied. Such research will help demonstrate if candidate confusion mentioned by the authors has been reduced. While there have clearly been changes in our figuration over time, issues concerning time to learn and apply The Spectrum and habitus of instructors and clients valuing traditional learning approaches seem to prevail to a greater or lesser extent.

References

Bradford, B., Hickson, C., & Berg, S. (2020). The teaching continuum. In B. Suesee, M. Hewitt, & S. Pill (Eds.), *The Spectrum of teaching styles in physical education* (pp. 152–165). Routledge.

British Association of Snowsport Instructors. (2008). *The BASI manual Alpine*. British Association of Snowsport Instructors.

Byra, M. (2006). Teaching styles and inclusive pedagogies. In D. Kirk, D. Macdonald, & M. O'Sullivan (Eds.), *The handbook of physical education* (pp. 449–466). Sage.

Byra, M. (2020). The Spectrum: My journey. In B. SueSee, M. Hewitt, & S. Pill (Eds.), *The Spectrum of teaching styles in physical education* (pp. 27–36). Routledge.

Culver, D. M., Werthner, P., & Trudel, P. (2019). Coach developers as 'facilitators of learning' in a large-scale coach education programme: One actor in a complex system. *International Sports Coaching Journal, 6*, 296–306.

Elias, N. (1978). *The civilizing process: The history of manners*. Basil Blackwell.
Elias, N. (1994). *Reflections on a life*. Polity Press.
Elias, N. (1998). The social constraint towards self-constraint. In S. Mennell & J. Goudsblom (Eds.), *Norbert Elias on civilization, power and knowledge: Selected writings* (pp. 49–66). University of Chicago Press.
Elias, N. (2009). Civilisation and psychosomatics. In R. Kilminster & S. Mennell (Eds.), *Norbert Elias: Essays III on sociology and the humanities* (pp. 180–186). University College Dublin Press.
Elias, N. (2013). *Interviews and autobiographical reflections*. University College Dublin Press.
Fitts, P. M., & Posner, M. I. (1967). *Human performance*. Brooks and Cole.
Grbich, C. (2013). *Qualitative data analysis: An introduction*. Sage.
Hewitt, M. (2020). Considering the application of a range of teaching styles from the Spectrum that promotes the holistic development of tennis players in a variety of learning domains. In B. SueSee, M. Hewitt, & S. Pill (Eds.), *The Spectrum of teaching styles in physical education* (pp. 60–72). Routledge.
Hewitt, M., & Edwards, K. (2013). Observed teaching styles of junior development and club professional tennis coaches in Australia. *ITF Coaching and Sport Science Review*, *59*, 6–8.
Hewitt, M., Suesee, B., & Pill, S. (2020). Introduction to the Spectrum. In B. SueSee, M. Hewitt, & S. Pill (Eds.), *The Spectrum of teaching styles in physical education* (pp. 1–13). Routledge.
Hopper, T. F., Madill, L. E., Bratseth, C. D., Cameron, K. A., Coble, J. D., & Nimmon, L. E. (2008). Multiple voices in health, sport, recreation, and physical education research: Revealing unfamiliar spaces in a polyvocal review of qualitative research genres. *Quest*, *60*(2), 214–235.
Kolb, D. (1984). *Experiential learning: Experience as the source of learning and development*. Prentice Hall.
Maguire, J. (2013). *Reflections on process sociology and sport: 'Walking the line'*. Routledge.
Manen, M. van. (1997). From meaning to method. *Qualitative Health Research*, *7*(3), 345–369.
McKay, J., Gore, J. M., & Kirk, D. (1990). Beyond the limits of technocratic physical education. *Quest*, *42*(1), 52–76.
McMahon, J., & Dinan Thompson, M. (2011). 'Body work-regulation of a swimmer body': An autoethnography from an Australian elite swimmer. *Sport, Education & Society*, *16*(1), 35–50.
Mosston, M., & Ashworth, S. (2008). *Teaching physical education*. https://spectrumofteachingstyles.org/assets/files/book/Teaching_Physical_Edu_1st_Online.pdf
SueSee, B., & Barker, D. M. (2019). Self-reported and observed teaching styles of Swedish physical education teachers. *Curriculum Studies in Health and Physical Education*, *10*(1), 34–50.
SueSee, B., Edwards, K., Pill, S., & Cuddihy, T. (2019). Observed teaching styles of senior physical education teachers in Australia. *Curriculum Perspectives*, *39*, 47–57.

17
FUTURE DIRECTIONS
Using The Spectrum in Coach Education

Shane Pill, Brendan SueSee and Mitch Hewitt

This chapter outlines how to use The Spectrum to analyse the pedagogical behaviour of coaches and explain how The Spectrum could be applied in coach education and development. We note that The Spectrum has been used previously to inform coach education and development, with Chapter 16 by Williams and colleagues an example. In this chapter we look at how tools to assess coach self-awareness of teaching styles and alignment between perceived and actual pedagogical execution can be used as coach development instruments.

Coach education that assists coaches to identify their perceived and actual teaching styles, in addition to exploring the underlying notions and explanations of such practice, is an avenue for coaches and coach developers open to self-reflection. Modifying, changing, or enhancing the practices of coaches requires recognition that the coach can identify their coaching behaviour and understand the assumptions that inform these behaviours. Identifying the teaching styles that coaches employ during coaching sessions and the underlying explanations of these practices permits a clearer connection between beliefs, assumptions, and practices (Hewitt, 2015). To this end, we suggest that The Spectrum will enable coaches and coach developers to clearly identify how and what learning the coach pedagogy facilitates during practice sessions and enable dialogue with coaches about the application of teaching styles during practice sessions for purposeful outcomes. We agree with Cushion (2010) that 'the most sophisticated understandings of coaching practice and advances in coach education would seem fruitless if coaches lack seemingly basic levels of self-awareness' (p. 44).

Survey Tool

Hewitt's (2015) investigation of tennis coaches teaching styles showed how to use The Spectrum as a survey tool for coaches to self-reflect on the use of teaching styles. The survey contained one question on each of The Spectrum styles. The question for each of the 11 teaching styles was as follows: 'How frequently do I use this landmark teaching style in my coaching sessions throughout the year?' A five-point Likert rating scale was used for participant ratings (Figure 17.1). The survey instrument, *Instrument for collecting coaches' self-identified beliefs in*

DOI: 10.4324/9781003041443-18

Landmark Teaching Style	Scenario Description of Landmark Teaching Style				
A	The students perform the task, selected by the coach, in a unison, choreographed, or precision perfomance image following the exact pacing (cues) set by the coach.				
How frequently do I use this landmark teaching style in my coaching sessions throughout the year?	Not at all	Minimally	Here and there	Often	Most of the time
	1	2	3	(4)	5

FIGURE 17.1 Scenario description from the description inventory of teaching styles showing the five-point rating scale used to measure how frequently a coach believed that the teaching style was used.

Source: Hewitt (2015), Hewitt and Edwards (2011) and Hewitt, Edwards and Ashworth (2011)

relation to the teaching styles they use during coaching sessions throughout the year (Hewitt, Edwards & Ashworth, 2011), is provided as Figure 17.2.

This instrument can be used effectively as Hewitt (2015) did as a self-assessment tool for coaches. The coach would read the scenario descriptors and reflect on their practice. This would allow the coach to draw conclusions about the coaching style they most/least frequently use and whether this aligns with their intentions. As some have found, there is often a lack of congruence between what coaches and teachers self-report using as a teaching style and what is observed as their practice (Hewitt, 2015; SueSee et al., 2019; SueSee & Barker, 2018).

The use of this instrument as a self-assessment tool can provide for a closer alignment between what the coach says they want to achieve as a coach and how they achieve this using a specific coaching style. The instrument may also highlight to the coach the behaviours or decisions that they need the players to make to achieve specific outcomes (e.g. use memory, discovery or creativity) and how the coach must change their instructional behaviour to achieve these outcomes from the player/s. By drawing the coach's attention to the decisions being made and the role that the decisions play in achieving specific player results or outcomes, the tool allows the coaching participants (both coach and players) to know exactly what they need to do (who will be making decisions 'when' and about 'what') to implement specific styles for specific task outcomes. We suggest that this contrasts with how coaches may draw naive conclusions such as, 'I ask questions and play games; therefore, I am using a GBA as questions and games are a feature of GBA's'. Whilst it is easy to see how a coach can make this naive conclusion, it does not highlight the instructional behaviours specifically which The Spectrum provides. For example, the scenario descriptor for Style G (Coaching by Problem Solving) mentions that the player previously did not know the answer and that they discovered the correct response. If all the player/s know the answer before the question is asked, then no one is discovering the answer. It is recall or the coach has used a form of 'retrieval practice'. What we highlight here is the specific nature of who (player or coach) needs to do what (recall, rehearse, discover, or create) for the behaviours to represent a coaching style and how The Spectrum can allow coaches to closely align their behaviour with the outcomes they want (recall, rehearse, discover, or create).

Scenario Style	Scenario Description of Teaching Style				
A	The coach selects the task that the player/s perform in a unison, choreographed or precision performance image following the exact pacing and rhythm (cues) set by the coach.				
How frequently do I use this teaching style in my coaching sessions throughout the year?	Not at all	Minimally	Here and there	Often	Most of the time
	1	2	3	4	5
Scenario Style	Scenario Description of Teaching Style				
B	The coach selects the subject matter tasks, the quantity, and the time limits so that player/s can practice individually and privately. The coach circulates among all player/s and offers private feedback. The player/s learn to set a pace to practice tasks within an allocated time frame.				
How frequently do I use this teaching style in my coaching sessions throughout the year?	Not at all	Minimally	Here and there	Often	Most of the time
	1	2	3	4	5
Scenario Style	Scenario Description of Teaching Style				
C	The coach selects the subject matter tasks and presents the expectations for player/s to work with a partner. One player (the doer) practices the task, while the other player (the observer) uses coach prepared criteria (checklist) to offer immediate feedback about the performance to the doer. When the first set of tasks are finished, the players switch roles and continue to the second set of tasks. The coach interacts with the observer to affirm the use of the criteria and the accuracy of the feedback comments and/or to redirects the observer's focus to specific performance details on the criteria.				
How frequently do I use this teaching style in my coaching sessions throughout the year?	Not at all	Minimally	Here and there	Often	Most of the time
	1	2	3	4	5
Scenario Style	Scenario Description of Teaching Style				
D	The coach selects the subject matter tasks and designs the criteria (performance checklist) for player/s. Player/s individually practice the tasks and check their own performance using the checklist. The coach privately communicates with player/s to listen to their self-assessment comments and either reinforces the player's use of the criteria or redirects the player's focus to specific performance details on the criteria.				
How frequently do I use this teaching style in my coaching sessions throughout the year?	Not at all	Minimally	Here and there	Often	Most of the time
	1	2	3	4	5
Scenario Style	Scenario Description of Teaching Style				
E	The coach selects the subject matter tasks and designs multiple levels of difficulty for each task. Player/s select the level of difficulty that is appropriate to their performance. If inappropriate level decisions are made, the player may change the level choice. Players check their performance using the coach prepared performance checklist (criteria sheet). The coach circulates to acknowledge the choices the players have made and to ask questions for clarification to affirm the accuracy of the players' assessment process and/or to redirect the learner's focus to specific performance details on the criteria.				

FIGURE 17.2 Instrument for collecting coaches' self-identified beliefs in relation to the teaching styles they use during coaching sessions.

Source: Hewitt (2015) andHewitt et al. (2011)

How frequently do I use this teaching style in my coaching sessions throughout the year?	Not at all	Minimally	Here and there	Often	Most of the time
	1	2	3	4	5
Scenario Style	Scenario Description of Teaching Style					
F	The coach asks one player a series of specific questions; each question has only one correct answer. The questions are sequenced in a logical pattern so that each answer leads the player step by step to discover the anticipated concept, principle, relationship or solution.				

How frequently do I use this teaching style in my coaching sessions throughout the year?	Not at all	Minimally	Here and there	Often	Most of the time
	1	2	3	4	5
Scenario Style	Scenario Description of Teaching Style					
G	The coach designs a situation or one question that has only one specific correct response—the situation or question is new, and the response is not previously known to the player/s. The players are given individual and private time to use their thinking and questioning skills to sequentially and logically discover the anticipated answer.				

How frequently do I use this teaching style in my coaching sessions throughout the year?	Not at all	Minimally	Here and there	Often	Most of the time
	1	2	3	4	5
Scenario Style	Scenario Description of Teaching Style					
H	The coach designs a single or series of problems, situations or questions that seek multiple solutions to the same problem. The task is new to the player/s; therefore, each player is invited to discover new possibilities, as they produce multiple responses to the specific problem. The coach acknowledges the production of multiple ideas, rather than any singular idea.				

How frequently do I use this teaching style in my coaching sessions throughout the year?	Not at all	Minimally	Here and there	Often	Most of the time
	1	2	3	4	5
Scenario Style	Scenario Description of Teaching Style					
I	The coach designates a broad subject matter/topic. Within that topic each player is responsible for producing an individual learning program that includes setting goals and the process for accomplishing the goals. The player/s design, implement, refine the program, and create performance criteria for their individual learning programs. The coach acknowledges the production of ideas and asks questions for information or clarification about the learning program.				

How frequently do I use this teaching style in my coaching sessions throughout the year?	Not at all	Minimally	Here and there	Often	Most of the time
	1	2	3	4	5
Scenario Style	Scenario Description of Teaching Style					
J	A player initiates a request to the coach to plan his/her own learning experience. In this experience the player makes all the decisions: selects the subject matter intent, designs, executes, and identifies the assessment criteria for the learning experience. The coach participates when and how the player requests. The coach acknowledges the learner's successful implementation of the plans and initiates questions where discrepancies emerge between the learner's intent and actions. It is not the coach's job to evaluate, rather to act as a reference source between the indicated intent and action when asked by the player.				

FIGURE 17.2 (Continued)

How frequently do I use this teaching style in my coaching sessions throughout the year?	Not at all	Minimally	Here and there	Often	Most of the time
	1	2	3	4	5

Scenario Style	Scenario Description of Teaching Style
K	The learner takes the role of both student and coach setting all learning objectives. The learner makes decisions about subject matter intent, design, execution, and assessment of the learning experiences. This style is independent of a coach and not initiated by a coach. Feedback from others occurs only IF the learner seeks it.

How frequently do I use this teaching style in my coaching sessions throughout the year?	Not at all	Minimally	Here and there	Often	Most of the time
	1	2	3	4	5

FIGURE 17.2 (Continued)

Observation Tool

Hewitt (2015) showed how the *Identification of Teaching-Learning Styles Instrument* (Ashworth, 2004) can be used to match coaches-observed teaching styles with vision of their coaching practice. The instrument contains the style scenario descriptions shown in Figure 17.2. It requires a coach developer or reflective coach to understand the teaching behaviour by focusing on subject matter (what is being coached) and learner behaviour. The observer is to firstly conclude if the subject matter (the task) induced reproduction or production thinking and then the teaching style being employed. For example, if a coach has given the subject matter to the player (whether verbally and/or with a demonstration), then they have asked the player to reproduce the movement, and feedback is provided, then this has the hallmarks of Practice Style B. Similarly, if the coach sets a problem (that the players do not know the solution to) and asks for a solution that requires a searching (trial and error) then it has the characteristics of Convergent Discovery Style G. Using the *Instrument for collecting coaches' self-identified beliefs in relation to the teaching styles they use during coaching sessions* provides an opportunity for the coach to reflect on if they are asking the players to recall known skills or strategies or if they genuinely need to solve an unknown problem.

Observation Coding

Hewitt (2015) used the *Instrument for Identifying Teaching Styles* (IFITS: Curtner-Smith, 2001) coding sheet in conjunction with the *Identification of Teaching-Learning Styles Instrument* (Figure 17.3) to determine the amount of time that coaches dedicated to employing various teaching styles. Coding requires a 10-second observation proceeded by a 10-second recording of this observation. In other words, every 20 seconds the coder decides which teaching style the coach was using or whether they were engaged in a session management activity. Session management is time the coach is involved in activity that is not directly related to teaching.

Interval	Teaching Style	OR	Session Management
1	A B C D E F G H I J K		M
2	A B C D E F G H I J K		M
3	A B C D E F G H I J K		M
4	A B C D E F G H I J K		M
5	A B C D E F G H I J K		M
6	A B C D E F G H I J K		M

FIGURE 17.3 An example of a section from the IFITS coding sheet to code a practice session.

Canopy Designs

Situated between the coaching styles A–K that we described in previous chapters are variations called canopy designs. Canopy designs share approximate but not precise learning objectives, decision structures and the developmental focus of the teaching style; rather, they approximate the style but do not exactly match the style. For example, if the observer noted Coaching by Command without direct pacing and timing of the activity by the coach, it would be Command Style A minus (−) pace and rhythm. The abbreviation for this notation is A−P&R. In this example, the episode follows the decision structure of the Command Style A while omitting the decision of pace and rhythm as the player made the decisions pertaining to speed or how quickly or slowly (pace and rhythm) they decided to perform the task or activity. Thus, the canopy design is labelled with a 'minus' (i.e., A−P&R) as a particular decision (i.e., pace and rhythm) varies the decision-making structure of the Coaching by Command (Hewitt, 2015). We suggest that the concept of canopies is particularly important to understand as people may view The Spectrum's styles otherwise in a versus manner—either I am doing a style, or I am not. This view can create conflict in the coach as they may see a style is not working 'fully' to achieve an outcome and may wish to adapt it. A canopy approach to a Spectrum of Coaching Styles avoids the potential for confusion concerning 'are they no longer "doing" Style B if they removed certain parts for a short episode?'; or if they are using a pure (called Landmark) version of the coaching style and succeed with the application of the style, but feel they failed the player achieving the 'best' learning outcome which could have come from a blended style. Canopy design is an area in need of future Spectrum of Coaching Styles research consideration.

The Spectrum and an Ecological Dynamics Perspective on Learning in Sport Coaching Settings

To date, explanations of The Spectrum have been mainly through cognitive psychological perspectives. We have drawn on this perspective several times when explaining aspects of The Spectrum and sport coaching for learning in the chapters. As is noted several times in this book, a philosophy of The Spectrum is a non-versus approach, and thus we recognise that pedagogical merit of the coaching styles we outline in this book might be equally well explained from a cognitive or an ecological perspective. However, to be transparent, we declare that we agree with Abernathy (2009), in that contemporary explanations of learning through cognitive models are not that different 'in practice' from ecological models of skill acquisition. Further, that from a pedagogical perspective, it is not immediately apparent to

The Spectrum of Coaching Styles

Coach (Maximum)   (Minimum)

----Who Makes the Pedagogical Decisions----

Player (Minimum)   (Maximum)

                    Command   Discovery

            Style A B C D E F / G H I J K

              Reproduction   / Production

A Varying Landscape of Affordances

<u>Highly specific activities</u>   <u>Varied activities</u>

Highly Structured Practice

                                  Informal Peer Coaching

        Coach-led activities   Guided Discovery

Direct Teaching --- Discovery Learning

                   A Varying Landscape of Affordances

FIGURE 17.4 The Spectrum (Mosston & Ashworth, 2008) alongside A Varying Landscape of Affordances model (Chow et al., 2020).

sport coaches how different theories, that while providing alternative explanatory positions, lead to pedagogical implications that are fundamentally different.

An area where ecological dynamics provides a basis for an explanation of The Spectrum is the model of A Varying Landscape of Affordances (Chow et al., 2020) that describes coach centred 'direct' and 'highly structured' pedagogy at one end of a 'spectrum' and at the other end guided and discovery pedagogy (Figure 17.4). Like The Spectrum, the A Varying Landscape of Affordances model shows a continuum of coaching 'methodologies' with a coach's focus on learning design. That learning design moves between different regions of an affordance landscape and mapping to 'methodologies' based on the learning need/s of a player/s (or athlete/s). In The Spectrum model, the movement 'along' the continuum of teaching/coaching styles is termed 'mobility ability', that is 'the ability of a teacher to comfortably shift from one teaching style to another to match changing learner objectives' (Mosston & Ashworth, 2008, p. 10). Both The Spectrum and A Varying Landscape of Affordances models describe coach directed pedagogy for highly structured practice activities at one end of the continuum and 'discovery' learning environments at the other end. We believe that the similarities in The Spectrum continuum and the recent A Varying Landscape of Affordances creates the potential for the latter to inform the former as an explanation of non-linear pedagogy.

Conclusion

The Spectrum has been of continuing relevance in physical education teacher education for over 50 years, however, it has only been in the last five years that Hewitt (2015) has applied it to the field of sport coaching. This is the first book to apply The Spectrum to the discipline of sport coaching. We suggest that there is much work to be done in the field of sports coaching and The Spectrum to empirically validate the claims made by Mosston and Ashworth (2008) regarding what each style can achieve. For example, in the sport of Australian Football (AFL) we have all observed Self-Check coaching (Style D) is commonly used in youth and senior AFL high-performance programmes, where players look at their game vision and information on the game from Champion Data to do a self-assessment against benchmarks set by the coaches, before the player talks with their line coach or development coach. As far as is known, the effects of this coaching style on player learning have not been researched. This is just one example of many, where coaches are already using the styles outlined in this book, but as an approach to learning, the coaching style has not been empirically tested. This may be due to the coaching style being called something else in the literature, or not being named at all.

The Spectrum not only provides the potential for a common pedagogical language for coaching styles, it also helps give the behaviours and deliberate decisions of the coach and players clarity. We hope that by translating The Spectrum from physical education teaching *pedagogy to a spectrum of coaching styles*, we have provided a *common pedagogical language* to assist a non-versus approach (from a pedagogical perspective) to skill acquisition, social development, cognitive development and coaching pedagogy discussions.

References

Abernathy, B. (2009). Some brickbats and bouquets for ecological approaches to cognition in sport. *International Journal of Sport Psychology*, *40*(1), 136–143.

Ashworth, S. (2004). *Identification of classroom teaching-learning styles instrument*. https://spectrumofteachingstyles.org/assets/files/articles/Ashworth2004_Description_Inventory_Of_Landmark.pdf

Chow, J. Y., Shuttleworth, R., Davids, K., & Araújo, D. (2020). Ecological dynamics and transfer from practice to performance. In N. J. Hodges & A. M. Williams (Eds.), *Skill acquisition in sport: Research, theory and practice* (3rd ed., pp. 330–344). Routledge.

Curtner-Smith, M. D. (2001). *Instrument for identifying teaching styles (IFITS)*. https://spectrumofteachingstyles.org/assets/files/articles/CurtnerSmith2001_IFITS.pdf

Cushion, C. J. (2010). Coach behaviour. In J. Lyle & C. Cushion (Eds.), *Sports coaching: Professionalism and practice* (pp. 43–62). Elsevier.

Hewitt, M. (2015). *Teaching styles of Australian tennis coaches: An exploration of practices and insights using Mosston and Ashworth's Spectrum of teaching styles*. Thesis submitted to fulfill Doctor of Philosophy. The University of Southern Queensland.

Hewitt, M., & Edwards, K. (2011). Instrument for collecting coaches' self-identified beliefs in relation to the teaching styles they use during coaching sessions throughout the year. In K. Larkin, M. Kawka, K. Noble, H. van Rensburg, L. Brodie, & P. A. Danaher (Eds.), *Empowering educators* (pp. 127–154). Palgrave Macmillan.

Hewitt, M., Edwards, K., & Ashworth, S. (2011). *Instrument for collecting coaches' self-identified beliefs in relation to the teaching styles they use during coaching sessions throughout the year*. https://spectrumofteachingstyles.org/assets/files/articles/Final-Survey-Questionnaire-5-for-Spectrum.pdf

Mosston, M., & Ashworth, S. (2008). *Teaching physical education* (1st online ed.). https://spectrumofteachingstyles.org/assets/files/book/Teaching_Physical_Edu_1st_Online.pdf

SueSee, B., & Barker, D. M. (2018). Self-reported and observed teaching styles of Swedish physical education teachers. *Curriculum Studies in Health and Physical Education*, *10*(1), 34–50.

SueSee, B., Edwards, K., Pill, S., & Cuddihy, T. (2019). Observed teaching styles of senior physical education teachers in Australia. *Curriculum Perspectives*, *39*, 47–71.

INDEX

Affordance/s 27, 33, 72, 129, 149
Alpine ski coaching 134, 135
Archery 26
Arnold, Peter 39, 43
Assessment 40, 43, 47, 51, 91, 123, 135–137, 139, 145, 146, 147
Athlete-centred 2, 5, 10, 60, 66, 88, 124
Australian football (AFL) 36, 56, 88, 109, 110, 113, 118, 150
Axiom 23

Baseball 31, 38, 44, 53, 60, 68, 75, 82, 88, 95, 118, 119
Battlezone 129, 130, 131
Bloom, Benjamin 3
Boxing 42
Brain networks 37
Bruner, Jerome 3, 7, 8
Bushwalking 90

Canopies 5, 118, 148
Canopy 1, 119, 120, 148
Canopy design 2, 22, 118, 148
Canopy of coaching styles 22, 118
Challenge point 16, 17, 37, 58, 59, 60–63
Check list 45, 46, 49, 55. 145
Coach-centred 3, 124, 128, 149
Coding 147, 148
Cognitive acquiescence 17
Cognitive dissonance 3, 4, 10, 17, 66, 72
Cognitive load 27, 54
Cognitive persistence 74
Cognitive representation 29
Commands 27, 32, 33
Community of learners 75

Cortical maps 37
Creativity 2, 4, 10, 11, 14, 19, 21, 22, 38, 71, 80–82, 84, 85, 92, 113, 115, 124, 125, 131, 141, 144
Cricket 31, 61, 62, 69, 89, 94, 102, 125, 129, 130
Cues 28, 31, 32, 38, 39, 40, 47, 48, 62, 65, 67, 95, 97, 113, 130, 144, 145

Debate of ideas 71
Decision making 2, 8, 9, 10, 13–16, 23, 24, 33, 36, 45, 54, 59, 60–63, 65, 77, 81, 87, 89–91, 96, 105, 106, 108–111, 113, 116, 120, 123, 131, 148
Declarative knowledge 24, 27, 71
Deliberate teaching 3, 8, 10, 114
Desirably difficult 60
Developmental channels 5, 10
Domains of learning 5, 43
Downhill snow skiing 38

Ecological 9, 27, 29, 72, 81, 128, 148, 149
Episodic 4, 22, 92, 101, 105, 108, 109, 118, 124
Equestrian 2
Explicit instruction 26, 27, 67

Feedback, augmented 29
Feedback, extrinsic 29
Feedback, intrinsic 29
Figurational 134
Folk pedagogies 8
Football (soccer) 36, 95, 112, 114, 118
Fraser, Neale 105
Freeze play 71

Game-based 1, 2, 4, 40, 66, 74, 75, 81, 109, 121, 123–127, 129, 131
Game play 70, 114, 116, 121, 129
Game sense approach 2, 65, 72, 81, 131
Goal orientation 59
GROW model 71
Guided inquiry 125

Hiking 30
Hopman, Harry 105
Hurdler 104

Idiosyncratic 1, 8, 9
Inattentional blindness 81
Inquiry 4, 17, 18, 19, 51, 66, 71, 75

Javelin 20, 26, 95, 101

Kayaking 30, 52, 67, 98, 99

Learning episode 4, 19, 33, 39, 40, 43, 66, 96, 97, 108, 118, 137

Memory 10, 11, 21, 22, 28, 33, 37, 40, 92, 97, 116–119, 124, 129, 131, 134, 135, 140, 141
Mental representation 29
Motivation 17, 20, 29, 52, 59, 60, 81, 88, 135
Motor memories 37
Mountain biking 30, 45
Movement cues 28, 130
Movement pattern/s 10, 11, 28, 29, 32, 37

Netball 39, 76, 82, 83

Outdoor pursuits 30, 38, 52, 61, 67, 77, 83, 90, 98, 104

Paralympic 88
Pedagogical 1, 2, 4, 9, 12, 14, 15, 20, 21, 23, 27, 29, 39, 63, 66, 70, 71, 78, 109, 123, 143, 148–150
Pedagogy 3, 5, 7, 9, 14, 24, 26, 65, 66, 71, 123, 127, 136, 143, 149, 150
Perceptual cues 111, 120
Perceptual representation 27
Play practice 125, 129
Play with purpose 124
Philosophy 2, 3, 7, 8, 22, 24, 66, 148
Physical education 1, 2, 4, 12, 15, 16, 39, 42, 49, 58, 65, 66, 119, 134, 135, 150
Physical learning domain 2
Physical literacy 5
Poomsae/kata 26
Pre-assessment 72
Principle of play 65, 66
Problem-based learning 75, 77
Procedural knowledge 24
Professional judgement 3, 24

Rate limiter 66
Roche, Tony 105, 106
Rock climbing 30, 61, 77, 83, 84, 102

School sport 43
Self-assessment 16, 20, 51, 52, 102, 144, 145, 150
Self-controlled 52, 100
Self-determination 52, 56, 88
Self-efficacy 42
Self-evaluation 52, 59
Shot 26
Skill acquisition 14, 27–29, 49, 67, 127, 130, 138, 148, 150
Skill establishment 27
Skill learning 14, 29, 33, 37, 52, 100
Softball 53
Sport coach as educator 3–5, 8, 10–12, 70
Strategy 11, 19, 20, 43, 65, 66, 69, 71, 77, 78, 81–83, 88, 89, 91, 111, 118, 121, 123
Surfing 96, 97, 104, 105
Symbolic representation 7
Synaptic reorganisation 27
Synchronicity 26, 32, 119
Synchronisation 29
Synchronised 26, 32, 33

Tactic 11, 65, 66, 124
Tactical creativity approach 80, 81
Tactical-decision learning model (TDLM) 125
Tactical games model (TGM) 125, 129
Tactical model 65, 72
Tactical timeout 49
Task card/s 37, 38, 47
Task cues 127
Task design 36, 37, 59, 60
Task difficulty 59, 60
Teaching games for understanding (TGfU) 65, 124
Technique 20, 29–31, 38, 39, 45, 46, 52, 54, 61, 67, 77, 84, 98, 99, 109, 116, 120, 124, 140
Tennis 1, 2, 5, 32, 33, 37, 39, 40, 47, 54–56, 60, 62, 63, 70, 77, 84, 91, 99, 100, 105, 117, 118, 143
Thinking players 2, 10, 11, 127
Toolkit 10
Touch football 44

Understanding by design 10

Video 20, 95, 98, 101, 102, 140
Video analysis 95
Verbal cues 33, 127
Visual cues 27, 33, 129
Visible thinking 10
Visual representation 38
Volleyball 47, 54, 59

Working memory 33

Yego, Julius 20, 95, 101